Dedicated to

Pearl Ann
Richard Allen
Charles Arthur
James Alec

and in loving memory to

John Charles Mills and to
Cecil Alec and Mable Crystal Mills

BLUE CATALINAS
of
World War II

BLUE CATALINAS
of
World War II

by
James C. Mills

Sunflower University Press®

1531 Yuma (Box 1009), Manhattan, Kansas 66502-4228 USA

About the Cover

Looking for Nagumo by Craig Kodera
© 1992, The Greenwich Workshop, Inc.
Reproduced with the permission of The Greenwich Workshop, Inc.
For information on Craig Kodera's limited edition
fine art prints call 1-800-243-4246.

In *Looking for Nagumo*, aviation artist Craig Kodera captures the form
and lines of the PBY-5a Catalina seaplane as remembered by airmen all
over the world who have flown her. Shown is 44-P-4 against the backdrop
of towering clouds, the favorite home of the Catalina.

On the fateful morning of 3 June 1942, Jack Reid and his crew set out
in a 44-P-4 looking for Chuichi Nagumo and the Imperial Japanese Navy
and found them. That crucial action gave an edge to the U.S. forces in the
pivotal Battle of Midway.

Copyright © 1995 by James C. Mills

Printed in the United States of America on acid-free paper.

ISBN 0-89745-190-2

Edited by Julie Bush

Layout by Lori L. Daniel

Contents

Maps

Acknowledgments

I would like to thank Dodd Meade and Company for their permission to include herein a bit of the work of Don Blanding, and the Greenwich Workshop, Inc., for permission to use on the cover *Looking for Nagumo* by Craig Kodera.

Without the help of the officers and crew of VP-44, this book would not have been possible. Through correspondence within the USS Patrol Squadron VP-44 Association of The Blue Catalinas of World War II, much of the material and most of the photographs were made available. Some of the material used is from discussions during our reunion in San Francisco in September 1993. The contributions of B. K. Vickrey, an honorary member of the association, are significant.

The status of the war in Europe, Africa, and Asia has been included to provide the reader with a perspective of world conditions and the war at the time the squadron was formed and at subsequent intervals of time. I am indebted to the authors of the books listed in the bibliography, which are sources of data for that information: Christy Campbell, Robert T. Elson, E. B. Potter, Robert Wernick, and *The World Book Encyclopedia* authors.

Thanks to Mel Crocker, Robert S. La Forte and Ronald E. Marcello, and W. E. Scarborough for data provided in their work.

Two works, rich in data on the Battle of Midway, have been valuable sources concerning the sequence of events, some flight-crew identification, and, in particular, results of the attacks by the Midway-based forces against the Japanese forces. Thanks to Robert J. Cressman, Steve Ewing, Barrett Tillman, Clark Reynolds, and Stan Cohen for data provided in *The Battle of Midway 4-6 June 1942* and to Gordon W. Prange for *Miracle at Midway*.

For over 50 years I have wondered about the mysterious and beautiful young Polynesian woman we rescued from New Georgia. I have wondered about the Australian scout at Segi Point with whom we talked briefly as we watched for enemy planes.

These questions were answered as my work led me to Walter Lord's *Lonely Vigil*. Lord helped me better understand the coast watchers and their mission and great accomplishments. His work is a source of data for the events on New Georgia immediately following our visit with Donald Kennedy, coast watcher extraordinaire, and the invasion of New Georgia as the U.S. forces started the push across the Pacific.

Last but not least, I wish to thank Barbara Funkhouser, retired editor of the *El Paso Times* and currently professor of journalism at New Mexico State University. Barbara spent many hours editing this work.

The errors remaining — corrections that dropped through the cracks or otherwise not implemented — are mine.

Introduction

WHEN I joined the Navy on 23 May 1941, I was eager for a new life, eager to experience the action that was to come. I wanted to learn of life at sea — a career in naval aviation. I could not know then that my dreams of high adventure and an opportunity to see other parts of the world would be fulfilled many times over.

I believed that my life had followed a path that had trained me for what lay ahead. My early childhood years were spent in the red bed plains country of Oklahoma, which grew wheat, corn, cotton, and oil well gushers. In 1932, my parents decided to move our family of four small children away from the city. They had the courage and foresight to trade our home for a farm in Arkansas. We felt fortunate to live, work, and grow up in the lands of the Poteau, Caddo, Petite Jean, Blue, and Boston Mountains, also known as the Ouchita and Ozark National Forests. We loved that beautiful land. I learned to hunt and fish in the waters of the Arkansas, White Water, Petite Jean, and Poteau Rivers.

We farmed for years in the small community of Center Point near Waldron, Arkansas. It was rural America, far from any large city. We had the opportunity to live and work with graceful, simple, and honest people who were dedicated to family, church, friends, and neighbors. We grew all our food and made enough money to buy the essentials we could not make or grow. The children farmed small plots set aside for them in order to earn money for clothing and Christmas gifts.

Later, my father operated a large farm at Cecil, Arkansas, near the Arkansas River. It was there that I learned to hunt. Barney, my constant companion, was an excellent hunting dog, and together we ran the trap line in the mornings and hunted raccoon, opossum, and fox on the cold winter nights. There were enough furs in the shed for Christmas spending money and more for clothes when the season ended.

It was in White Oak, near Ozark, Arkansas, where Mr. Austin, teacher and coach, taught us basketball on an open-air earthen court, marked off by rocks along the border. He taught us the joy of hard work, careful practice, and teamwork; the art and power of the follow-through; and the secrets of the zone defense.

My father then settled on the small farm of his dreams near Waldron. It was there that the glorious seasons of football and basketball competition followed. Under our school principal and coach, L. R. Sawyer, the Waldron Bulldogs added football, basketball, and track trophies to the display case in the gymnasium every year.

One day I walked to town on an errand for my mother during the school lunch hour. As I passed the Baber Drug Store on Main Street, I heard the strange sounds of a radio broadcast in German. Adolf Hitler was addressing the German people, and the program was being carried by networks across the United States. Though I did not speak or understand the language, the message was ominous. Hitler had already conquered part of Europe and apparently intended to conquer the rest.

It was then that I recognized the necessity of joining the Navy at the end of the school year, though I wanted to get two years of college work and take flight training for a career in naval aviation. However, we did not have the money for college, and things were moving so fast in Europe that there was no time for two years of school anyway. The alternative was to enlist and work toward a flight career from the ranks.

I could not know at the time that my future would lead to a U.S. Navy Patrol Squadron, the USS VP-44, which flew Consolidated's PBY Catalina, a true flying boat. The Catalina was destined to provide the Navy with most of the oceanic surveillance required during World War II in both the Atlantic and Pacific Oceans.

As I look back on the days of Patrol Squadron 44, 51 years after the tour in the Pacific, I am only now able to place the role of the PBY-5 Catalina of World War II in its proper perspective. Since completing the work on this manuscript, I have a better appreciation of the plane and crews and their contribution to the successful execution of the war against the Axis powers.

A Navy patrol plane maintained long and lonely vigils over vast stretches of endless ocean. It worked alone. Its duty was to search a large sector of the sea, which may have extended hundreds of miles deep into enemy-held territories, and to report the presence of any enemy forces. Contacts with enemy planes were likely when patrolling contested waters.

Perhaps the lonely nature of the work performed by the Catalinas and their crews accounts for the lack of documentation on their part of the action during World War II. Certainly, the mission of a single patrol craft hundreds of miles from base is less spectacular than waves of bombers attacking a munitions factory. And indeed, most of the work performed in the Pacific by patrol craft was boring surveillance of miles of empty ocean. However, assurance that supposedly empty ocean was in fact empty was also vital information.

In the battles of the North and South Pacific, fights with enemy patrol craft would become almost a daily occurrence for the crews of VP-44. Yet the enemy land-based bombers of both Wake Island and the Solomon Islands soon became wary of attacking the PBY. Though the Imperial Japanese Navy patrol bombers had a two-to-one speed advantage over the Catalina, they learned not to press the attack unless they found one of the PBY's .50-caliber guns to be jammed or inoperative.

Of all the Midway-based planes launched against the Imperial Japanese Navy during the 3 June 1942 night torpedo attack conducted hundreds of miles from base, only one PBY, commanded by Lieutenant W. L. Richards of VP-44, hit and inflicted damage on one of the enemy oilers, the *Akebono Maru*. The Battle of Midway, 4-6 June 1942, had PBY patrols everywhere. They fanned out to the east of the Midway atoll from the island of Kauai and also to the north, west, and south from Midway. They located, tracked, and maintained Fleet position data on the enemy forces before and during the battle. During this time, only one Catalina was shot down and four planes of VP-44 were damaged in fights with twin-engine enemy bombers operating from a base west of Midway. Many of the downed airmen were rescued by PBYs as the battle raged on and afterward.

The open-sea rescue missions in the Solomon Islands performed by "Dumbos" — the U.S. Navy's code name for PBYs on such sea rescue missions, named for the Walt Disney cartoon elephant with huge ears — are legend. A number of fliers of the U.S. Army Air Forces, U.S. Marine Corps, and U.S. Navy owe their lives to the rescues performed by the Catalinas. In many cases, rescue missions occurred under fire from enemy-held islands. In addition, surveillance of the disputed oceans was maintained during that campaign. The coast watchers, a unit of the Royal Australian Army (RAA), operated from lonely outposts in the Solomons, providing movement data via radio on Japanese forces. Supply and transport for the Solomon coast watchers, many times deep into enemy-held territory, was a vital function. These missions were frequently conducted in weather conditions so bad that other aircraft dared not venture out.

Admiral William F. Halsey said that the coast watchers saved Guadalcanal and Guadalcanal saved the Pacific. The PBY Catalina was the coast watchers' best friend.

What follows is not a scholarly history of the patrol squadrons of World War II. It is, rather, a record of one of the many patrol squadrons that flew the Patrol (P) Bomber (B) designed and built by Consolidated Aircraft (Y) of San Diego, California. It is presented in the terms expressed by the men of the squadron — what they saw, what they did, and how they felt about the job they were assigned. It is a story of men who flew missions at any time in any kind of weather, often against far superior forces; most often they lived to file their combat reports and fly again.

The account of Heavier Than Air (V) Patrol (P) Squadron 44 presented here is representative of the record of other PBY squadrons that served in both the Atlantic and Pacific. Taken together, these squadrons provide an exciting and glorious chapter of the book of World War II. It is a record worth preserving.

This material was assembled so that my grandsons can know of the values of those men who devoted a part of their lives to serving their country during the 1940s, men from all walks of life, from across America. A few experienced hands trained the many new hands and formed an efficient unit capable of undertaking any assignment. Not one individual ever hesitated for an instant in taking on a mission, regardless of the odds against returning. Each man was custodian of some government property, and he guarded and cared for it as he would his own; each performed to the best of his ability and was as much concerned with the survival of his shipmates as he was of his own. These men and those of the other squadrons were men of honor, and they acquitted themselves accordingly.

My presentation of the events is a salute to the men of the PBY squadrons and a gesture of thanks for the time shared with them.

ARM1c James C. Mills, San Diego, California, 1943.

Chapter 1

Seattle and San Diego

1939-1940 — Winds of War

THE winds of war were sweeping across Europe. Hitler's Germany had annexed Austria in 1938 under an agreement with Britain's Neville Chamberlain, Premier Edouard Daladier of France, and Benito Mussolini of Italy. Czechoslovakia lost the Sudetenland to Germany; then, Germany occupied the remainder of Czechoslovakia.

Much earlier, Benito Mussolini's forces had swept through Ethiopia, easily conquering and slaughtering the crudely equipped Ethiopian forces. On 1 September 1939, German troops invaded Poland, and two days later Britain and France declared war on Germany.

Russian troops invaded Finland on 30 November 1939.

Germany, Italy, and Japan were allied in what was known as the Rome-Berlin-Tokyo Axis. Later in 1940, they would sign a military aid pact.

Japanese forces had invaded and conquered Manchuria. They also conquered parts of China, including the cities of Hankow and Canton, and controlled many of China's port cities.

In Mountain Home, Arkansas, old men sat in front of the Mountain Home Mercantile and argued, some in anger, about the apparent military buildup in the United States. Some thought it wrong to put America's young men in the large Army barracks being built in Texas and other parts of America, believing that their morals would be destroyed. Most thought their country had no business "pulling British chestnuts out of the fire" during this war. These men seemed to reflect the attitude of most Americans. The United States was at peace with the rest of the world. The country was trying to recover from a deep recession, and times were still hard. Nevertheless, young men — boys near high school graduation and those in college or planning college — were trying to determine the course their lives should take in view of the alarming news from Europe and Asia.

USS Patrol Squadron 20, under the control of Fleet Air Wing Four, operating out of Seattle, Washington, was under the command of Lieutenant Commander W. D. Johnson. The squadron manned the PBY Catalinas, which were flown by Johnson and the 13 pilots under him: five lieutenants and eight aviation cadets. (One of the lieutenants, R. A. "Rosy" Rosasco, was later to command the squadron, designated VP-44.) The squadron conducted extensive training exercises while operating out of Seattle.

On 1 July 1939, the squadron was redesignated VP-44. Lieutenant Commander Johnson remained as its commanding officer and thus gained the distinction of being the squadron's charter commanding officer. During the remainder of the year, VP-44 continued to conduct regular training exercises.

The Nazis attacked Denmark on 9 April 1940. Denmark and Norway were conquered by Germany in a campaign that lasted less than two months, at a relatively small cost except for the losses to the German navy: Admiral Erich Raeder lost half of his fleet to the British navy during the Norwegian campaign. This loss was to prove disastrous because without sea power, the Nazis could not launch a ground invasion of England.

One positive effect of the Norwegian campaign was the long-overdue replacement of British Prime Minister Neville Chamberlain with Winston Churchill. On 10 May 1940, Churchill presented his new government to the British Parliament while Germany's long-awaited assault began on the Western front. German forces smashed their way through the Netherlands, Belgium, and Luxembourg.

On 23 May, the commander of the British Expeditionary Forces (BEF), General Viscount Gort, ignoring orders, decided to retreat to Dunkirk and thus made the decision that saved the BEF. Germany's General Heinz Guderian and his panzer divisions were closer to Dunkirk than was Gort.

They were stopped at the Aa Canal on 24 May, a scant 12 miles from Dunkirk. On 25 May, a few of Guderian's tanks were roaring their way across the canal when Hitler, feeling confident of victory and desiring to conserve armor, ordered the advance to halt. Thus, he made it possible for the BEF to escape to England.

On 5 June, the Nazis launched a new offensive against France. Within four days the French were in hopeless retreat. On 10 June, Mussolini entered the war on the side of Germany to share in the spoils.

France signed an armistice on 22 June with Premier Philippe Henri Pétain, a Nazi puppet, setting up a government in the unoccupied part of southern France at Vichy. Brigadier General Charles de Gaulle became a leader of the Free France movement and called for the French to continue to fight. Nouvelle Caledonia, an island in the southwest Pacific, 800 miles east of Australia, was in the column of the Free French Possessions and would later become an important U.S. Navy base.

Italy invaded the British Somaliland and swept into Greece. Hungary and Romania joined the Axis.

On 22 September, Japan pushed into French Indochina. Japan had waged war in Asia since 1937. By 1940, the armies there were deadlocked, and Japan turned to other areas to expand its empire.

The reports of the heroic rescue of the Allied forces by the British armada at Dunkirk spread across the United States and touched the heart of its people. There was a feeling of kinship developing in the minds of the Americans with the 338,226 British, French, Belgian, and Dutch troops who escaped. Many came to believe the lend-lease of U.S. destroyers to the beleaguered British was necessary. America was building military training camps, ships, and airplanes.

However, some people on America's West Coast were alarmed at the amount of scrap metal leaving its ports destined for Japan. Many in Long Beach, California, thought that each tin can and junk automobile manufactured in the United States was stacked on wharves awaiting shipment.

In America, the feeling developed that all of Europe might fall to the Nazi army before anything could be done. The words Junkers, Stuka dive-bomber, Messerschmitt fighter, and panzer divisions became feared household words. Blitzkrieg took on the meaning of a powerful army, efficient down to the last sharpened pencil. It came to mean a highly developed army, pounding its way across Europe with crumbling British and French forces in front of it.

Young men across America began defining the plans for their future. Those who had strong preferences for the military services were taking the necessary steps for joining a branch. They were completing schoolwork in specialty fields or making plans to join defense-related industries to avoid the draft. Everyone began to think about their particular role in the "war effort."

USS Patrol Squadron 44 (VP-44) continued intensive training exercises in the home port of Seattle until November 1940, when the squadron was redesignated VP-61 and the home port changed to Naval Air Station (NAS) Alameda, California. The squadron would later deploy to Norfolk, Virginia, and be redesignated VP-82, VB-125, and finally VPB-125 while conducting operations in the Atlantic.

1941 — Forming a Squadron

On 3 June 1941, the second squadron to be designated VP-44 was commissioned at the Naval Air Station in San Diego, serving under Fleet Air Wing One (FAW 1) with six PBY-5 Catalina aircraft assigned.

Lieutenant Commander R. C. Brixner assumed command of the squadron in October 1941 with Lieutenant (jg) W. L. Richards as the executive officer. Other senior officers were Lieutenant Donald G. Gumz, Lieutenant (jg) C. E. Olson, Lieutenant (jg) R. L. Summers, Lieutenant (jg) Robert S. Whitman, Jr., and Lieutenant (jg) Shelby O. Cole. The remainder of the staff of commissioned pilots were ensigns who had completed college and recently earned their naval aviator wings, qualifying for the PBY aircraft. They came from all walks of life across America.

Ten of the enlisted personnel were veterans of the first VP-44 from NAS Alameda who had served before the squadron was decommissioned in 1940. They were Frank Alford, Raymond Derouin, Anthony Fornataro, John Gammell, Lloyd Griffin, Alexander Jocius, Joseph Meagher, Jack Reid, Earl Robinson, and Zygmunt Zydak. Jack Reid had

served in VP-44 at the time of the unit's commission and thus had the distinction of being a "plank owner" of VP-44.

Of the early complement, 17 were trained and seasoned old hands who would in turn train, guide, and make sailors of the young seamen coming into the squadron. They were chief petty officers (CPOs) in the specialties of machinist, ordnance, and radio. The group included the veterans Cesare Cavadini (in charge of the radio shop), Charles Coffin, Stephen Leflar, Carl Lundquist, Kenneth McCardle (the squadron's leading chief), Francis Musser, Vinton Pease (who would be instrumental in training the young radiomen), Earl Robinson, Angus Rose, Joel Stoval, Arcia Turner, and Ralph Williams.

The squadron personnel complement also included another group that would be influential in squadron operations. These men were enlisted pilots with the petty officer rating aviation pilot (AP); they were experienced pilots and navigators. This group of APs included Clifford Adams, Julius Cox, John Gammell, Armido Mancini, Fredrick Panetto, Jack Reid, Roy Robinson, Richard Umphrey, and Samuel Wideberg.

In the ensuing years from commissioning, the complement of VP-44 personnel would vary depending upon the deployment, deployment conditions, and the squadron mission. In 1941, the squadron would build to a level of 286 enlisted personnel: 10 chief petty officers, 10 aviation pilots, 148 petty officers (POs), 7 seamen first class (Sea1c), 102 seamen second class (Sea2c), and 9 seamen apprentices (AS).

27 October 1941 —
The Fleet Air Wing School Group

In late August 1941, excitement began to build among us young recruits of the San Diego Naval Training Facility boot camp who had arrived in May. We had drilled, marched, carried rifles, worn leggings, and worked through the rifle range for nearly three months. We knew and liked the two chief petty officers, Chief Signalman Albright and his assistant, who had worked and drilled us so hard but were fair and honest. Training would soon be finished, and there would be shore liberty.

The bulletin board listed the ships, stations, and

PBY-5a Catalina over Tarawa, *circa* 1944. (Thomas G. Monahan)

other units where there were openings for recruits. Of special interest was a list of openings for the Fleet Air Wing School, NAS North Island, San Diego. Those of us interested in the school met daily after hours to discuss the possibilities of being selected and to exchange information with each other.

Representatives of the organizations and ships conducted interviews on the scheduled date. One week later, the names of candidates selected were posted. We who were chosen for the aviation school on North Island were overjoyed and began the formation of friendships and a camaraderie that would, in many cases, carry through two wartime tours in the Pacific and on to successful Navy careers. A number of the friendships would last through entire lifetimes.

When we joined the Fleet Air Wing for training

in the PBY-5 Catalina aircraft, we were joined by others from the Great Lakes NAS training facility, in northern Illinois, and other facilities. During following weeks, those striking for the aviation machinist mate (AMM) rating studied aircraft maintenance and aircraft engine maintenance. Those who were pursuing a career in aviation radio and electronics for the aviation radio mate (ARM) rating, as I was, studied electronics, aircraft electrical systems, and hours upon hours of Morse code practice. The aviation ordnance mate (AOM) training covered all aspects of aviation ordnance, including the secret Sperry bombsight.

In October, 15 recruits, including Monroe Nelson of Seattle, Patrick Mahon of St. Louis, Sherman Moore, Willard Nicks of California, Walter Mitchell, George Newcombe, Edwin Olsen and Rex Swinnford from Dallas, Jim Pearson, Robert

Totten, Angus Rose and John Watts of Portland, Reid Wilson and Lloyd Wood from Illinois, and myself, transferred to USS Patrol Squadron 44 (VP-44). Others with similar training and background joined the FAW school group and ultimately joined VP-44. This later group included John J. Klopp of Cleveland, Keith K. Wilkason of St. Louis, and Clifford V. Troland of Portland.

These men of the FAW school group who joined VP-44 were representative of the thousands who had planned and worked to arrange their schooling and personal affairs to join the service of their choice in a technical field to their liking while war clouds were still storming across Europe and whispers of war were rippling across America.

During the fall of 1941, representatives of another group of young men who had planned their careers and trained through the college Naval Reserve programs came to San Diego to join VP-44. They were commissioned officers with the rank of ensign. As college students, their goals and ambitions led them to their commissions, Naval Aviators Flight School, flight wings, and the opportunity to qualify for the PBY Catalina aircraft.

3 November 1941 — The PBY-5a Aircraft

During the first week of November 1941, the peacetime Navy routines of maintenance and training were in effect. During that week, training flights for the Fleet Air Wing school group started with the planes of USS Patrol Squadron VP-44. Less than half of the pilots and crew of the squadron were experienced, yet it was up to them to provide the many hours of flight training, navigation for the pilots, operations and maintenance, gunnery practice, and safety procedures for the new recruits of the FAW school. Each of the new pilots and enlisted crew members had his own moment of personal reflection as we climbed up the ladder, through the Plexiglas blister, and into the waist hatch of that grand seaplane. We were joined by a common thread of the emotional recognition that life would forever be different. Each person knew that the act represented the culmination of youthful dreams and plans, and all were in awe of this magnificent Navy airship, a true "flying boat."

The plane was the latest version of seaplanes in naval aviation's proud history and was the mainstay for the Navy's oceanic surveillance. The first delivery to the Navy was made in 1940, under the designation PBY-5 Catalina, the same designation used by the British under a purchase in 1939. The aircraft was painted light blue and white and had a gross weight of 35,000 pounds. The wingspan was 104 feet, with retractable wingtip floats. The wings, equipped with racks for depth charges, torpedoes, or bombs, could carry 4,000 pounds of explosives. The wing after-section and the rudder were cloth-covered. Two wing struts on each side of the hull and a tower at the wing center connected the wings to the fuselage.

A catwalk ran the full length from the nose section to the tail. The nose section contained an anchor, a platform for a bombsight, navigation access ports, and mounts for twin .30-caliber machine guns and was the domain of the ordnance mate air bomber. Aft of the nose section bulkhead was the cockpit with elevated seats, controls, instrument panels, and throttles; the pilots could see forward, to port (left), and to starboard (right). Next was the navigation and radio compartment. Along the port side was a porthole and a navigation table with accommodations for maps and navigation gear. Across the catwalk was the radio operator's position with a table, typewriter, Morse code key, radio transmitter, radio receiver, frequency meter, and radio direction finder (RDF) equipment. Aft of this compartment bulkhead was a large compartment containing a galley, four bunks, potable water tanks, tools used in flight, and access to the tower. The tower was an aerodynamically neutral foil connecting the fuselage to the giant wings that held the fuel tanks. It contained a seat, foot rests for the crew member, fuel-control valves, and flow meters and was the domain of the crew plane captain.

Through the hatch, aft of the bunks, was the waist hatch compartment with one of the plane's distinguishing features: two large Plexiglas blisters, one on each side of the hull, which were just below and aft of the wing trailing section. There was a fold-down seat at the forward bulkhead on each side providing excellent visibility fore, aft, to port, and to starboard. It was an ideal position for the .50-caliber machine gun — one in each blister — with a concave walkway around the gun mount for the gunner. It provided stowage for the life raft, sea

6

A close-up view of the Catalina with plane commander Lieutenant Thomas G. Monahan, plane captain John J. Klopp, and her crew, later on Tarawa, in July 1944. (Jim Klopp)

anchors, and Very pistol, and on the bulkhead was a Klaxon — a loud, electronic horn — for calling general quarters (meaning all hands should immediately take up their assigned duty stations and be prepared to engage the enemy) and battle stations (engage the enemy).

Every compartment of the ship was functional, including the tail section. Access to the tail section was through the aft hatch at the waist compartment. It contained a tunnel hatch with a .30-caliber machine gun, safety belt, flare and smoke-bomb launcher, commode, and stowage for disposable paper bags. All crew positions connected to a common interphone system.

On the exterior, the radio communications antenna connected from the upper tail section to the wingtips, forming an open "V" pointing forward. The antenna fed through an insulator at the starboard side of the hull to a point aft of the wing. The radio direction finder antenna was located on the wing between the two engines. The pilot voice radio antenna fed through the hull near the copilot position to the forward edge of the starboard wing.

To see her taxiing on the water is to be reminded of a cross between a boat and a submarine with a giant wing attached at the conning tower. To observe takeoff for the first time is to forever dispel any doubts about the capability of the two Pratt and Whitney R-1830-32 engines that develop 1,200 horsepower each. First, the surface water in the vicinity of the ship flattens. Next, a wake develops as she gains speed, and a large plume of water develops and lengthens to hundreds of feet. As she goes up on the step — the "jog" in the hull provided to help break the vacuum between the hull and the water — only the center section is cutting the water. Then the water beneath her flattens again as she lifts with nose pointed upward, gaining altitude at the rate of hundreds of feet per minute.

It is no mystery that the crews of the Catalina would grow as fond of her as they were of their own homes. Indeed, many of them would spend much of their lives in the plane during the ensuing years. When circumstances required, they could, and many would, live in the ship for days and even weeks at a time without leaving her.

As flight training and ground instruction continued for trainers and trainees of VP-44 at North Island Naval Air Station, San Diego, the British Isles had been mercilessly bombarded nightly. Sweeping into Russia were 150 Nazi and other Axis divisions. All the Balkan nations were under German and Italian control. War raged in North Africa. In October 1941, a German submarine had torpedoed and sunk the destroyer *Reuben James*, making it the first U.S. naval vessel to be lost by enemy action in the war.

7 December 1941

Life in the peacetime Navy was pleasant for those personnel of the naval units located at the facilities in San Diego in the summer and fall of 1941. The climate was mild and sunny, and the new personnel of the squadron were sightseeing and enjoying southern California, many for the first time. For them, Balboa Park, the San Diego Zoo, the museums, and the old sailing ship *Star of India* tied up at the city pier were great attractions.

On Sunday, 7 December 1941, some of the squadron personnel were visiting relatives and friends in other cities along the California coast. Others were enjoying liberty ashore while the activities at the tennis courts and swimming pools at the Naval Air Station were beginning to pick up. Many of the "old-timers" of VP-44 were at their homes in San Diego or in nearby communities with their families.

I was visiting a cousin and aunt in Long Beach. As we sat quietly reading the Sunday papers, the radio that had been playing popular music of the time suddenly became quiet. An announcer came on and in a clearly agitated voice said, "Please stand by for an emergency announcement." The message was repeated, and a long silence followed. At last the voice announced, "The Japanese have attacked Pearl Harbor, the Japanese have attacked Pearl Harbor." The message was repeated and additional information became available: swarms of planes had attacked the fleet at Pearl Harbor, where battleships were being bombarded and torpedoed. Hickam Field was under attack, and all planes were destroyed. The Navy Air Field on Ford Island was also destroyed.

My cousins and I looked at each other in speechless amazement and then intuitively stepped outside the house and into the yard. Other neighbors who had heard the radio message also flocked outside, unconsciously looking toward the ocean and the skies. My aunt's car came into the drive, and she exclaimed, "The Japs have attacked us! I knew they would, and I just bought vegetables from them." She went to the back of the car, took out three bags of fresh vegetables, and put them in the garbage can.

Everyone was perplexed. People knew that matters were serious in Europe, but no one had expected a sneak attack from the Japanese on the island fortress of Oahu and upon the Navy's Pacific Fleet that was riding quietly on the waters of Pearl Harbor.

A young officer, Ensign William H. Cullin, had completed training in Nevada and was en route to San Diego to report to VP-44 for duty. He was traveling with his mother and sister. They stopped at Needles to purchase gasoline.

The station attendant saw the new officer's uniform with the bright ensign strip that was on a hanger in the automobile and commented, "I see you're rushing back to your station."

"Well, I am going to San Diego," the officer replied, "but why do you ask?"

"Haven't you heard?" the attendant asked. "The Japanese have attacked Pearl Harbor." The mother and sister began to weep softly.

Kenneth H. McCardle, leading chief of Squadron VP-44, left home immediately upon hearing the shocking news. He was experienced and knew what needed doing. That day and the days to come would be busy ones for those in leadership positions in the squadron. His wife and daughter drove the chief to the Navy pier.

Seaman Patrick J. Mahon, one of the new graduates of the Fleet Air Wing school, was on watch duty from 12:00 to 4:00 p.m. on that day. At 1:00 p.m., the petty officer of the guard rode up on a bicycle and advised him that the United States was at war with Japan and to be alert. Half an hour later he rode up again and gave Pat a clip of .45-caliber ammunition for his side arm. He then waited to see if he knew how to install the clip in the gun.

Ensigns J. J. "Jiggs" Lyons, Robert A. "Bob" Swan, Henry S. "Hank" Noon, and Ralph C. Donaldson shared an apartment in the town of Coronado near the Naval Air Station. After a night

out, they were sleeping soundly when the telephone rang.

They were ordered back to duty, and three of them dressed and left immediately. Jiggs Lyons, thinking it was a test, did not go; he was much more interested in sleeping. He received two more calls to report to duty without any explanation. The officer then dressed and took the ferry to San Diego with the intention of checking into a hotel to get some sleep. On the ferry, he learned of the attack and reported to duty as quickly as possible.

Confusion reigned on the seaplane ramps of Patrol Squadrons VP-43 and VP-44. The seaplane ramps were hard-surface areas used to park the planes. One side of the ramp let down into the ocean to provide a means of launching the aircraft into the water. Planes were spotted — or parked — on these ramps and bombs were put in place on the wing bomb racks. Only one 500-pound bomb was available for each plane.

Machine guns were installed on the planes, and as they were readied for flight, crews went aboard. VP-44 was first over the side, into the water, with its planes, although two of them did not have the two .50-caliber machine guns in the waist hatches. The planes of the two PBY squadrons took off that Sunday afternoon on the first West Coast wartime patrols of World War II.

Lieutenant (jg) Shelby O. "Pappy" Cole and Ensign Bob Swan, pilot and copilot respectively, were assigned an antisubmarine patrol sector. A short way into the flight, they received a radio message from pilots of scouting and observation planes, who reported that they were attacking a submarine and asked for assistance in the form of a bombing run on the target. Pappy Cole arrived on the scene and made a pass over the target, but then informed the pilots to hold their fire. The planes were attacking a whale.

By 4:00 p.m. that day, a dozen motor whaleboats — uncovered craft, 16 to 20 feet in length, equipped with seats for approximately 16 people — were standing by off the pier at the Navy landing in San Diego. Others, three and four at a time, loaded personnel bound for the North Island Naval Air Station. Personnel, by the hundreds every hour, were streaming back to the Navy shipyards and air station from all over southern California.

That afternoon, patrol schedules were established for the southern California waters. By that evening, a squadron muster was held and a wartime status declared. Night watches were posted for sentry duty on all seaplane ramps and squadron areas. America had started mobilizing for war.

The Naval Air Station at San Diego was a beehive of activity. The week following the attack seemed to be an eternity for squadron personnel. Monday morning, 8 December, Squadron VP-44 received orders to dispatch its six aircraft to NAS Alameda for patrol duty off the coast at San Francisco. Numerous accounts of enemy activity had been reported in those waters.

By Tuesday, the Naval Air Station was operating under blackout conditions. All buildings, including hangars, administrative offices, and living quarters, were blacked out. Small blue Christmas tree lights illuminated the Bachelor Officer's Club and mess halls. Meals served at night for personnel on duty were almost impossible to see. Hundreds of Marine Corps and Army troops reported to the station and installed antiaircraft artillery. Sandbagging of the facilities was in progress during all daylight hours.

The following Thursday, 11 December, the rest of our squadron received orders to pack all personal and squadron gear and be ready to move out by 2:30 p.m. All squadron tools and spare parts, including one of the large Pratt and Whitney engines, were transferred by truck and ferry boat to the platform of the Santa Fe Railway Station in downtown San Diego. At 5:00 p.m., all personnel arrived with gear. At 9:00 p.m., all equipment was stowed in a freight car, and the special five-car train pulled out (the scheduled trains did not have the room to accommodate the squadron). The working hours had been long and hard.

The trip represented the first opportunity we had had to rest and relax. There was, however, little food on the train, and no one had eaten since breakfast that morning. That night, the cars transferred to the Southern Pacific Railway. Good food was available, and the remaining portion of the trip was pleasant.

Special trucks and buses were waiting at the railway station in Oakland, California, when the train arrived. Personnel and gear debarked, including the one-ton aircraft engine, and were soon at the new base, NAS Alameda, California.

Chapter 2

NAS Alameda

WE who had traveled to Alameda by train learned that the six planes dispatched to Alameda earlier in the week had received a "warm reception" in the Bay Area. They had left late in the afternoon on Monday, 8 December, and as they approached San Francisco that evening, the entire Bay Area began to black out and was soon in virtual darkness. At the shoreline, the incoming planes began receiving antiaircraft fire from the gun batteries guarding San Francisco, who were unaware that the planes were "friendly" and who perhaps had "itchy" trigger fingers and a fear of any incoming planes. It was necessary to abandon plans to land in the bay at the seaplane base. Instead, each crew had to select a lake or cove in outlying areas for a landing place. The following day, after many communications, it was decided that the five planes that were able would again take off to land at the seaplane base. The sixth plane had landed on a mud flat and was stuck. The crew and the area Coast Guard had tried in vain to free it.

As soon as the ground personnel arrived at NAS Alameda on 12 December, a detail was formed to rescue the stranded plane. First, it was necessary to remove the fuel in the tanks. Next, all equipment that could be taken out was transported to the air station. Considerable digging to orient the plane's heading and to create a pathway toward the water followed. With only a small amount of fuel on board, an effort by the engines, and a great undertaking by the rescue team, the plane inched its way into a turn in the direction of the water and eventually made its way there. At last the plane was afloat, with enough fuel aboard to make the short hop to the seaplane base. Thanks to the inaccurate fire of the gun batteries guarding San Francisco and enough moonlight to make a landing, the crews of the seaplanes had been saved to fight and to help guard the approaches to San Francisco.

The young officers and we new enlisted personnel then had an opportunity to visit the San Francisco area and to learn more about the country we were serving. It was a limited opportunity, however, because work and training schedules left little free time. Shore liberty was granted occasionally, and we looked forward to visiting San Francisco, Oakland, and other communities in the area. Some would later return and marry the young women they met on these infrequent visits ashore.

Within a few weeks, flight crews went to San Diego to pick up new planes for the squadron, increasing our number from 6 to 12. The crews also exchanged the PBY-5 seaplanes, which could land only on water, for new PBY-5a amphibians, which could touch down on water and on land. Ensign Robert Swan was a member of the detail sent to San Diego to receive the new planes. He was also designated to sign for the aircraft when received by the Navy representatives. Bob reported that it gave him great satisfaction to sign for several hundred thousand dollars worth of airplanes, particularly because his total personal fortune was minus $1,000, the amount he owed on his automobile.

The new planes appeared to be awkward at first on the landing strip, but the crews soon adjusted to landing the amphibians and grew to like them as much as they had the seaplanes. All pilots soon qualified for amphibian operations in the new PBY-5a aircraft.

There were intensive training sessions for the mechanics, radio technicians, and ordnance men in addition to regular aircraft preventive maintenance schedules. For the radio technicians, there was an added requirement to learn cryptology because all continuous wave (CW) radio transmissions would be encoded. Morse code CW practice classes were held regularly for the FAW radio group.

The new planes came equipped with the .30- and .50-caliber machine-gun armament in place with ammunition canisters ready for use. The large aircraft hangars, where squadron headquarters offices and shops were located and where ground operations were conducted, accommodated two of the large amphibian aircraft. As soon as the kits for the wing racks used for mounting torpedoes, depth charges, or bombs were received from Consolidated Aircraft Co., they were installed on the planes.

The hangars were noisy during daylight hours due to workers and machinery. One morning there was a loud clatter as one of the 500-pound bombs accidently fell from its rack to the concrete deck. In an instant, except for the distant air-pressure pump, the noise ceased and the hangar became utterly quiet. The next sounds were sighs of relief from across the entire hangar. The bomb had not exploded.

Once we had arrived at Alameda, regular patrol schedules were established for the California coastline. People along the coast were justifiably afraid of shelling by submarines, but the regular flights of the seaplanes around the Bay Area did much to allay their concern, according to local radio stations and newspapers. All planes on patrol flight carried a full complement of depth charges. These regular patrols served the dual purpose of flight crew training and surveillance.

One of our games at the time was guessing which of the squadron's crews would fly under the Oakland Bay Bridge or the Golden Gate Bridge. Later it developed into a game of guessing which crew would fly under both. Soon, though, crews were regularly flying under the bridges when the heavy fog had lifted high enough to expose the bridge supports and surface water. After passing under the Golden Gate, the seaward course could be held while gaining altitude through the heavy fog.

Operating regular antisubmarine patrols out of the San Francisco Bay could be done only at great risk to planes and crews. One patrol was forced to land at sea because of fog. They taxied to the Golden Gate Bridge and across the bay to the seaplane base at Alameda. Ensign Bob Swan noted that the plane had more taxi time than air time on the engines that day.

The defensive element of the training mission of the squadron while at Alameda was not entirely in vain. Lieutenant (jg) Pappy Cole and his crew did sight a Japanese submarine in the waters near the San Francisco harbor entrance. They attacked immediately by dropping two depth charges, but both failed to explode and the submarine safely submerged and escaped.

Apparently, the city of San Francisco unknowingly had an efficient submarine defense system, for later, as reported by Ensign Cornelius D. "Neil" Brislawn, a city garbage barge and scow hit and sank a submarine. The barge was under tow on a long line by a tugboat. The submarine apparently came up to investigate the strange echoes received and was struck by the barge. It sank, and a large oil slick developed on the surface. Neil states that the incident was reported in the local papers.

In April 1942, Squadron VP-44 was ordered to report to Naval Air Station Ford Island, located in Pearl Harbor, Hawaii. One six-plane section flew to San Diego from Alameda. There the landing gear was removed and shipped to Ford Island by surface vessel. This reduced the weight of the plane and provided space for the rubberized fuel tanks, which were installed in each side of the wheel well. A cover plate was placed over the well, but because it was not water-proofed, water filled in around the tanks during taxiing and takeoff. All of San Diego Bay plus some of the open sea at the approach to the harbor were used for takeoff. When the planes finally lifted from the surface, they left a long stream of seawater in the air from the water around the rubber tanks.

All went well on the transition flight from San Diego to Pearl Harbor, considering the inexperienced crews who were flying. Ensign Robert Swan was assigned as navigator on Lieutenant (jg) Donald "Don" Gumz's plane. During the flight, Bob found that he was showing a position behind the other five planes in the section; that is, it appeared that their plane had not traveled as far as had the other five. Gumz came back to the navigating table and dressed Bob down, advising him to wait until the others had reported and then to give a position in the center of the other reports.

Bob did that, but he continued to plot the aircraft position according to his calculations. When according to the other reports Gumz and his crew should have arrived at the expected location of the Hawaiian Islands, they were not there. The lead plane and four others wanted to set up a box search, but Bob, knowing he was right, stuck by his guns and argued with Gumz, recommending they stay on course for an additional 180 miles. Don accepted Bob's recommendation, they remained on course, and later the islands came into view.

On 19 April, the second section of six planes also made the transition flight from San Francisco. Ensign William "Bill" Cullin, flying with this section, was also perplexed at his position reports. He

was navigator in the lead plane with the squadron commander, Lieutenant Commander R. C. Brixner, and was showing about 30 miles difference between his and the average of the reports from the other planes. He invited Brixner to check his star sights. Brixner, having been in the cockpit for some time, got up and stepped back to the navigation table, stretched, and said, "Son, I don't know how to use that thing." But Cullin's navigational errors were slight, and the plane maintained good flight position with the other five aircraft.

All went well for both sections. One plane was forced to land at Molokai because of low fuel. The others landed in the bay at Pearl Harbor with little fuel left. Later, Gumz apologized to Swan at a meeting of pilots and navigators. He then established classes for the junior pilots and made Bob the instructor and assistant navigation officer.

By 20 April 1942, the transition for all 12 aircraft from the West Coast to NAS Ford Island was successfully completed with an average flight time of 20.3 hours.

All other squadron personnel crossed by ship, on the *Lurline*, formerly a Matson luxury liner on the San Francisco-Hawaii route. We boarded the ship at a San Francisco pier and were able to observe, from a passenger deck, the loading of squadron gear, which had been trucked from Alameda. Loading occurred for four days, 24 hours per day, and although we were still tied at the pier, the slight motion of the ship made hundreds of the Army personnel seasick.

Any thoughts we had entertained of a luxury crossing were soon dispelled. The squadrons were assigned quarters consisting of a section of deck boarded off with plywood to keep out wind and rain. Temporary toilet facilities nearby were used by hundreds of men.

At the outset, the food on the *Lurline* was good. As hundreds of military personnel streamed aboard, the length of time the meals were served was extended to the point that food was available during nearly all daylight hours.

Judging from the sights during the embarkation, it was clear that the United States was mobilizing for war. A tremendous number of personnel and equipment had been loaded aboard the *Lurline*, and she was only one of the many ships departing every week for the Hawaiian Islands from that port.

Late on 25 April, we saw the lines being cast off and felt the movement of the ship as tugs moved her from the pier. Then came the sound of her engines moving her toward the Golden Gate.

Time passed swiftly. As the coast of the U.S. mainland receded, there were reflections on the past and anticipation of what the future held. This trip represented, for many of us new hands, the first time aboard ship and the first time outside the continental United States.

The Fleet Air Wing school group soon found that the uppermost deck of the superstructure, where the signal flag locker was located, was the best vantage point to observe the ship and ocean. Except for meals, we spent all daylight hours there.

In slightly more time than it had taken to load the ship, she had crossed the Pacific, and a thrill swept through the passengers as land was sighted to port side. Molokai slipped past to stern and Diamond Head came into view to the starboard side. As the ship rounded the Diamond Head point, it became clear why the blind poet Don Blanding had described Diamond Head as "a setting for a giant jewel, the sun."

For this voyage, the *Lurline* was not met by bands, hula dancers, and flower leis. Instead, she was met by acres of buses and trucks waiting to take the human and material cargo. VP-44, the first squadron on the ship, was almost the first off. Buses took the squadron personnel to a large field on one of the military reservations.

Chief Kenneth McCardle mustered the crew and marched us into a large circle. The next orders came as a surprise. "All right, all hands, drop your pants." Thereupon he unbuckled his belt, and his trousers fell to his ankles. There was no alternative but to follow suit. It must have been quite a sight to passersby on the adjoining road to see an entire squadron standing in a great circle with their pants down. It was an agonizingly long wait for a single doctor, accompanied by a hospital corpsman, to inspect each man.

The final leg of the journey to NAS Ford Island was to bring a feeling of shock, dismay, and anger to the men. As the motor whaleboats began plowing through the waters of Pearl Harbor, each and every one of us began to understand that we were going

to witness something we had heard of but could never have prepared ourselves to see firsthand.

To starboard lay the battleship *Arizona* with only her long, curvilinear hull exposed. It was an emotional experience to reflect that 1,103 men of her crew were still aboard, that only five months ago they were alive and well and looking forward to their futures, just as we were. To the port side, along battleship row, were superstructures of great ships, some canted at a strange angle. The battleships *Nevada, Tennessee, West Virginia, Maryland, Oklahoma,* and *California,* tied there with the *Neosho* and *Vestal,* were principal targets of the Japanese attack. Three torpedoes had hit the *Oklahoma,* which capsized. Dive-bombers had hit the *Maryland, Oklahoma,* and *Nevada.* Bombs had penetrated the deck of the *California* and exploded. The *West Virginia* was sunk. Only the *Nevada* had gotten under way, and the crew had beached her. She had been hit by one torpedo and three bombs. The *Tennessee* had taken two bombs. Debris and damaged ships were everywhere.

Farther on, more damage was in evidence in the dry docks. However, something new and exciting came into view. The great cranes of two of the dry docks were in constant operation, and ships inside the docks were swarming with men. Brilliant flashes of arc welders all along the ships' sides and decks twinkled like a field of stars at night.

Suddenly, there was a feeling of pride: the Fleet was being rebuilt, the damage would be repaired, and those who had wrought this terrible destruction would answer for it. They would never have the opportunity to invade these islands again.

When the boats pulled up at the dock near the seaplane ramps, we could observe that the hangars appeared to be new and ready for occupancy. Some of the squadron planes were parked on the apron. The crew's quarters were new and comfortable. As VP-44 had trained its crews and readied its planes to take up patrol duty on the island, the facilities had been rebuilt and were ready at the time of arrival. VP-44 continued to move toward its destiny.

In the European Theater, on the Russian front, snow, mud, and cold had stalled the German armies. Field Marshal Fedor Von Brock's troops had stormed to within 40 miles of Moscow, but the Russian troops had thrown them back to winter defensive positions. They would resume their attack in May 1942.

In the North African campaign, German and Italian armies were fighting a seesaw campaign with the British troops. In May 1942, General Erwin Rommel's Afrika Korps would begin a campaign to capture Tobruk in Libya and start a dash to Egypt.

Japanese conquests in the Pacific continued. Manila fell to invading Japanese forces, which had also landed in the Netherland East Indies in January 1942. Their forces also took the port of Rabaul, New Britain, and established a powerful naval base there. Bataan was surrendered to the Japanese on 8 April 1942.

In early 1942, Admiral William F. Halsey's task forces, the carrier groups of the *Enterprise* and *Yorktown*, raided the Marshall and Gilbert Islands. The *Enterprise*, Halsey's flagship, took heavy risks and successfully raided the Kwajalein and Roi atolls while part of Admiral Raymond Spruance's covering force attacked the Wotje atoll. The *Enterprise* task force included one oiler, seven destroyers, and the heavy cruisers *Chester, Northhampton*, and *Salt Lake City*. While the *Enterprise* planes attacked Kwajalein, Captain Thomas M. Shock's *Chester* and two destroyers held Taora Island under fire. Admiral Frank Fletcher's *Yorktown* and cover-

ing forces, the second prong of the two-pronged attack group, was kept in an unexposed position while aircraft raids were conducted on the Mili, Jaluit, and Makin atolls.

When the *Enterprise* entered Pearl Harbor on 5 February 1942, battle flags flying, after the raids on the Marshalls and Gilberts, it was met with a wild reception. In contrast, one day after this tumultuous greeting, Admiral Fletcher's *Yorktown* force, which had kept out of harm's way and accomplished very little, entered the harbor without much notice and with ships unscathed.

Halsey had brought back to Pearl Harbor America's first victory of the war. After news accounts of the battle were released, Halsey earned the name "Bull Halsey" and the title of a fighting "American Hero."

On 18 April, one of the most daring raids attempted by any element of the U.S. Armed Forces was launched. Under the command of Lieutenant Colonel James H. Doolittle, 16 North American B-25 Mitchell Army Air Forces bombers sped off the deck of the carrier *Hornet* to bomb Tokyo. The carrier was operating in Admiral Halsey's Task Force 16 and was commanded by Admiral Marc A. Mitscher. One effect of the raid was to reinforce the plans of Admiral Isoroku Yamamoto, who foresaw a strike on Japan, to capture the two islands of the Midway atoll in the central Pacific Ocean.

Chapter 3

Ford Island, Pearl Harbor

FLIGHT patrols that provided surveillance for the oceanic approaches to the Hawaiian Islands became effective when all VP-44 planes and personnel arrived at Ford Island. Regular flight schedules and flight crew assignments set the pattern for flight duty and liberty hours.

The organizational structure for the Scouting Forces in April 1942, comprised of the PBY aircraft based in the Hawaiian Islands, was formed into two groups, designated Patrol Wing One and Patrol Wing Two, which were located at NAS Kaneohe Bay and at the Fleet Air Base, Ford Island, respectively. Patrol Wing One included five squadrons of approximately 12 aircraft each. VP-11 operated the PBY-5 seaplane, and the other four squadrons — VP-12, VP-14, VP-72, and VP-91 — operated the PBY-5a amphibian. In Patrol Wing Two, VP-23 operated the PBY-5 seaplane, and the other three — VP-24, VP-44, and VP51 — operated the PBY-5a amphibian.

The chain of command for squadron comman-

ders was Patrol Wing, Commander Patrol Wings Pacific Fleet, Task Force 9 (Naval Air Base Defense Force), and Commander in Chief of the Pacific Fleet. The chain of command was not as cumbersome as it might first seem. Rear Admiral Patrick Bellinger held the titles of COMPATWING Two, COMPATWINGSPAC, and Com Naval Air Base Defense Force. In addition, Patrol Wing One was administered from Patrol Wing Two.

VP-44 occupied the various maintenance shops and office spaces in the hangar dedicated to the squadron and made them operational. At 7:30 a.m., all officers and men attended muster for orders of the day and calisthenics. Within a few days, the heavy flight patrol schedules and aircraft maintenance schedules became routine. The ordnance, metal, machine, and radio shops were humming with activity.

The younger and more junior officers were becoming experienced pilots and navigators. The aviation pilots continued to make progress and were assuming more advanced positions among the ranks. Julius Cox, Jack Reid, Fredrick Panetto, and Richard Umphrey received commissions in April. Chief Petty Officers Cesare Cavadini, Vinton Pease, and Joel Stoval, with other experienced petty officers, directed the radio shops in maintenance activities and training for the younger and less experienced radio personnel. Likewise, training and advancements continued in Chief Petty Officer Arcia Turner's ordnance group and in other groups throughout the full range of the squadron's flight, maintenance, and support activities. Kenneth H. McCardle, squadron leading chief, became much better known and well liked for his handling of squadron matters. We men of the FAW school group then held ratings of petty officer 3rd class.

During and preceding spring 1942, the U.S. Fleet Aircraft Scouting Force, Patrol Squadrons, carried a full ship's complement of personnel including staff support, medical, maintenance, storekeeper (SK), and mess attendants (Matts). (In addition to seagoing vessels, land bases and aircraft squadrons were commissioned as "ships," and all personnel were referred to as ship's company.) Senior officers included Lieutenant Commander R. C. Brixner commanding, Lieutenant W. L. Richards as executive officer, and Lieutenant Donald G. Gumz. Junior officers were Lieutenants (jg) C. E. Olson, R. L. Summers, R. S. Whitman, and J. E. Cox. Forty officers held the rank of ensign for a total of 48 officers. The enlisted personnel included 176 petty officers, of which 20 were chief petty officers and 8 were naval aviation pilots. There were 68 seamen and 64 seamen apprentices and seamen recruits, or apprentice seamen. The grand total strength of the squadron was 356 officers and crew, representing a cross section of America's middle and upper middle class, from most of the states. First and second flight crews contained a mix of experienced and inexperienced personnel for training purposes. (Normally, first flight crews were made up of more experienced personnel and usual-

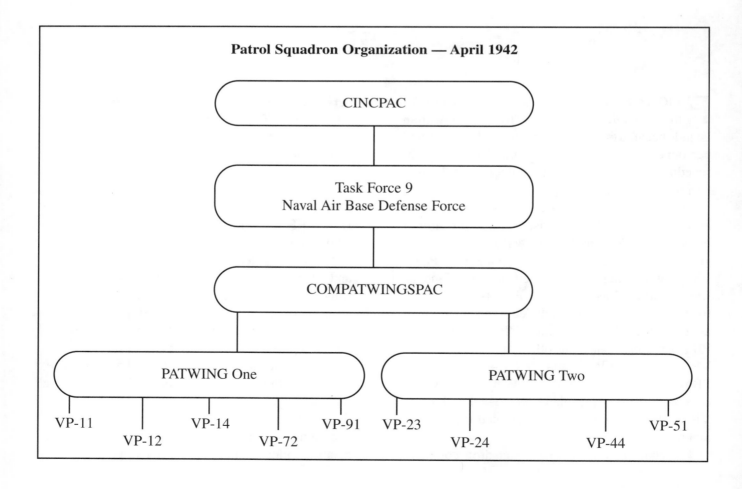

Patrol Squadron Organization — April 1942

CINCPAC

Task Force 9
Naval Air Base Defense Force

COMPATWINGSPAC

PATWING One

PATWING Two

VP-11   VP-12   VP-14   VP-72   VP-91   VP-23   VP-24   VP-44   VP-51

At Waikiki, April 1942. Left to right: Cliff Troland, Jim Mills, and Reid Wilson. (Reid Wilson)

ly flew patrol missions, while second flight crews were made up of less experienced personnel and served as alternates.) Work schedules soon established a routine that provided two days on standby and maintenance, one day on patrol, and one day liberty.

At one end of Waikiki Beach were its two hotels, the Royal Hawaiian and the Ala Moana, and open beach extended from the hotels to Diamond Head at the other end. Swimming at Waikiki, occasionally a lunch or dinner, and sightseeing were popular activities. The men seemed to be well groomed at all times. Most of the barbers in Honolulu were young and pretty Chinese and Japanese women and provided a welcome change from the ship's service barber shops.

Quickly, the days fell into a busy but pleasant routine. Those on the maintenance schedules could observe the activities in the harbor. It was a special thrill when one of the ships that had been badly damaged or sunk in the 7 December raid made its way past Ford Island for the States and further repairs. There was more excitement when ships or submarines entered the harbor, especially when flying the battle flag. We could hear the welcoming bands playing at the dock when they tied up.

When the *Saratoga* came in, it was clear that she was in bad shape. There was a mighty list to port side and a huge weight hanging from the flight deck midway to the waterline. A large hole appeared in her starboard side and just below the normal waterline when upright. All hands on her flight and lower decks were at the rail and at attention, her band was playing, and the battle flag was flying from the mast. It was an impressive sight.

Debris from the 7 December raid was deposited along the shoreline of Ford Island. Among the wreckage were parts of Japanese aircraft that were attractive to souvenir hunters. Many of the spark plugs found in the engines of the wrecked Japanese planes carried markings of U.S. manufacturers. Others carried Japanese markings that added to their value as souvenirs.

An electrical junction box from a Japanese plane was found. We were astounded to discover that the wiring was several times larger than the required diameter to carry any of the possible electrical currents necessary for aircraft meant to operate off an aircraft carrier. The engine mounts were designed specifically to the dimensions for an American Pratt and Whitney engine. It was very easy to develop a strong desire for revenge just by examining these parts and then glimpsing up to observe the destruction in the harbor that the Japanese planes had wrought.

McCardle shattered the calm during muster in early May 1942. He announced that the squadron would prepare immediately for advanced base duty, training under adverse conditions to prepare personnel for operations under difficult circumstances. McCardle gave the orders for packing personal gear and departure following Lieutenant Commander Brixner's reading of the advanced base orders. "Current patrol and maintenance schedules are to be maintained. Six-plane sections will be rotated to the advanced base to complete the training," the orders read.

The first detachment of six planes departed Ford Island at noon on 8 May. It was a short flight to the base known as Barbers Point, Ewa, Oahu. On landing, the planes parked in a clearing near the airstrip. The assigned barracks were two clusters of eight-man tents for the officers and crew.

That afternoon, some of us who were free toured the area and found that the term "advanced base" was appropriate. First, the location was on the leeward side of the island with no cooling sea breeze. It was hot with high humidity, which made life miserable. In addition, there were swarms of mosquitoes everywhere. On a tour through the brush we found that to move or shake one of the bushes was to stir up additional millions of the miserable insects. They were ravenous. The terrain appeared to be composed of lava rocks and bushes that, in appearance, were similar to the mesquite of West Texas. We sighted several of the large Hawaiian mongoose.

If daylight hours were miserable, nighttime was torture. It was hot both day and night. The tents were large and clean with netting sides, but it was impossible to get the mosquitoes out of it. Sleeping cots had mosquito nets around them, but to get into the cots, it was necessary first to drive out the mosquitoes. Next, you had to expel those that came in with you. Last, the netting had to be tucked under the edge of the mattress to keep the pests out. To leave a knee or elbow against the netting at night was to have it eaten raw.

Lieutenant (jg) C. E. Olson ordered watches posted for the planes at night. To stand watch at night outside the aircraft, it was necessary to wrap a towel around the head and neck and wear a jacket and gloves. Some sentries tried standing watch from inside the aircraft. To do that, they had to use a "bug bomb" (insect spray) and then open one of the aircraft hatches to breathe the outside air. The temperature inside the planes was insufferably hot. Within a few minutes, it filled with mosquitoes again and the spraying process needed repeating.

To say that there was some grumbling about conditions would be a monumental understatement. At muster on the third morning, Ensign J. M. Scott, personnel officer, noted that the continuous night-long complaining and cursing did not reflect well on the squadron. He acknowledged that conditions

were not the best but asked that the profanity be reduced. Most of the crew tried, but it was not easy to distinguish any reduction in verbal abuse directed against the noxious insects.

Patrol flights continued from Barbers Point. Flight duty was much sought after. It was an opportunity to get aloft, out of the oppressive heat and away from the insects, and to be able to breathe freely.

Suddenly, on 15 May, orders at the daily muster came to pack personal gear and leave at 8:30 a.m. It was a happy departure as each of our six planes lifted off the runway for Ford Island, leaving behind a mosquito-filled dust cloud. That evening, we of the incoming crews discussed some of the experiences with those who were going out the following morning. At first, the new crews were led to believe that they were headed for a wonderful experience. The truth came out, however, and they learned that ahead of them lay one of the most miserable experiences of their lives. But the time we spent at Barbers Point did lead to new perspectives, for each man seemed to feel he was in a better position to take on whatever tasks might lie ahead.

At the regular morning muster at Ford Island on 19 May, Lieutenant Commander Brixner announced that the squadron would stand by for further orders. The news was electrifying, for we sensed we were going into a battle zone. "Flight crews will be posted," he announced. "All personal gear will be packed and ready to go. All matters pertaining to squadron movements are classified secret and are to be treated accordingly," he continued. "All shore leave canceled immediately." Chief McCardle read the orders of the day for the crew, and all hands were dismissed. The next muster was set for 1:00 p.m.

It was clear that the advanced base exercises had not been without purpose — but what was it? That was the question in the minds of both officers and crews. There was suddenly a new sense of determination, an exhilarating feeling of anticipation, and more importantly, a new feeling of confidence. With the advanced base experience, everyone seemed to feel that whatever mission was assigned to the squadron and whatever conditions it imposed, it could be handled with ease. Would there be an opportunity for combat? Where would it be?

USS *St. Louis* (CL-49), Mare Island Navy Yard, 6 March 1942. (National Archives)

These questions lingered only briefly. Personal gear and the aircraft spare parts needed packing.

At the 1:00 p.m. muster, orders were to complete preparation for departure. Three musters were held on the following day. At the conclusion of each one, McCardle's words were, "Stand by to stand by to stand by." The phrase "stand by" was added in repetition on each of the following days and at each muster.

Chapter 4

USS
St. Louis

THERE was a determined look on the faces of the officers and men who boarded the motor whaleboats at the Ford Island dock on the afternoon of the squadron's departure, 22 May 1942. There was not much talking other than Chief McCardle's few brief orders. Each man, as he stepped onto a boat, had his own thoughts about the future. They shared a feeling of anticipation and excitement along with a grim conviction to "see this one out." Uppermost in the thoughts of all were questions on the nature of the new mission and the squadron's destiny.

As the line of motor whaleboats plowed through the waters of Pearl Harbor, the sailors looked at the ships and docks. They unconsciously compared what they saw with the scenes they had viewed when they had first entered the harbor little more than a month before. There had been many changes, and more were occurring daily. Several moments of silence were observed as the boats filed past the battleship *Arizona*, oil slicks still rising from her as she lay silently on her side.

Excitement began to mount as the whaleboats turned into berth C-4 where a mighty cruiser was tied up. The excitement heightened as someone said "the cruiser *St. Louis*."

Most of us "aviation sailors" (commonly referred to as "Airedales") had never served on or even boarded a man-of-war surface vessel, and particularly one of such grandeur. It is one thing to see such a ship from the pier or passing through the harbor, but to see it from the waterline, at the ladder, is awesome. The ship became even more impressive as we climbed the ladder and saluted the colors and officer of the deck. A quick glance from the bow to the stern made the statement that here was an entirely new and different world and a seat of power of the oceans.

A yeoman (Y) with Chief McCardle checked each man off a list as we boarded, while other members of the ship's company logged each of us on board. We stood by until all hands boarded and then filed along the superstructure and assembled near one of the mighty gun turrets at the stern of the ship. At muster, a bosun mate (BM) issued life jackets and escorted us through a deck hatch and down a ladder to assigned quarters. Little was left of daylight hours after boarding and adjusting to the new surroundings.

Another group of military personnel started streaming aboard: Marines were carrying huge packs of personal gear and fighting equipment and lugging cases of ball ammunition. From their appearance, we surmised that there was the possibility of ground fighting, which heightened speculation as to the location of our squadron's destination.

Evening chow was a new experience, but the food was good aboard the ship. In short order, everyone had turned in with the visions of the day's sights and anticipation of coming assignments. Later, there was the unaccustomed feel of motion and then the throb of the ship's mighty engines and subtle feel of the screws pushing her. The USS *St. Louis* (CL-49) escorted by the destroyer *Case* (DD-370) set out late that evening.

Squadron VP-44 at that time had approximately 55 percent of the earlier personnel complement. First flight crews were either en route to or at their destination, and the rest were at sea, heading to the same location.

Seventy-eight men of VP-44 had boarded the *St. Louis*. The five officers included Ensigns C. J. Bachtel, G. H. Hardeman, J. M. Scott, R. R. Sparks, and R. C. Trejo. There were 6 mess attendants, 12 seamen apprentices, 10 seamen, 40 petty officers, and 5 chief petty officers. Many of the seamen and some of the petty officers had been dropped from the rolls. The reduced force seemed indicative that less emphasis was to be placed on training and more on action. With the plane crews, the squadron strength was at about 200 officers and enlisted men, which did not include those temporarily in sick bay at Pearl Harbor and gunnery school at Kaneohe Bay. Among the sick were ARM3c Reid Wilson, who had a serious throat infection, and AMM2c Loren Judas, who had been wounded during gunnery practice.

Sleep came fast and sound that first night on board but was shattered shortly after it started, or so it seemed. A call to general quarters sent us tumbling out of bunks, quickly dressing and stumbling up the ladder to attention on the deck.

"My God," I thought, "under attack before arriving." But we learned that general quarters was always called during the early and late daylight hours. The squadron stood at ease and watched as the sun rose from the sea into a cloudless sky. Seeing the morning unfold from our perspective on deck, near the gun turret with its mighty artillery overhead, was an experience not to be forgotten.

The Marines who had boarded with us were also at ease on the ship's fantail near the launch rail and crane that launched the ship's scouting and observation plane. After sunup, chow was served, and then a pleasant surprise came as the bosun's whistle sounded and he announced a muster for Squadron VP-44 personnel.

For once, the fellows eagerly scrambled topside and into formation. It suddenly occurred to us that we would learn about our destination. Present at muster were five officers of VP-44, an officer whom we had never met, and 68 enlisted personnel. Chief McCardle called the group to attention and saluted the officer in charge, Lieutenant (jg) W. L. M. Snead, A-V(S) USNR, and gave the muster report. The officer was not a member of the squadron and apparently was serving as an escort for the detachment on the ship. Snead took an envelope from his jacket pocket and read the orders. The aircraft departures for VP-44 planes had been given with orders for radio silence, and orders for the aircraft crews were to be read when they were airborne. As it turns out, six planes of the squadron had left Ford Island the previous day, 22 May, for their then-unknown destination, and the remaining six were leaving that day, 23 May. The ground detachment was to board the *St. Louis*, which we had done, for transport to the same destination. The squadron would report to the commanding officer at Midway Islands for an extended period to conduct patrols from that location. The news pleased everyone. The general feeling was that conditions on Midway could never be as bad as on Barbers Point.

The next two days were agreeable for squadron personnel. There were no duties except for muster at general quarters morning and evening. The food was good, the ship was neat and clean, and the ship's crew was pleasant, though we seldom saw them because they were busy at their duties. The daily pattern followed during daylight hours was a visit with the Marines of C and D Company of the 2nd Raider Battalion, Carlson's Raiders, at the ship's fantail.

The Fleet Air Wing school group had maintained its identity and enjoyed the camaraderie established from boot camp and the FAW school. All of us were assigned to positions in second flight crews and were becoming adept at our specialty ratings and at gunnery with the .30- and .50-caliber machine guns. For the first time in many months, we were free for a while and could visit and recount our Navy and civilian life experiences. Many threads in the fabric of camaraderie of the group were woven during the voyage.

Talking with the Marines during the morning hours after battle stations was immediately a favorite pasttime. They had many stories to tell. Their training in fighting, particularly night fighting, fascinated us sailors. They were adept with knives, weighted piano wires, chains, chokers, and, of course, the guns they carried. One of them in particular, Old Red, was a great talker.

The afternoons were also pleasant for several of the FAW group who gathered forward and lounged underneath the great gun turret. We exchanged stories from the cities, towns, and farms across America. The top of the gun turret and the long gun barrels formed the top frame of a view of the ocean. The long curvilinear bow of the ship formed the bottom of the frame. The long bow slowly rose to point at the white fleecy clouds above. It then slowly lowered toward the bottom of the trough of the sea as the ship rode the long swells of the ocean surface. The rhythmic throb of the engines and propeller would change predictably as the course of the ship altered to form a zigzag pattern toward Midway Islands.

These were not strange waters to the sailors. Our surveillance patrols had frequently taken us along the Hawaiian Island chains and atolls of Gardner Pinnacles, French Frigate Shoals, and others, but never as far west as Midway. The feeling was that every flying fish in this part of the ocean had been counted hundreds of times, but this was the first time to observe them at sea level.

On early 25 May, word was that the ship would dock at Midway. All personal gear was carried topside for prompt debarking. The sailors of VP-44 and the Marines of Carlson's Raiders were having their last visit aboard the USS *St. Louis* when we sighted land that morning. Old Red was in top form. There was a case of .30-caliber ball ammunition at his side as he sat on his pack telling us stories of the Marines. A ship's bosun came by, looked at the ammunition, and told Red, "You better get that gear below deck."

Old Red looked at the sailor and said, "By God, the major told me to bring that up, I worked like hell to do it, and nobody but the major tells me to take it back." He then stood, walked to the ship's rail, and spat a big wad of tobacco juice into the ocean.

The thoughtful bosun gave a good-natured grin that turned into a large smile and said, "Sure," and walked away.

We would later learn of the 2nd Battalion raid on Wake and Tarawa Islands. The Raiders went ashore from submarines, attacked the island installations, and then re-boarded the submarines. Old Red was wounded while in the brush going in. He lay there while his buddies conducted the raid.

They picked him up on their way out. His flesh had separated from his chest and lay on his stomach. While he was alone in the brush, Red had spit tobacco juice on his chest, then folded the skin back in place and tied it down. Reportedly, he completely recovered in three weeks and was ready to go again.

The presence of the Raider Battalion on board had seemed to be an indication that ground fighting on Midway was a possibility. That possibility seemed to be a serious omen as the small coral atoll came into full view. If it came to ground combat on the two little islands, every one of the squadron sailors wanted to be either airborne or in the near vicinity of the Raiders. The aviation personnel of the Fleet Air Wings were not issued side arms or rifles. Depth charges, bombs, torpedoes, and .30- and .50-caliber airborne machine guns were our only weapons.

Chapter 5

Midway Islands

25 May 1942 — Dig In on Eastern Island

THE deck of the USS *St. Louis* provided a vantage point to view the Midway atoll. A large circular coral reef enclosed a lagoon with two small islands at the southern part. Large breakers formed off the southern reef, grew larger as they approached the reef, and then crashed over the jagged coral heads. The frothy white seawaters then rushed madly toward the sandy beach of the easternmost island, gradually losing strength. The waters gently slid up the sand only to recede and flow smoothly back toward the reef until the next huge breaker crashed and the process repeated.

The entrance to the lagoon was through a natural break in the center of the reef, along the southern boundary, called Brooks Channel. The *St. Louis* moved slowly through the channel heading north with Eastern Island just off the starboard side and Sand Island just off the port side. In short order, the ship tied up at the pier, and VP-44 personnel debarked with their personal gear and assembled on the dock. Next, small boats arrived and the squad-

ron boarded for the short trip, across the channel, to Eastern Island.

From the channel, Eastern Island appeared low and flat with a control tower and a few buildings along the northern shore. At the eastern end, there were some large sandbagged bunkers. Along the runway were many coral sand aircraft revetments, particularly along the lagoon side that was the northern shore of the island. The airstrip control tower and all buildings were also located along the northern shoreline.

Three aircraft runways were the central feature of Eastern Island. The two long runways crossed near the center of the island. For a takeoff in the westerly direction, these runways appeared to have a heading of approximately 225 and 260 degrees, respectively. The third runway, the shortest of the three, had a heading of about 315 degrees for takeoff in the northerly direction. It crossed the other two near their eastern ends. Packed coral made an excellent surface.

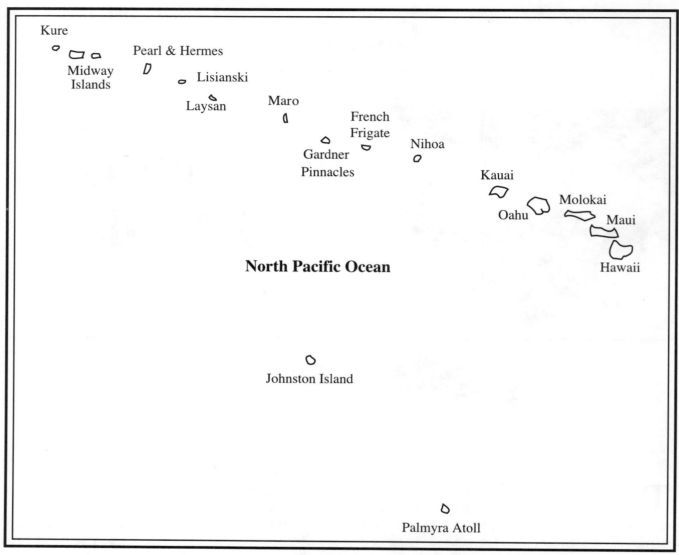

Hawaiian Islands.

Sand Island seemed appropriately named. It was hilly rather than flat, and the hills appeared to be sand dunes. There was a seaplane ramp and aircraft hangars. Several buildings that looked like they housed the island's military industrial activities were located along the southern and eastern shore. Barracks, mess hall, and administrative buildings occupied the central part of the island. Trees and bushes covered the northern shoreline.

Shortly after landing on the dock at Eastern Island, a muster was called and orders were issued for drawing supplies and setting up living quarters.

Food was served from the Marine Corps mess hall located near the small control tower. Four-man tents with cots and mattresses were issued from the Marine supply building near the tower.

Midway had been developed as a Navy base, and a full complement of sailors was stationed there. In addition, Marine fighter and bomber squadrons and a Marine company that manned the antiaircraft batteries made up the permanent station personnel. They had been on Midway for many months.

Four of us from the Fleet Air Wing radio school — Clifford V. "Cliff" Troland, Edwin L. Olsen,

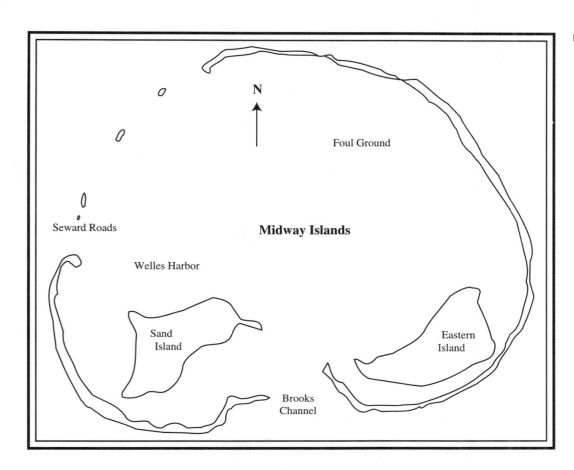

Midway Atoll.

Sherman J. "Earthquake" Moore, and myself — elected to bunk together. We decided to explore the island before picking out a place to set up a tent.

The southern shoreline of Eastern Island appeared to be more attractive. On the northern side was the mess hall and a post exchange operated by the Marines. Along the north-south runway and eastern side of the island were the large sandbagged bunkers that housed the Marine Corps Command Post. Just south of the long runway and near the crossing with the short runway was a large coral sand revetment containing an abandoned SB2U Vindicator aircraft — a scouting bomber — that appeared to be out of commission and beyond repair. West of the revetment was an area clear of brush. Other than this one revetment, there appeared to be no development along the southern boundary of the airstrip.

It was there in the clearing, near the revetment, that we decided to erect our tent and set up quarters. Hundreds of birds, at first glance, appeared to be the only occupants of that side of the island. The

southern shoreline seemed less than 75 yards away and the reef beyond about 50 yards more.

By the time gear was checked out and the tent set up, it was near the end of the day. Driving tent pegs in hard coral rock proved difficult, but the effort was worthwhile. We set up a comfortable tent with two cots along the back and one on each side with plenty of room for seabags and personal gear.

A Coleman gas lantern was hanging on the tent center pole, and the tent opening faced south toward the reef and crashing breakers. The coral sand was clean. Shaking clothing and bedding outside the tent freed it of the sand. That night we went to sleep with the sound of the great breakers crashing over the shallow reef. The rush of the waters rolling to the shoreline followed.

The next morning, Ensign Scott ordered all hands to build a good and secure slit trench for protection from enemy attack. The trench was to be built in a zigzag pattern so that only one person would be hit in the event of strafing. He also informed us that there was some certainty that a

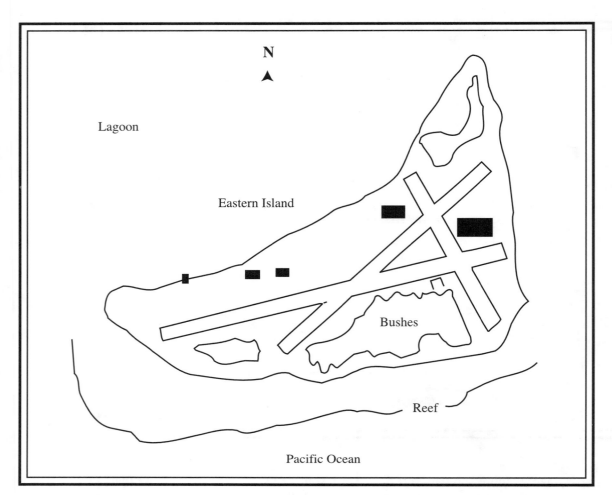

Midway — Eastern Island.

Japanese fleet was bearing on our location and was expected to invade Midway, the Aleutian Islands, or the Hawaiian Islands.

Because the hard coral rock was almost impossible to dig with small hand tools, we decided to build the trench in the small clearing between our tent and the bushes. The design selected was a double row of sandbags built from the surface of the ground up rather than a dug-out trench. It formed an elongated "Z" with a covering of sandbags; entrances were on the top at each end of the center section. Two people could go in at each entrance, one to the end and one to the center section. Filling the burlap bags with the packed coral was not practical, but it was easy to shovel the loose coral sand from the edge of the revetment. When the walls were completed, the trench appeared to be indestructible. Nevertheless, we elected to build a cover over it. We obtained 6 x 6 and 2 x 4 timbers

to construct a frame for the cover. The 2 x 4 timbers were placed crosswise along the top of the trench and the large timber along its center length.

The large timber was cut into three pieces to fit along the two end sections and the center section of the "Z." Two rows of sandbags were placed along the top, with one end of the bags on the large timber and the other end on the top of the sandbag walls. When the trench was finished, we considered it a masterpiece and believed it would survive anything other than a direct hit.

The first flight crews were flying regularly, which meant that those of us who came to Midway on the *St. Louis* had very light duty. We who were not flying usually got out early to watch the other crews assemble, warm up the aircraft, and take off. When the last PBY cleared the field, we had breakfast at the Marine Corps mess hall. There was some discretionary time until the flights returned that afternoon, and most of the ground personnel were always on hand along the parking areas to see them come in.

26 May 1942 — A Field of Bombs

Our FAW radio group had some free time on our second day at Eastern Island, 26 May, to walk around the area and become more familiar with it and to observe the population of birds. To our dismay, we learned that the brush-covered area that ran along the southern side of the island was one of the world's largest bomb dumps. There were five-feet-high stacks of 500-pound bombs, almost as tall as the bushes; another pile of bombs was within 50 feet of our tent. After some consultation, we decided to leave the tent and slit trench where they were. If the bomb dump ignited, most of the island would be blown up with it anyway.

But the bushes along the southern side also contained most of the island's small birds along with a share of the albatross, or gooney birds, which covered the island by the thousands. The huge birds were fun to observe as they were great clowns, and they had little or no fear of people. Beautiful little birds lived in the bushes alongside the slit trench. They had red beaks and white feathers with black bands around the lower part of their necks. They chirped incessantly with a light musical sound and became fast friends with the new residents of the tent next door. They were called "Chinese love birds," which seemed to suit them. It quickly became a routine each day to sit for a while on the slit trench and watch and listen to them. They never took any of the food from the mess hall offered to them.

With the living quarters and trench completed, our four-man radio group decided to build a machine-gun emplacement in the clearing in front of the tent. Determined to make a pit, we checked out a pick and shovel. After a full day's labor, we had a hole two feet deep. We ringed the hole with a double row of sandbags three feet high. A large timber installed vertically provided a mount for the gun. When the gun pit was completed, Ensign Scott came by to inspect the installation. He believed it to be an excellent gun emplacement but could only wish us good luck on finding a gun. No such luck happened.

Ensign Scott advised that Navy headquarters fully expected the Japanese invasion forces to strike Alaska, Midway, or Midway and the Hawaiian Islands simultaneously during the first week of June. When asked if there were supporting elements of the U.S. Fleet deployed to meet the threat, Scott replied honestly, "I don't know. Midway may or may not be on its own. We need to be in a position to prepare ourselves and make the best defense possible."

To our relief, some reinforcements were coming in. On 29 May 1942, four sleek B-26 Army Air Forces bombers landed — Martin Marauders, each with a Navy Mark IV torpedo. They were new to the VP-44 sailors but looked as though they could do the job. Eight more PBY-5s of VP-23 also came in and landed in the lagoon. Under their wings, each carried a torpedo. A buildup was under way.

30 May 1942 — Dogfights

Eight lumbering Army B-17 Flying Fortresses landed on Eastern Island on 30 May as additional reinforcements. They appeared to us sailors to be as awkward as the PBYs, and with the PBYs they took most of the parking space alongside the landing strip. The bombers could be used for search, but they appeared to be no more effective than the PBY when deployed against attacking surface vessels. High-altitude bombing against surface vessels with these planes did not seem to be practical.

The aircraft of VP-44 and VP-23 were by then all flying long daily patrols to an arc of 700 miles to

Approximate Distance and Bearing Relative to Midway		
Name	Bearing (degrees)	Distance (miles)
Kure Island	284	60
Wake Island	253	1,181
Tokyo, Japan	295	2,565
Pearl & Hermes Reef	104	100
Lisianski	119	314
French Frigate Shoals	112	765
Pearl Harbor, Oahu	107	1,301
San Francisco, CA	63	3,202

the north, around to the west, and to the south. First flight crews were manning most of the flights; secondary crews were filling in on flights when needed. Midmorning on 30 May, Midway received contact reports from two PBYs. Each of the patrol planes had encountered and engaged Mitsubishi bombers. The Japanese planes were land-based twin-engine bombers that were assumed to be operating off Wake Island.

At 9:50 a.m., Patrol Plane Commander (PPC) Lieutenant Forest A. Roby and crew — Ensign Robert B. Felmuth, Ensign Harry A. Sorenson, Samuel R. Wideberg AP1c (NAP — Naval Aviation Pilot), Wilbur V. Lamson AMM1c, Anthony R. Fornataro AMM2c, R. D. Scott AMM3c, John W. Griffith ARM1c, J. F. Morrison RM3c (Radio Mate), and Clifford A. Olin AOM3c — were patrolling in plane number 44-P-10 at 800 feet in a cloudless sky. "Plane closing fast on the port quarter," came a report from Anthony Fornataro in the port blister.

Sam Wideberg, who operated the twin .30s in the bow, reported that the bomber, a type also identified as a Betty, came upon them from the starboard quarter and passed close by the waist gunner while looking them over, bringing all his guns to bear. The waist gunner did not fire, although he had his sights dead on.

Wideberg, however, did not wait for orders to shoot. As the Japanese bomber pulled up forward into his field of fire and he recognized the big red "meatball" on the fuselage, he cut loose with the twin .30s. Experiencing a searing pain across his chest and stomach, Sam thought he was hit, but as he felt with his hand to determine where he was wounded, he found no blood. Instead, his chest and upper bare stomach were swelling with burn blisters from the hot brass shells of the machine gun.

From that point, the dogfight continued for about 30 minutes with the bomber making attack runs and the PBY taking evasive action. Roby was mindful of the 20-mm cannon the Betty carried and did an excellent job of staying clear of it.

At 10:05 a.m., the lookout in the port waist of 44-P-3 reported an aircraft at about five miles on the port quarter. Flying with PPC Lieutenant (jg) R. B. Hays that morning were Ensign W. E. Headly, Ensign P. W. Vannoy, Clifford A. Adams AP1c

(NAP), F. O. Scofield AMM1c, R. A. Lux AMM2c, Francis E. Ford AMM3c, Richard E. Brandt ARM1c, D. D. Capps RM3c, and George W. Newcombe AOM3c.

Hays took a defensive position at low altitude while the plane, identified as Japanese, closed in to about 150 yards, firing its 7.7-mm machine gun. The enemy stayed abeam the PBY so that only one American gun could bear on him. The .50-caliber gun in the PBY's port waist hatch fired one canister, 60 rounds, at him on the attack. Some of the tracers were seen entering the nose of the enemy plane.

Following that first attack, the Mitsubishi kept a greater distance. He climbed to about 300 feet and made a series of turns, apparently trying to bring tail guns to bear. Bob Hays used defensive skidding turns at low altitude. The Mitsubishi had a speed advantage, giving him the initiative. After the first attack, he never came within the PBY's machine-gun range.

Nevertheless, first blood was drawn at Midway: Machinist Ford was wounded, though not seriously. Hays's plane collected three hits in the starboard gas tank, one in a control cable, and several in the wings, tail, and hull.

In the early afternoon, 44-P-3 came in and parked on Eastern. Ford was treated on the spot and then taken to the hospital for further examination. A short time later, 44-P-10 came into the pattern for a straight-in approach landing. She was clearly in trouble; the propeller on one engine was feathered. But the plane made a clean landing and taxied into a parking position.

Bullet holes are never easy to count with great accuracy on a large plane. The average of several quick counts yielded 175 holes in the wings, engines, propellers, hull, and tail. One bullet had hit a cylinder of one engine, causing the engine failure. Oil from the engine had streamed off the wing.

The crew of 44-P-10 had used 400 rounds of .30-caliber and 300 rounds of .50-caliber ammunition. The plane was declared unfit for service but could be patched up and sent back to Ford Island for overhaul. Amazingly, none of the crew was injured.

31 May 1942 — Determination

Another B-17 Flying Fortress from Oahu landed

on Eastern Island carrying ammunition for VP-44 on 31 May. It was clear to everyone that an invasion of Oahu was likely and imminent. If taking Oahu was the objective of the Japanese force, then Midway would not be bypassed. If Alaska was the objective, then only a feint toward Midway was a possibility.

The PBY patrols were flown by the first flight crews, who had flown the planes to Eastern. They were fortunate because they were busy. For the maintenance and second flight crews, the daylight hours passed slowly. There was time to observe the daily activities on the airstrip and for meditation on the possible consequences of the upcoming battle.

If an invasion force approached Midway, one or more of the patrol planes would spot it. In that event, a tragic outcome for the plane and crew was a possibility. Only luck and good judgment could help them get out a contact radio message and avoid an engagement.

If an attack and invasion force hit the island, then the outcome could be disastrous for the offensive and defensive air crews and ground personnel. A massive force, such as the one that had struck at Pearl Harbor, Hickam Field, and Kaneohe Bay, would surely be victorious in an invasion attempt.

Determined though they might be, the forces at Midway would never be able to do more than momentarily slow a large power bent on taking the little atoll. The Marine pilots of the fighters and bombers would fight to the death. The PBY crews would locate invasion forces and then take any possible offensive action. And we sailors believed that the Army B-17 force would also take any offensive action possible. However, because high-altitude bombing in the B-17 or the PBY did not seem to be practical against fast-moving surface vessels, the small force of B-26 bombers equipped with torpedoes appeared to be the best support for the Marine forces.

These thoughts crossed our minds, as well as thoughts about our individual prospects. I believe that each person considered the way that he would like to handle the situation in the final end game. Certainly, most felt that this was the occasion for which they had trained.

From all appearances, each man, whatever his duties, was determined to do everything possible to prepare while remaining cheerful and resolute. It is likely that no one on Midway was willing to consider being taken alive. It is also likely that every man felt he must make a fight of it, with bare hands if necessary, in the final moments of his individual part of the action.

Reinforcements continued to arrive. The latest to touch down and park along the crowded airstrip on Eastern consisted of nine additional B-17 Flying Fortresses.

1 June 1942 — More Contacts

Occasionally, extra hands were needed on the patrol flights. It was my good fortune to be selected from the volunteers for the crew of 44-P-7, flown by Ensign Richard Umphrey, on 1 June. Two of the patrols, 44-P-6 and 44-P-7, were destined to engage enemy bombers on that day.

Flying with PPC Ensign J. J. "Jiggs" Lyons on 44-P-6 on the morning of 1 June were Ensign George W. Hanthorn, Ensign Fredrick S. Panetto, Ensign Frank H. Jarrel, Dean A. Ferbrache AMM1c, Zygmunt F. Zydak AMM2c, Richard G. Watson AMM2c, Charles F. Buchanan AMM2c, Leo G. Black ARM2c, and George W. Grove Sea2c (volunteer).

At 9:40 a.m., a twin-engine land-based Japanese bomber tried to make a surprise attack by coming up from the port quarter on 44-P-6. On that first pass, the PBY's port .50-caliber gun was inoperative, but the bow guns did have an opportunity to return fire. Using the superior speed advantage, the enemy made one pass over the seaplane and dropped five 100-pound bombs. Fortunately, none of them hit their target. The twin-engine bomber made 11 additional passes from the port and starboard quarter. When he learned that the port .50-caliber gun was inoperative, he made all passes from that position. The crew then moved the .30-caliber gun from the tunnel hatch and placed it in the port waist. On the twelfth run, the little .30-caliber fired about 50 more rounds. With that pass, the enemy broke off and Lyons made it to cloud cover. His crew had used over 300 rounds of ammunition.

One man was injured. George Grove had been hit in the stomach by shrapnel from the CO_2 bottle in his life jacket, which had been hit by a 7.7-mm bullet.

At 10:30 a.m., Ensign Richard Umphrey, flying 44-P-7, sighted a twin-engine land-based bomber dead ahead, bearing directly on him. He hit the Klaxon horn and took evasive action by diving. The crew — Ensign Russel W. Neil, Ensign Robert R. Sparks, Mathias J. Vopatek CAP (Chief Aviaion Pilot) (NAP), Edward E. Garner AMM1c, Conrad E. Smith AMM2c, Edward C. Roark AMM3c, James A. Fielder ARM1c, George B. Johnson Sea2c, and myself — were ready. As the bomber, with its red meatball, flashed past, both bow guns and the waist gun got off good bursts at him. The bomber then made an approach from below and rear and another parallel to bring his waist guns to bear.

When the Klaxon had sounded battle stations, I was on radio watch. Ensign Robert Sparks, navigator, gave me a precoded message to send out. I sent the message, a contact report, and received an acknowledgment from the Midway radio operator. I realized later that the message was the first I had transmitted from a PBY, except for training work. The message was sent out during wartime and in the heat of battle. The long hours of training had paid off, for the radio contact work went smoothly.

After closing with the Midway operator, I had an opportunity to follow the action. Watching the pilots made it possible to tell where the attacking plane was located. Each time Umphrey looked back and left and then turned into the attacker, our guns started firing. There is a great deal of comfort in the sound of your guns when you are under attack.

When Jiggs Lyons, in 44-P-6, broke out of cloud cover at 10:25, he saw our Catalina under attack. He immediately headed for the fight, and his crew was able to bring the bow guns and the starboard waist gun to bear on the target. They used an additional 100 rounds on this engagement. With that, the enemy bomber broke off the fight with our plane, 44-P-7, and left the area. Dick Umphrey estimated that our crew had made 50 hits each with the .30- and .50-caliber guns. We used 320 rounds of ammunition.

In the early afternoon, our two PBYs came in for landing on Eastern. Umphrey reported only two holes in the forward part of the hull; Lyons reported five holes in the structural part of the plane. Together, the two planes had fired over 600 rounds of ammunition. The PBY aircraft and their crews had acquitted themselves very well in spite of a firepower and two-to-one speed disadvantage.

When 44-P-6 landed, an ambulance pulled up alongside the plane. Two hospital corpsmen went aboard. They came out with a stretcher bearing George Grove.

"Hey gunner," Cliff Troland shouted, "what did they do to you?"

"Well," Grove replied, "I was using this .50-caliber here and the CO_2 bottle in my life jacket exploded. I guess you could say that I got hit by my life jacket." From that day forward, George Grove was known in the squadron as Gunner Grove.

While our two PBYs had been engaged with the enemy, two flights of three Navy TBF-1 torpedo planes each had come into the landing pattern at Eastern Island. They were a welcome sight. These six carrier-based planes taxied into position along the airstrip. Additional PBYs from a Kaneohe-based squadron also came in and taxied into a parking space, ready to take up flight patrol assignments. Four damaged PBYs were returning to Ford Island for repairs.

The VP-44 crews had an opportunity to become acquainted with their counterparts in the Army Air Forces, who had arrived on Midway only days before. One of the Army gunners showed CPO Francis Musser, of Ensign Jack Reid's crew, their ammunition for the .50-caliber machine guns. It was identified by a blue color at the nose tip and was designed to explode upon impact. Musser and the ordnance man placed some of the rounds at strategic locations in the ammunition belts of their .50-caliber guns in the PBY.

At this time, the airstrip on Eastern Island was not the only location bearing heavy traffic. During the previous few days, the traffic in the harbor at Sand Island also had been heavy. We learned that additional supplies of aviation gasoline had been delivered. That was good news, because a large supply of gasoline had been accidentally ignited and lost weeks earlier. With the B-17s flying frequently and PBYs flying long patrols, huge quantities of fuel were gulped every day. There was some concern that the fuel supplies would not last through the battle if there was to be one.

A Navy Douglas R4D transport plane landed on

Crew of VP-44, plane 44-P-4, 6 June 1942. Top row, left to right: R. J. Derouin, Francis Musser, Gerald Hardeman, PPC Jack Reid, and R. A. Swan. Front row: John Gammell, G. Goovers, and P. A. Fitzpatrick. (Jack Reid)

Eastern on 2 June 1942 with ammunition and other supplies. The ammunition consisted of 5,000 rounds for the aircraft machine guns. About one-quarter of it was transferred to VP-44, and the rest went to the Marine aviation squadrons.

The island was a continuous beehive of activity. There were slit trenches and tents in every conceivable location not taken up by buildings, aircraft taxiways, or parking spaces. The exception was the southern side of the island. Perhaps the hundreds of bombs stacked up there had discouraged settlers in that area.

3 June 1942 — Looking for an Encounter
On 3 June, 22 PBY crews rolled out at 3:00 a.m.

They had their favorite breakfast of bacon, eggs, and toast with mugs of hot coffee. They left the mess halls directly for the planes to run through a preflight check for the long patrol. Plane captains (PCs) — those enlisted men responsible for keeping the plane in good order — picked up the large boxes that held the crews' lunches.

Ten of the crews were from VP-44. Others were from VP-23, who were operating PBY-5 seaplanes out of the lagoon. Since arrival at Midway on 22 and 23 May, the VP-44 crews had flown long ten-hour patrols every day. They were under strain but appeared to be fresh and ready to fly.

PPC Ensign Jack Reid of 44-P-4, his copilot, Ensign Gerald Hardeman, and navigator, Ensign

Bob Swan, attended the preflight briefing while other crew members — John Gammell AP1c (NAP), Francis Musser ACRM (Aviation Chief Radio Mate), Raymond J. Derouim AMM2c, George Goovers, Jr. AMM3c, and Patrick A. Fitzpatrick AMM3c — put aboard the day's provisions of food and water and checked out the aircraft. Their sector for the day was west by southwest, which was in the general area for a possible encounter with the twin-engine medium Mitsubishi bombers operating out of Wake Island. They hoped for an encounter for revenge as well as for an opportunity to try the explosive bullets obtained from the Army Air Forces plane crew.

At about 4:00 a.m., they took off with the other crews for the long and lonesome patrol. As they left that morning, there were only high, scattered clouds and a light easterly breeze. The weather forecast Jack Reid and Bob Swan received at the briefing was favorable. Visibility for the mission promised to be satisfactory. They did not take the search altitude of 800 feet but rather held to about 500 feet, in order to practice firing the aircraft machine guns, until they were clear of Midway by about ten miles. Both Jack and Jerry Hardeman checked the surface of the ocean for any vessels, and, there being none, Jack called into the intercom, "Release the smoke bomb."

Pat Fitzpatrick, being familiar with the routines established and practiced for many months, was at his station in the tunnel. He lifted a smoke bomb from the rack and the cover plate for the smoke bomb launcher tube, pushed the bomb into it, and announced, "Smoke away." Pat then lifted the tunnel hatch and locked it open, unlatched the .30-caliber machine gun, swung it out, and locked it in place.

With his safety belt on, Pat then took off his hat, grabbed the sides of the hatch to stick his head out, and looked out at the broad expanse of the ocean, which tilted, from his perspective, at about 20 degrees. There, about 500 yards away, a plume of smoke was beginning to rise from the ocean. The plane was in a loose turn to port; then it circled back for a gunnery practice run on the smoke bomb. John Gammell had the bow turret open and the twin .30s in place and was tracking the rising column of smoke. The plane made a low-altitude run on the

target at a range near 200 yards with Raymond Derouin at the .50-caliber in the waist hatch and Fitzpatrick in the tunnel; they each squeezed off, in turn, about three bursts of four rounds each. The objective was to fire a short burst, check impact, and squeeze the trigger again.

By using an aim, shoot, check and aim, shoot, check technique, a greater accuracy was possible and use of the precious ammunition was more effective. The plane then made a banking turn to starboard, and Frances Musser at the other .50-caliber squeezed off about 12 rounds in successive bursts. He took great care that none of the blue-tipped ammunition obtained from the Army Air Forces was in the belt for the practice run.

During this time, George Goovers was in the tower checking flow meters, valves, and fuel levels. From his vantage point, with portholes to both starboard and port sides, he had an opportunity to observe how well his buddies had done on the gunnery run. As the plane started climbing to the cruising altitude, Patrick secured the tunnel gun and the hatch. Both waist guns were secured into locked position, and hatches were closed. Patrick and George exchanged places, and lookouts took positions in each side of the waist hatch. The lookouts' and mechanic's tower positions would be rotated during the long patrol.

Bob Swan was busy at the navigator's table. He laid out the maps and course, checked compasses and wind direction from the ocean surface whitecaps, and was ready to continue plotting the aircraft course and distance from Midway.

Musser, the chief radio mate, had set out the chronometer used by him and Swan and made the limited checks possible in keeping with radio silence on his radio transmitter. Using the frequency meter, he checked his radio receiver and the pilot's voice radio communications gear. Just to make sure he could get radio direction finder position data in the event of trouble, he ran a check on his direction finder gear. Derouin, the PBY plane captain, was busy checking flight gear and equipment stowage and preparing all materials that would be needed.

By that time, the crew was into the flight routine for the day. Operating positions would be switched around for a change, and occasionally one of them might have an opportunity to stretch out on one of the four bunks for a quick rest. The weather was perfect for an oceanic surveillance mission. The winds were light and visibility was unlimited in all directions. But there was one significant factor in the morning's weather that could be a disadvantage: if there was an engagement and trouble developed, there was no cloud cover in which to hide. It would be a fight until the enemy broke and ran, or it would be a fight to the death. Any aircraft in the Japanese Navy, except the Kawanishi flying boat, was faster than the PBY.

Most of the squadron personnel in the second crews had not flown a single mission. The pattern of activities for us had not changed since our arrival. We normally watched the aircraft take off, had breakfast, then checked the bulletin board. During the day we washed clothes or wrote letters. Some inspected the Army planes. Two of the sailors met Second Lieutenant Thomas H. Weems, bombardier, who was pleased to show them the sleek B-26 bomber and its torpedo.

But our routine suddenly changed. Two Japanese ships had been sighted southwest of Midway by Ensign James P. Lyle and his crew, who had taken off at 4:00 a.m. that morning. They had spotted the two vessels and took the Catalina down for a better look. A dispatch was prepared and sent out by Lyle's radioman at 8:43 a.m. At 9:04 a.m., they reported two converted minesweepers 470 miles from Midway to the southwest. The force was one-half of the four-minesweeper Japanese force allocated to the Midway expedition that had sailed from Wake Island on 31 May. There was some speculation by those on the Eastern Island flight line that the sighting may have been an error in ship identification. It certainly did not represent a force capable of attacking Midway. Many thought it likely that they were friendly forces, but that optimistic speculation was soon shattered.

For the crew of 44-P-4, it had been an uneventful patrol as they neared the end leg of the flight. As Ensign Swan prepared to give the patrol plane commander the heading for the dogleg to return to Mid-

way, Musser urged him to check to see if they could go any farther. Swan studied the remaining fuel supply and their position and briefed Reid. They could go 20 to 30 minutes longer on the present heading. Reid responded, "Just tell me when we have to turn." He wanted an encounter with the enemy just as bad as the rest of the crew did.

As the time expired for the extended search heading, Swan started to give Reid the heading for the new course. At that instant Reid spotted specks on the horizon. He gave the binoculars to Hardeman saying, "Are those ships? I think we hit the jackpot." Hardeman concurred. Moments later John Gammell, in the nose compartment, sang out, "Ships dead ahead, about 30 miles dead ahead." Francis Musser's radio message, "Sighted main body," went out at 9:25. Minutes later, a second message, "Bearing 262, distance 700," was sent. Midway was the target of the Japanese force, which was only 700 miles away.

Musser, the radioman, and Swan, the navigator, worked steadily in their joint compartment on position and message preparation. The messages on ship type, speed, bearing, and course went out in Morse code when approved by Reid. Gammell, the bow gunner, stood by with guns out and at the ready; the guns in the tunnel and waist hatch were also manned. The copilot remained on lookout and responded to orders from the flight commander. All were tensed and ready to respond in an instant.

Jack Reid, the plane commander, was the busiest person on the crew, and yet he was the coolest. He was responsible for the aircraft, the crew, and the decisions for the plan for reconnoitering an imposing hostile force. He was also responsible for ensuring that data on the enemy force got to Midway. He knew full well that if detected, they would be hit by anything from a sky full of Mitsubishi Zeros to a large force of scouting seaplanes. Yet they had to search out the forces and file their dispatches. It was a tall order.

Coolly and calmly, Jack Reid scouted the force for over two hours. He kept the Catalina at low altitudes and came up from different positions, counting the sightings at each one and radioing the results. The long wakes in the ocean from the steaming armada led him to either port or starboard positions of the ships. Reid's flight logbook, entry dated 3 June, cryptically reads: "On routine patrol out of Midway. Sighted first body of Japanese fleet in battle of Midway. Fleet consisting of 17 ships, Battleships and Cruisers, Destroyers, Troop transports. Tracked for two hours and returned to Midway." The entry reflects none of the electrifying emotions, tense hours of work, or pools of sweat that every person in the crew must have left in the bilge of 44-P-4 that day.

The aircraft landed in the afternoon with little fuel to spare. When asked how they managed to stay aloft for an additional three hours, Swan replied, "Raymond Derouin has three dependents — a wife and two daughters. He always puts in an extra 50 gallons of gas for each dependent."

Speculations about the possible invasion forces and possible targets were then dispelled along the flight line; another PBY had reached the vicinity of the Japanese force spotted by Jack Reid and gave a contact report of two cargo vessels and two smaller vessels heading toward Midway. It was clear that there was an invasion force out there and its target was Midway. Every person, whether on a flight crew, standby crew, or maintenance, faced the stark reality of an engagement with enemy forces that were far superior in numbers to everything the island could muster and throw at them.

Several first-line fighting ships were bearing down on the island at about 20 knots, complete with an invasion force and support and supply vessels. No one had yet sighted Japanese carrier groups, but surely they were in the area. The unknowns were their location and whether there were any U.S. Fleet units in the vicinity. When that question came up, Ensign J. M. Scott's words were, "We had better plan on being ready and going it alone."

During the noon meal, those who served and those who were served knew the invasion was imminent. All accepted the likelihood of bombardment on the night of 5 June and the landing at daylight the next morning. It was a sobering experience. No one was cheering at the prospects, but no one showed any sign of fear or regret that the events of their lives had brought them to these islands at that point in time. Rather, there appeared to be a will to make the best possible effort, whatever the circumstances.

The B-17 bombers began taking off while lunch was being served. The first one, on a spotting mission, left several minutes before the main group began taxiing out for takeoff. They carried 600-pound bombs and bomb-bay gasoline tanks for long-range bombing missions.

That afternoon, information received on the flight line indicated that their mission had been highly successful with direct hits on many of the targets. The news came as a surprise, for the raid was carried out at an altitude of several thousand feet. If the reports were true, then the bombsights they were using were far superior to the Norden sight used in the PBYs. Later, however, one of the crew on a PBY spotting mission indicated that it appeared that the B-17 attack was a complete waste of good bombs.

It was learned later from Japanese records, as reported in *Battle of Midway* (Cressman *et al.*) that the best scores attained by the B-17 mission were near-misses of 100 to 200 yards, not bad at all for high-altitude free-falling bombs against moving ships. These occurred near the *Argentina Maru* and the *Kiyozumi Maru*. Apparently, the Army Air Forces bombers, operating at very high altitudes, seemed to their crews to be doing a much better job than they actually were.

Four additional PBY-5a planes arrived on Midway from Pearl Harbor, each carrying a torpedo beneath the wing. The crews ate supper and rested in their aircraft for a short while. One crew member indicated that they expected to make a torpedo run that night. Three of the planes were from VP-24 and one was from VP-51. The crew members were:

24-P-12
Lieutenant (jg) O. P. Hibbard
Ensign A. L. Mills
Ensign J. C. Boyden
T. Roadbuck ARM3c
J. S. Gordon ARM3c
J. N. Hughes AMM3c
D. L. Ellis AMM2c
C. D. Ream AMM1c

24-P-11
Ensign G. D. Propst
Ensign B. L. Amman

24-P-11 *(continued)*
H. C. Smathers CAP
D. M. Zeck AMM3c
G. C. Harrison AMM3c
E. L. Kline AMM3c
V. Abate ARM3c
H. W. Hex ARM3c
J. K. Bwyer ARM3c

24-P-7
Lieutenant (jg) D. C. Davis
Ensign R. J. Ney
J. I. Foster AP1c
K. K. Anderson ARM2c
T. T. Kimmel AMM2c
W. M. Thompson RM2c
W. C. Henderson AMM3c
C. L. Hunt AMM3c
R. H. Neuman AMM3c

51-P-5
Ensign A. Rothenberg
Lieutenant (jg) Nolan
Ensign J. O. Adams
C. G. Lawler AMM2c
C. C. Roberts AMM3c
O. M. Spanr ARM2c
P. F. Arcidiacono Sea2c
M. R. Sugg AOM3c

At 5:00 p.m., Lieutenant William L. Richards, executive officer of VP-44, and Patrol Plane Commanders Lieutenant Hibbard, Lieutenant Davis, Ensign Propst, and Ensign Rothenberg were called to a preflight briefing on the advancing Imperial Japanese Navy. They were told that an enemy force consisting of about 12 large ships and several smaller ships had been contacted that morning at a point bearing of 261 degrees true from Midway at a distance of 700 miles. The force consisted of transports, an aircraft carrier, several cruisers, and destroyers. The large ships were steaming in a line of two columns on course 081 degrees at a speed of 18 knots. The force had been attacked during the afternoon by U.S. Army Air Forces bombers, leaving one of the ships ablaze.

Richards was in charge as flight commander.

Orders given to him were to locate the force, deliver a torpedo attack, and return to base. Richards would lead the flight from Lieutenant Hibbard's plane, 24-P-12.

Not one person of the four crews of VP-24 and VP-51 hesitated to make the flight. Although they had made a ten-hour journey from Pearl Harbor that morning, every officer and man was willing to embark on an all-night combat mission.

The four PBY-5a Catalina seaplanes, equipped with a Mark XIII Mod I torpedo, took off from Eastern Island at 9:15 p.m., rendezvoused, and proceeded on a course of 261 degrees.

Meanwhile, the runway lights were burning as an aid for the returning B-17s in locating the island. The lights had been switched on at 7:30 p.m. The Flying Fortresses began arriving at 9:30, and the last one on the bombing mission touched down at 10:30 p.m. The crew members of the flight who discussed their mission with the sailors on the flight line seemed to believe that they had crippled the Japanese fleet, though they did admit that there were some elements still on a course to Midway. As hopeful as the stories sounded, however, there remained some skepticism on the part of the sailors about the effectiveness of high-altitude bombing against moving targets.

As the runway lights switched off that evening, my tentmates and I, camped near the south shore, were turning down the valve on the Coleman lantern and climbing into our cots. The Chinese love birds were quiet at night, and the runway, too, was quiet after a busy day. Lying there in the still night, with only the familiar and soothing sound of the distant breakers crashing on the reef, it was only natural to speculate on coming events. After some silence, Edwin Olsen said, "Well, do you suppose they will be landing tomorrow night as we estimated?"

"No doubt about it," said Sherman Moore.

"Riding those breakers in on a landing craft is a perfect way to hit our shoreline just south of the tent," Cliff Troland commented.

"Let's locate a machine gun for our pit the first thing tomorrow morning," I added.

The consensus in the tent was that it would take more than a few B-17s and torpedo-equipped PBYs to stop the Japanese invasion armada, but it did seem possible that the Marine bombers on the island might be able to stop it.

It was difficult to go to sleep that night with the visions of landing boats and barges riding the crests of those giant breakers on the reef.

Lieutenant W. L. Richards and his four Catalinas flew through mixed weather conditions on the course toward the columns of the Japanese armada. At midnight, the last moments of 3 June, 51-P-5 was not in contact with the group, having disappeared while flying through heavy clouds. A short while later they also lost contact with 24-P-11. Only Lieutenant (jg) Douglas C. Davis in 24-P-7 remained in contact with Lieutenant Richards in 24-P-12.

The planes carried a new and prized electronic device — radar. This four-plane unit was the first of the PBY patrol craft that the Fleet Air Wing Patrol Commands had provided for radar installation. The radar system was Canadian-built and designated CVE-1 and used an array of three Yagi antennas (composed of several elements of half-wave dipole antennas designed to yield better performance than a single dipole antenna): one above the navigation and radio compartment, covering the area straight ahead, and two along the wings of the plane, covering the areas of the port and starboard beams. The antennas were constructed of Model J antenna wire and insulators between vertical supports from the surface of the plane. They had not been used by the patrol craft in battle up to this point. Without the radar, the mission that night would have been impossible.

At 1:15 a.m. on 4 June, Aviation Radio Mate J. S. Gordon of 24-P-12 reported radar contact 12 miles on the port beam. Radar blips indicated ten or more targets. Turning 90 degrees on the targets and tracking them on the forward antenna, 24-P-12 homed on the targets until some of them were in full view at about seven miles ahead.

Richards then formed the course for attack. He came upon the largest silhouette on the moon path at reduced speed and fired the torpedoes and machine guns at an altitude of 100 feet and 800-yard range. He then banked and pulled up in a turn

over the ship's stern. Machinist Mates J. N. Hughes and D. L. Ellis, who were operating the .50-caliber machine guns in the waist hatches, reported a huge explosion and heavy smoke as their fish struck the bow of the ship. They would learn later that they had damaged the oiler *Akebono Maru*, killing 11 men and wounding 13. The PBYs of VP-24, under the command of Lieutenant W. L. Richards of VP-44, had struck first in the battle for Midway.

Lieutenant (jg) D. C. Davis started setting up his run in 24-P-7 at the same time as Richards. He did not fire until his second run on the target, which was just ahead of the *Akebono Maru*. His gunners in the waist hatch did not report a hit, but Machinist Mate T. T. Kimmel swept the deck of the ship with his .50-caliber gun. They would later learn that they had probably attacked the *Kiyozumi Maru*, injuring eight of the ship's crew. By the time they attacked, the antiaircraft crews were busy, and the plane suffered hits in the bow, fuselage, wings, and tail section.

In the meantime, Ensign Gaylord D. Propst and his crew of 24-P-11 had located the armada. Propst set up his attack, fired, and then banked sharply to the left. A single enemy plane tried to intercept them, but they avoided it by making for cloud cover. The crew thought they had a hit but would later learn from Japanese records that they had missed their target.

Lieutenant Richards in his "Report of Night Torpedo Attack of June 3-4, part 14," states:

> Lieutenant Richards landed at Laysan at 1045 Hours. Fuel remaining less than 50 gallons. Time of flight 13.5 hours.
> Lieutenant (jg) Davis, 24-P-7, landed at Laysan at 10:00 a.m.: fuel remaining 10 to 20 gallons. Time of flight 12.8 hours.
> Ensign Propst, 24-P-11, landed at sea in the vicinity of Lisianski out of fuel. Time of flight 13 hours. The crew was rescued about 6:30 p.m. on June 6. The plane was beyond salvage and was sunk by gunfire.
> Ensign Rothenberg, 51-P-5, landed at Laysan at 1105 hours. Fuel remaining 10 to 20 gallons. Time of flight 13.8 hours.

During the 31-hour period ending 11:00 a.m. on

PBY plane commanders of torpedo attack, 3-4 June 1942. Left to right: Ensign Allen Rothenberg (VP-51), Lieutenant (jg) Douglas C. Davis (VP-24), Lieutenant William L. Richards (VP-44), and Ensign Gaylord D. Propst (VP-24). (National Archives)

4 June, these crews, except for Richards, had been in the air for 23½ hours. Then followed an all-day and all-night wait on the water in adverse weather conditions. The crew of 24-P-11 was down at sea for approximately 53 hours before being rescued. Then the crews made another flight to Pearl Harbor on the following day.

The mission these men performed took them from Midway on 3 June across the international date line on 5 June to a fight with a sizable invasion force and a return to the Hawaiian Island chain on 4 June 1942. The distance had been 560 miles from the departure point to the targets.

They received well-earned awards for their part

in the battle. The commendation noted that this was the first instance of a night torpedo attack and the use of radar on moving ships by U.S. Navy patrol planes. Richards and the four patrol plane commanders received the Silver Star. The other commissioned officers and enlisted pilots received the Distinguished Flying Cross. The enlisted crew members received an advancement in rating for their part in the mission.

4 June 1942 — Attack and Attack

The PBY crews rolled out early again on 4 June as they had every morning for what seemed to be months without change. For most of them, it was the thirteenth day of their extended patrols on a semi-battle stations alert status. It also marked the day when they knew before takeoff that contact with enemy forces was a strong possibility. Each knew that the patrol sector plans for the day would take one or more of the planes to a rendezvous with elements of the Japanese forces. Every sector was important, whether it contained empty ocean or an armada. The information on whether a sector contained only empty ocean was vital to those who would be directing the air battles that day.

Every member of the crews of VP-44 and VP-23 was well aware of the possible outcome of his part in the action, which was only hours away. Each, in his few moments of private thought, considered his chances for a fatal encounter, but outwardly, everyone went about breakfast and preparations for the day's flights with cheerful determination and purpose.

Patrol Plane Commander Lieutenant Shelby O. Cole and his navigator and copilot, Ensigns Ralph Donaldson and Richard Klinge, arrived at the revetment where their Catalina was parked and, as usual, found the plane outfitted for the flight and ready for engine start-up and checkout. Aviation Chief Machinist Mate (ACMM) Earl H. Robinson and AMM3c Allen J. "Tommy" Thompson had made fresh coffee and were in the waist hatch with the rest of the crew — AP2c Roy Robinson (NAP), Aviation Chief Ordnance Mate (ACOM) Arcia O. Turner, ARM1c M. R. Ubben, ARM2c Jack L. Bohner, and AMM2c C. E. "Bill" Harmon.

The pilots each got a cup of coffee and started to walk back to the waist to enjoy it with the rest of the crew while waiting for orders to take off. As Pappy Cole stepped through the waist hatch, the aircraft tilted downward and the tail section gently came to rest on the coral sand with the nose section about eight feet in the air.

Startled, yet knowing the problem, Cole shouted, "Bill Harmon, move forward slowly and stop when I shout. No one else move, even an inch." Gingerly, Harmon, who happened to be in one of the compartments toward the front of the plane, moved forward. When the plane began to settle slowly nose-down, Lieutenant Cole ordered, "Bill, stop and go back a half-step."

The plane nose wheel gently settled onto the

coral sand. Cole and the crew went forward to their flight positions, knowing that had the load shifted forward quickly, the nose wheel would have crashed through the nose compartment, disabling the plane for the most important flight of its life.

Earl Robinson, the plane captain, and Bill Harmon, second mechanic, inspected the underside of the tail section, nose wheel, and nose wheel compartment as Tommy Thompson climbed into the tower to check out that position during engine warmup and checkout. When Robinson gave an "all OK" report to Cole, the plane commander breathed a deep sigh of relief.

Farther along the flight line, Ensign Jack Reid and his crew were checking their plane, 44-P-4, for another long day on the far reaches of the assigned patrol leg. There was one change in crew assignments: Lieutenant Donald G. Gumz had assigned himself to the crew for the day as he considered their sector the most likely to offer an opportunity to meet the enemy.

The crew of 44-P-12 — Patrol Plane Commander Lieutenant (jg) Robert S. Whitman, Copilot Ensign Walter H. Mosley, Navigator Ensign Lee C. McCleary, Ensign Jack H. Camp, ACRM James W. Adams, AOM2c Philip L. Fulghum, AMM1c Virgil R. Marsh, AMM2c John C. Weeks, AMM3c Clarence J. Norby, and RM3c William H. O'Farrell — were in the adjoining revetment to 44-P-4, readying their plane, as were the remaining crews of VP-44 and VP-23 in the lagoon where their planes were tied up at seaplane buoys.

At about 4:10 a.m., the B-17s and PBYs were lifting off the island airstrip, following the fighters that had taken off to provide cover for the bombers and patrol planes. The PBYs of VP-23 were lifting off the lagoon.

One of the flight crews of a Catalina detached from NAS Kaneohe was shorthanded that morning and needed a volunteer bow gunner. George W. Newcombe AOM3c, one of the FAW school group who had joined the squadron on 27 October 1941, volunteered. Another squadron also needed a volunteer that morning. The pilot of one of the detachments of six planes of Grumman Torpedo Squadron VT-8, AMM1c Darrel "D" Woodside (NAP), needed a replacement for AMM1c William L. Coffey, who had flown with him from Ford Island.

AOM3c Lyonal J. Orgeron of VP-44 volunteered to fly as turret gunner with VT-8. It was reported that Orgeron had previously served with Woodside and they were pleased to fly together again.

For us four radiomen living near the lone aircraft revetment on the south side of the island, morning came late — 5:00 a.m. Moore's alarm clock was off that morning. We dressed hastily and went outside to find the airfield relatively quiet. Several men were about, but the PBYs and many of the B-17s were gone, and some of the planes that had been warming up were then having their engines shut down. We made the decision to go back to the tent and doze off until time for breakfast or until something happened. It was not long until there were new developments.

At 5:20 a.m., Ensign Howard P. Ady of VP-23 reported by radio the sighting of the main body of the Japanese naval attack force consisting of two carriers, three battleships, and six to eight destroyers. Lieutenant (jg) Chase of another PBY of VP-23 reported, "Many planes headed [toward] Midway, 100 miles, north by northwest." Following the PBY reports, radar reports started multiplying. In all, the carrier strike force of the IJN had launched 36 Zero fighters and 72 carrier bombers and carrier attack bombers to form the first attack wave against Midway.

The air-raid alarm for Eastern and Sand Islands sounded at 5:58 a.m. The Marine fighters of VMF 221, consisting of 24 F2A-3 Brewster Buffalos and F4F-3 Grumman Wildcats, scrambled to intercept the enemy planes headed for Midway. The Navy Grumman TBF Avenger torpedo bombers and Army B-26 aircraft were starting their engines.

The crews of the VT-8 detachment from Ford Island were the next to become airborne. The small force of TBF-1 Avenger torpedo bombers taxied out with Lieutenant Langdon K. Feiberling leading the first section of three planes with Ensign Albert "Bert" Ernest and Ensign Charles E. Brannon. Flying with Ernest was turret gunner AOM3c J. D. Manning and ARM3c Harold H. Ferrier. The second section of three planes was led by Ensign Oswald J. Gaynier with Ensign Victor A. Lewis and Aviation Pilot Darrel "D" Woodside (NAP). Woodside's crew that morning included Ptr2c (printer)

Arnold T. Meuers, tail gunner, and AOM3c Lyonal J. Orgeron, turret gunner, from VP-44.

Following the Grummans off the field were the four Army Air Forces Martin Marauder B-26 bombers, each carrying one Navy torpedo. Plane commanders were Captain James F. Collins, First Lieutenant William S. Watson, First Lieutenant James P. Muri, and First Lieutenant Herbert C. Mays. The crew flying with Collins that morning included Second Lieutenant Colin O. Villines, Second Lieutenant Thomas H. Weems, Sergeant Ernest M. Mohon, Jr., Sergeant Jack D. Dunn, Technical Sergeant Raymond S. White, and Corporal John D. Joyce.

Next, 28 Marine VMSB 241 dive-bombers took off — Douglas SBD-2 Dauntlesses and Vought Sikorsky SB2U-3 Vindicators, each carrying a 500-pound bomb.

After the last dive-bomber headed out for rendezvous and the sound of his engine faded out, the island for the first time in many days seemed quiet and almost deserted. The four of us — Moore, Olsen, Troland, and I — at our slit trench near the wrecked and abandoned SB2U-3 marveled at the strange stillness. The only sounds were those of the Chinese love birds in the nearby bush and the distant drone of a gasoline-powered generator that we had never heard before.

"I have a feeling that this is the calm before the storm," said Edwin Olsen as we continued to scan the skies.

The silence on Eastern Island did not last long; it was broken around 6:30 a.m. by the distant sound of aircraft, though none were visible. Suddenly, there was the sound of explosions from Sand Island.

"Plane spinning in!" shouted Sherman Moore, and there, high overhead to the north, were several "V" formations of planes, one of them leaving a spiral of smoke as it twisted earthward. The explosions on Sand Island were then recognized as anti-aircraft fire. The guns continued to pound furiously at the enemy aircraft. A second plane smoked and started falling, then a third.

At that point, Cliff Troland shouted, "Look out,

they're coming out of the sun!" Toward the sun, just risen over the ocean skyline, was what appeared to be a cloud of insects. They were growing perceptibly larger by the second. The four of us quickly filed into the covered trench we had so carefully constructed, hoping it would never be used.

The first machine-gun fire from Sand Island started just before the first bomb hit it. Next, several bombs exploded, and furious machine-gun anti-aircraft fire accompanied each blast. The first bomb then struck Eastern Island, and the local machine guns began chattering nearby. Bombs started falling in rapid succession, and with each of them, the earth seemed to buck.

A pattern of the action began to develop. As the machine guns on the western side of the island opened up, a bomb would explode. Then machine-gun fire shifted, following the attacker from the west to the eastern side of the island. The bombs began hitting closer to the trench.

"They're trying to hit the old dive-bomber in the revetment," Troland said. As the machine guns opened up again, there was an explosion that rocked the earth and knocked the breath out of the four of us.

Moore and I, in the north end of the trench, were facing each other on hands and knees. We thought the trench had collapsed. We tried to hold the 6 x 6 timber up with our backs. Likewise, Troland and Olsen in the southern end thought they were holding the top up. Edwin Olsen delivered a clear and sincere prayer.

After that, the bomb blasts seemed to be more widely spaced. I slowly lowered my back, and the timber overhead remained firmly in place. "The trench held," I shouted. "It's in good shape." The pattern of attack then changed. The bombs ceased, but with the opening of the defensive machine-gun fire at the edge of the island came the sound of the attacking plane with its engine noise and strafing gunfire. Then the sound of the enemy receded as the defensive machine-gun fire swept across the island following it.

Suddenly it was quiet. The last of the attackers sped to the northwest. Moore stuck his head out, and the silence on Midway was again eerie. Each of us climbed out of the trench, which had proven to be a good bomb shelter.

The only sound on the island was a road grader traveling down the runway, pushing debris from the bombed buildings and an enemy plane that had crashed on the runway. What devotion to duty. The operator must have been beside his grader during the raid and dashed out with it while the last plane was still in view. The sight of that lone sailor and his machine rolling down the airstrip increased our respect for the ship's company at Midway. As we climbed out of the shelter, we noted that the little Chinese love birds were silent. Several were hanging head-down on the bushes with blood dripping from their beaks. The tent was gone. Beside the trench, a corner of the tent showed from underneath a ring of coral sand around a deep bomb crater. The center of the crater was midway between the place where the tent had stood and the edge of the aircraft revetment.

In the distance, a huge column of black smoke was beginning to rise over Sand Island. Glowing orange flames could be seen around the base of the column. We began to walk slowly around the revetment, still cautiously watching the sky. Then looking into the revetment, we saw that one of the old dive-bomber's tires had been shot and that it now sat at a tilted angle. It seemed likely that the target of the enemy bomber was the old plane. The pilot had missed by about 60 feet, but he did get a tent.

On the other side of the revetment, some sandbags were laid out in a rough form of a slit trench. Some had been tossed about by a bomb blast. There, lying between the scattered bags, was the body of a young soldier airman. He was face-down with a gas mask on, lying in the center of an open Bible. The slit trench had not been there late the last evening. He must have come in during the previous day and laid out the sandbags filled with the loose coral sand that night.

Beside the airman, near the sandbags, was his .30-caliber rifle and several slings of ammunition. I gently lifted the rifle and ammunition belts from the sandbags and carried them over to the bomber for cleaning and use later that night if necessary. I vowed silently to use the rifle during the coming invasion, to the last round, with the feeling that the ghost of this young man, whom I had never met, would be there to cheer me on.

As the four of us walked on to the north-south

crossing runway, AOM3c Arthur Arsenault came toward us to see if we had been hit. None of the squadron personnel in his area had been hit.

But there was damage. The buildings along the northern side of the airstrip were gone. Packages of cigarettes and other materials from the post exchange littered the area. The invading plane that had crashed into the runway had left a scattered trail of debris from the impact point up to the Marine command bunkers, where its engine had come to rest with a part of the fuselage about 15 feet away. On the side of the fuselage was the battered red meatball marking. Several Marines were going over the wreckage and were also examining the body of the pilot.

Stories of the attack were soon spreading across the island by word of mouth. Some had seen a U.S. pilot of one of the fighters bail out of his badly smoking plane. They watched in horror as one of the attacking Zeroes made several passes at the man dangling from the parachute. One plane appeared to come down and strafe the point where the parachute and pilot had landed. There were several reports of the PT (patrol torpedo) boats — small, high-speed vessels capable of launching torpedoes at surface ships — that were still active in the lagoon, and of the very effective defensive fire they had put up.

Arcia O. Turner, when he had not been flying, had erected a .50-caliber machine-gun pit at mid-island, near the shower and supply buildings. Turner was an expert in ordnance and gunnery. During the raid, the nearby buildings were blown up, but the gun emplacement was spared. One of the bombers came in on a course in the gun sights. It was a target that the gunner at the emplacement could not miss. The bomber crashed on the northwest end of Sand Island.

On the day of 6 June, Turner took Cornelius "Neil" Brislawn to see the wreckage of the plane. He gave Neil the pilot's navigation plotting board as a souvenir. Neil has the plotting board to this day.

Of the 24 F2A-3 Buffalo and F4F-3 Wildcat fighters that had taken off at 6:00 a.m., very few returned, and those that did were seriously damaged. Reports circulated that they were badly outclassed by the Zeros of the attacking force. When a

Zero got on their tail, their most effective maneuver was to slow down, making a sitting duck of themselves, then nailing the attacker with fire when he sped away — if they were still alive, that is.

Few of the dive-bombers of VMSB 241 returned from the mission against the carrier force. Those that did were badly shot up.

AOM1c V. R. Evans was found lying face-down in his slit trench on the northern shore of the island. He had refused to move when his friends in VP-44 told him the raid was over and to get up. He thought he had been mortally wounded, and as the raid had progressed, he decided his leg had been blown off. The friends examined him and told him his leg was all right. He slowly and gingerly rose, and there beside his leg was a can of Spam. Though badly bruised, his leg was fine. He had been hit by the can of Spam when the mess hall blew up. We did not laugh.

The crew of 44-P-12 knew that the search sector assigned to them — or for that matter any sector assigned to the PBY squadrons — faced combat that day, 4 June. Their sector gave an outgoing course of 269 degrees true heading.

Patrol Plane Commander Lieutenant (jg) Robert S. Whitman had not seen combat but knew that they might on that day. His copilot, Ensign Walter H. Mosley, was an experienced combat veteran who had reported to VP-44 only a few weeks earlier.

Mosley's distinguished service record included patrol duties with VP-22 out of Port Darwin, Australia. On 19 February 1942, he had been copilot for Lieutenant Thomas Moorer (later to become Chief of Naval Operations and Chairman of the Joint Chiefs of Staff) when they were shot down by Zeroes operating from a carrier. The plane, though burning rapidly, landed without a loss of life. The crew had been rescued by a tramp steamer loaded with ammunition for the Philippines. The steamer, however, was sunk, and everyone swam to a nearby island, to be later picked up by an Australian gunboat. They eventually returned to Pearl Harbor.

The rest of the crew in 44-P-12 had not experienced the initial baptism of fire, but most were experienced hands. Third pilot was Ensign Jack H.

Camp; Ensign Lee C. McCleary was navigator. The enlisted men, though not combat-experienced, were old hands with Squadron 44. ACRM James W. Adams shared the radio/navigation compartment with McCleary and operated the radio equipment. AMM2c John C. Weeks was an experienced bow gunner and mechanic. Plane Captain AMM1c Virgil R. Marsh operated the tower. AOM2c Philip L. Fulghum and AMM3c Clarence J. Norby were stationed in the waist hatch at the .50-caliber machine guns. RM3c William H. O'Farrell operated the .30-caliber gun in the tail section.

During the early morning period of flight, Whitman and Mosley watched the horizon for surface vessels. Weeks and the two waist hatch lookouts also kept a sharp eye out for aircraft and ships, knowing that they could expect an attack from any quarter.

At around 7:15, about three hours into their flight, Mosley shouted, "There they are!" On the horizon was the Japanese armada. Quickly, Lee McCleary and James Adams readied the contact report and sent it out. At that time Philip Fulghum's voice came over the intercom reporting a plane on the port quarter. In an instant, the .50-caliber started barking.

Another report gave the position of a second aircraft, another float plane, and as Whitman and Mosley twisted and turned the PBY, three planes from the enemy carrier *Chitose* were attacking them. One broke off and fell away, leaving a trail of smoke. The two remaining Petes — Zero float planes — continued the relentless onslaught as Adams sent out the combat attack message.

As the plane turned and banked, the crew fired the .30- and .50-calibers. The firing shifted from the bow to the tunnel gun and from port to starboard. They were giving a good fight. McCleary was torn between marking their position and looking for the attackers. He decided to open the small hatch above the navigator's table to spot the seaplanes for the pilots. As he lifted himself up on the table, he felt a sting on his leg. The sting was at the spot where his body would have been had he not climbed on the table. He never opened the hatch. As he glanced at Whitman, he realized the pilot was dead. Adams was sending out the plain language radio message, "Down, down, down." Fulghum continued to fire at

a float plane. Then, seeing that his aircraft wings were on fire and knowing that the crash was imminent, he went forward to release the two 500-pound bombs.

Lee McCleary saw that Mosley was also dead. He died holding the yoke close to his chest trying to come out of the dive. He would have been successful even in death had the fire not burned out the control surfaces. McCleary braced himself for the impact. Chief Adams, who had earlier adjusted the screw on his Morse code key so that it was closed, was also dead and slumped over the desk. His radio was sending out signals as an aid for radio direction finders.

The crew then hit the ocean in a steep dive, afire from the end of one wing to the end of the other. At impact, the nose section broke off across the radio navigation compartment, about at the location of the propellers. McCleary found himself somewhere below water, possibly 12 feet. Although wounded, he struggled to the surface. The bow section was gone, and the plane tilted nose-down with the tail section high but slowly settling. The gasoline-fed fire was roaring.

Virgil Marsh retrieved the life raft from the waist hatch in spite of the raging fire. John Weeks, though wounded himself, helped Marsh repair the bullet holes in the damaged raft. Fulghum assisted the other wounded men, Camp and McCleary, into the raft.

Lieutenant Whitman, Ensign Mosley, AMM3c Norby, RM3c O'Farrell, and ACRM James Adams died in their bullet-ridden plane. The five men in the life raft watched as the plane sank and the fire on the surface died out. Three of the men were wounded — John C. Weeks, Lee C. McCleary, and Jack Camp, who was seriously injured by machine-gun bullets. Marsh and Fulghum set about putting the raft in order.

Francis Musser of Ensign Jack Reid's crew in 44-P-4 picked up the radio signals from Chief Adams in Lieutenant Whitman's crew and passed the data to Ensign Swan and Ensign Reid. All hands knew the full implications of the series of messages from 44-P-12 and wanted badly to cross over and make a rescue. But to do so would have been contrary to orders and was impossible. All they could do was hope the crew would survive the impact and be rescued later. Any enemy forces in their sector must be spotted.

At about the time that 44-P-12 was meeting its fiery death, Captain James F. Collins and his B-26 force and Lieutenant Langdon K. Fieberling with his TBF-1 force were simultaneously trying to thread their way through the screening ships, thick antiaircraft fire, and swarms of defending Zero fighters. Their targets were the carriers reported earlier that morning by Ensign Howard Ady of VP-23. Most of these men would also meet a violent end. Of the ten planes in the small B-26 and TBF-1 force, all but three were destined to hit the water at high speed, consigning the crews to eternal rest in the Pacific Ocean.

With only small pieces of debris and shrapnel littering the runway, the Eastern Island airfield was still fully operational. Fifty-gallon drums of gasoline were being used to refuel the planes. The hospital corpsmen with an ambulance picked up the dead and wounded.

Planes that had gone out to attack the carrier force were straggling back around 9:15 p.m. In the air were two of the Army B-26 attack bombers. One coming in on final approach appeared to be in trouble. As soon as the plane touched the sand, it lurched slightly as the port landing gear seemed to shatter with a flat tire. The pilot did a good job of lifting the wing until the speed was reduced. He then lowered the plane, and she skidded along the runway, curving to port in a good parking spot, having done no damage to the field or facilities.

The second B-26 came in, also in obvious trouble. Both wing landing gear were down, but there was no nose gear in sight. The pilot was making what appeared to be a stall landing with the tail down. The plane touched the surface, still tail-down, and rolled along the runway with nose up. Slowly the nose went down, then the plane skidded along the runway, veering to port side. It also came to rest in a pretty good parking spot, considering the pilot had an incomplete set of landing gear. Both of the craft were well-peppered with cannon and machine-gun bullet holes.

"Look out!" Cliff Troland shouted. "Plane com-

ing in with bad gear." One of the TBF-1 Avengers was on final approach. The plane was wobbling and obviously had trouble with the controls. Yet, it landed smoothly on one landing gear, and as the wing touched down, the plane ground-looped to port, making a full circle before coming to rest on the runway. The moment the plane stopped, the ambulance and fire truck pulled up beside it.

It too was covered with cannon and machine-gun bullet holes. The elevator had a large round hole, and much of the gun turret appeared to be shot away. The .50-caliber machine gun pointed out at an awkward angle rather than aft as in the landing and stowed position. The pilot appeared wounded as his back was covered with blood. One of the crewmen, apparently badly wounded, was then taken out. Next out was the machine gunner in the turret. He was dead, and to the bystanders who could see, his body appeared to be in almost two parts. Both Ensign Bert Ernest and ARM3c Harold Ferrier were wounded, and AOM3c J. D. Manning had been killed in action. Plane 8-T-1, Ensign Ernest's, was the only plane to return to Midway of the six of Torpedo Squadron VT-8 that had lifted off that morning.

That meant that AMM1c Darrel Woodside and his crew of plane 8-T-5 did not make it through the barrage of antiaircraft and the defensive Zero fighters protecting the IJN attack fleet. Woodside and Ptr2c Arnold T. Meuers of VT-8 and AOM3c Lyonal J. Orgeron of VP-44 were killed in action, along with the other four crews of VT-8. None were reported to reach a target in the fleet close enough to launch their torpedo except Ernest, who jettisoned his torpedo at a cruiser but got no indication of a hit.

The pilots and crews of the two Army B-26 Marauders that returned to Midway felt lucky to be alive. They had also flown through swarms of Zeros and heavy antiaircraft fire to launch at one of the enemy's long aircraft carriers. They each thought they had hit the target, but there was no confirmation.

Of the 28 men who had taken off that morning in the B-26 bombers, 14 were killed when the planes were shot down. The two returning planes, piloted by Captain James F. Collins and First Lieutenant James P. Muri, had returned to Midway with the planes and propellers literally riddled with bullets.

Second Lieutenant Thomas H. Weems, navigator on Collins's plane, recounted the mission:

We arrived [at Midway] about noon on May 28. . . . Two additional planes joined us . . . from the 22nd Bombardment Group, making a total of four planes in the B-26 group on Midway.

While on the island, I wanted something to do. I met a short man, an Annapolis man, I think, named [Donald G.] Gumz, and asked him if I could go out on one of the PBYs the next day. He said sure and told me where the plane was parked. The reason I didn't go was because I overslept that morning. I did go out on a B-26 that morning, for the navigator of [James F.] Collins's crew had taken sick. I volunteered to take his place and made the flight.

We were in our planes that morning and had the engines turning up when a messenger came by and told us to take a heading about northwest to carriers at about 225 miles, as I remember it. We took off a little after 6:00. The TBFs were in front of us, and we followed them out. About 50 miles out we spotted a PBY hovering around the clouds, and he had dropped a flare parachute. We learned later that he was a spotter for enemy aircraft and had dropped a parachute flare as a warning to Midway. In over an hour we spotted the fleet, and there were plenty of them. Captain Collins selected a carrier and released the torpedo at it. I am told that we were the first to contact the fleet that morning by a few seconds. We were under heavy antiaircraft fire going in, but no planes attacked us until we released the torpedo and then went over the carrier.

We hadn't been hit until that time. The planes attacked us after we went over the carrier. I saw one coming right at us. He did most of the damage with a 20-millimeter cannon and blew up the nose wheel. . . . Collins did a good job by getting right down over the water. We finally got up into the clouds.

On the way back, we saw some Japanese planes headed back to the carrier from Midway. They made no attempt to bother us. Shortly, we got back to Kure Island and could see the smoke from Midway and knew then that we were home-free. When we got ready to land, Captain Collins had everyone get in the back of the plane, copilot and all, except me and I stayed in the navigator's chair. We came in on two wheels [and] stayed up a long time before the nose went down. Finally it went down and there was a lot of noise, but I have had rougher landings.

I counted the holes in the plane after we landed, and there were 75. Nine of the holes were in the propellers. . . . It was funny that the man I replaced on the flight had completely recovered from his sickness by the time we returned.

I returned to Hawaii on June 6, . . . I believe on a C-47. We learned later that the crew we flew back with was lost on a flight from Midway about seven months later.

By 9:30 a.m., the B-17 Flying Fortresses were beginning to straggle in. The crews seemed to be in high spirits and indicated again that they had scored several hits and many near-misses.

"Not a chance," said AOM3c Arthur Arsenault. "It is a waste of good bombs." The laborious process of refueling the B-17s started again. Because another raid was likely, they were ordered to refuel, rearm, and go back to the targets.

Later, records would show that the B-17 bombing efforts were no more effective than the previous day's work on the IJN invasion force. Most of the bombs missed by a wide margin with a few near-misses. Because they were working at such high altitudes, the overly optimistic crews of the bombers possibly mistook near-misses for hits. But the effort was not a total loss, because the invasion fleets engaged in many maneuvers to avoid the big bombers.

On the southern side of the airstrip, where the bushes were filled with hundreds of bombs, there was great activity. Small tractors pulling bomb carts were making trails through the brush and hauling out bombs to put into the bays of the large Army Air Forces planes. Some of the ordnance personnel of VP-44 assisted the soldiers in that effort to learn more about the Army planes and to help occupy the time.

To sailors and other personnel on the flight line, the outlook for Midway was dismal. The islands had taken a pounding, although the airfield was still operational. The supplies of aviation gasoline, which up to then had seemed inexhaustible, were being rapidly diminished. Nothing serviceable remained of the four B-26 and six TBF planes. Few of the fighter aircraft defending the islands were left from the raid that morning, and few of the dive-bombers had returned. Even if there was gasoline to fuel them, there were not enough planes left to repel the invading attack reported to contain two carriers, battleships, heavy cruisers, and many destroyers bearing in from the northwest. In addition, an invasion force to the west with troop transports, supply ships, and escort cruisers and destroyers was headed for the islands at high speed. No one yet had confirmed reports of damage to either of these fleets.

There was some good news. The flight of the four PBYs that had left Midway late on 3 June on their torpedo run, led by Lieutenant W. L. Richards, apparently had landed at French Frigate Shoals.

Around 10:30 a.m., Sherman Moore reminded Cliff Troland, Edwin Olsen, and me that our tent was buried under the edge of the bomb crater, so we set out to find a shovel and some tools. Only one corner of the tent was visible, but digging it out proved to be an easy task because the coral was soft and loose. The tent was just slightly damaged, having a split about four feet long on the side facing the center of the crater. We shoveled off the coral above the tent. The cots, bedding, and personal gear beneath it suffered no damage, but loose coral sand had infiltrated everything. Cleaning up proved to be little trouble, except for the time it took to shake out the sand. We rotated with the shovel until a clear place near the original location of the tent was smoothed out, and the tent was set up again.

Sherman, Cliff, and Edwin left to return to the runway flight line. I stayed behind to clean the rifle I had found that morning beside the young American airman who had died.

The raiders of Midway that morning had not paid a high enough price for the damage they had inflicted. No official count had been received, but three planes had been seen falling from the enemy formation while the antiaircraft firing was first active. One plane was known to have crashed on Sand Island, and one had scattered debris over the end of the runway on Eastern Island when it crashed. Unofficial reports indicated that the defensive fighters had shot down some of the attacking planes but far less than the enemy attackers had taken. A few of the dive-bombers from Midway had also shot down attacking fighters from the carriers.

The crew members of Jack Reid's 44-P-4 continued on assigned patrol as they received radio reports of the tragic end of 44-P-12. They scanned the skies for aircraft and the sea for surface vessels. They kept abreast of some of the action as ACRM Francis Musser copied reports from the PBY communications radio frequency and gave them to Ensigns Reid and Swan.

The flight was uneventful, however, until the return leg of their search sector. Smoke and surface vessels appeared on the horizon. They tracked a force of two battleships, four cruisers, four destroyers, and a burning aircraft carrier as Musser sent out the radio contact reports. There was sufficient cloud cover to hide in, which permitted them to come out from different positions to snoop on the fleet below. Each time they came into view of the ships, they were greeted by heavy antiaircraft fire.

The runways on Eastern Island were busy around noon on the 4th. The Flying Fortresses were landing and taking off. Several were being refueled and bombs were being loaded through the long bomb-bay doors. An air-raid alert sounded. Antiaircraft guns fired until the incoming planes were recognized as friendly SBDs.

To the men on the flight line at Eastern Island, the events of the course of the battle were just beginning to unfold. First, the follow-up raid by the attacking enemy aircraft carriers had not materialized as expected. From the reports sent in by the PBYs, the invasion force to the west was still on a course to the island. It could arrive that evening, and a bombardment of the island could begin sometime after nightfall, to be followed by landing forces. And there were some new elements to the reports. The last SBD aircraft to land on the island was from an aircraft carrier. That a U.S. Navy aircraft carrier was participating in the action was good news to the men on Midway. Further, one of the PBYs from VP-44 had reported a burning enemy aircraft carrier, which was assumed to be one of those spotted by Ensign Howard Ady of VP-23 much earlier in the day. The best estimates from comments heard on the flight line was that the outcome of the battle in progress hinged on there being a sufficient naval force in the area to repel the invasion.

Traffic on the airstrip and congestion by the B-17s made entry by the returning PBY patrol planes difficult. Several of the VP-44 craft landed in the lagoon and were pulled up on the ramp by the VP-23 beaching crew. Lieutenant (jg) Pappy Cole's plane made a good approach and turned with the tail into the ramp. Lines were attached and the tractor tug pulled the plane toward the ramp. For some reason, perhaps because the plane was amphibious rather than a seaplane and had a different center of gravity, the plane's tail dipped toward the water and knocked one of the ramp crew unconscious. Unfortunately, no one else in the beach crew saw the incident, and the crewman disappeared beneath the surface. Tommy Thompson called until he got the attention of another crewman, who then swam under the plane and found his buddy.

Later in the afternoon, 2:55 p.m., the patrol planes returned and were refueled and readied for flight while the patrol plane commanders were being debriefed. Several of the younger sailors gathered around 44-P-4 when it had parked and were talking to Francis Musser and others in the crew. Edwin Olsen asked Musser if he could have a drink of water from the plane. Musser said, "Sure, go ahead." The other sailors, for the first time, realized that they had not had food or drinking water since the day before.

At 3:58 p.m., Ensign Ted Thueson of VP-23

radioed in a sighting of three burning enemy ships. At 4:00 p.m., six B-17s from Midway and four vectoring in from Hickam Field reported attacking an undamaged aircraft carrier with several direct hits and near-misses. Records would show later that there were no hits and that luck had still eluded the high-altitude bombers. At 4:09 p.m., Theuson reported two cruisers, and at 5:45 p.m., he reported that the three burning ships were Japanese aircraft carriers and that he was setting a course for Midway.

During the late afternoon, the B-17s were again gulping great quantities of gasoline and consuming time on the airstrip. Of the huge supply of bombs on the southern side of the island, there were enough left to load only six B-17s on the following day. Crews of the Midway-based Marine Corps bombers were preparing their planes for another mission at around 5:45 p.m. They were delayed until near nightfall because there was no fighter cover for them. Experience from the morning raid had clearly indicated that bombers, when unescorted by fighter cover, were doomed. The Marine Corps crews gassed and readied their planes for an attack and took off at 7:15 p.m. With the departure of the planes of VMSB 241, the last attack launched from Midway that day had taken off.

Moore, Olsen, Troland, and I crossed the airstrip to our tent and laid down on the cots. There was no thought of undressing. Although we did not realize it, we were exhausted and hungry.

"I wonder when they will get here?" Edwin Olsen said.

"Before morning," replied Cliff Troland.

"No one can say we haven't done our part in this thing," mused Sherman Moore. "Taken together, we have saved the Navy the cost of 12 meals today."

For the first time the island seemed quiet and peaceful. There, once again, was the soothing sound of the breakers a few yards to the south as they crashed on the reef and waters rolled up to the shoreline. There was also something solemn about the sound, for the mental pictures of landing craft coming in on those breakers were particularly vivid that night.

The night bombing mission by VMSB 241 returned from the search for the "burning carrier" without results. They had not located the target. There was a brief alert and some antiaircraft fire until they were recognized as friendly.

5 June 1942 —
Battle Stories Unfold and Rescues Begin

At 1:30 a.m., there was a crash of a cannon and the island alert sounded. Troland, Moore, Olsen, and I tumbled off the cots and toward the slit trench. I came out last carrying the .30-caliber rifle and ammunition slings. I laid them on the end of the trench opposite the ocean side. "They're right on time," commented Troland. We heard another cannon report, and the shell seemed to ricochet off the landing strip and scream with a lower pitch as it sped off over the lagoon. Surprisingly, it did not explode.

"We should have dug this trench into the ground," said Olsen. "Those shells are coming in horizontally." There were two or three more shots, and again, one of them seemed to ricochet off the airstrip. Then it was quiet once more, and soon the all-clear sounded, indicating that at that moment the enemy was no longer a threat. For some reason, the heavy bombardment and landing had not materialized.

Lieutenant (jg) Pappy Cole and his crew did not sleep much the night of 4 June and the wee hours of 5 June. Part of it was spent in the bunker on Sand Island. His crew and two others had landed in the lagoon on 4 June due to crowded conditions on Eastern Island. But he and his crew in 44-P-10, along with the other planes of VP-44 and the seaplanes of VP-23, rolled down the seaplane ramp at 4:00 a.m., 5 June, into the lagoon waters of Midway. Flying with Pappy Cole was the same crew that by then had flown hundreds of hours together — Copilot Ensign Richard Klinge, Navigator Ensign Ralph Donaldson, AP2c Roy Robinson (NAP), ACOM Arcia O. Turner, Plane Captain ACMM Earl H. Robinson, ARM1c M. R. Ubben, ARM2c Jack L. Bohner, AMM2c Bill Harmon, and AMM3c Tommy Thompson. Their sector for the day was northeast at about 50 degrees, the area where burning carriers had been reported. Confident that they

had an opportunity for combat, they took off at 4:00 a.m., about the same time as others of VP-23 and VP-44 on Sand Island and the planes of VP-44 on Eastern Island had left for the patrol.

PBY reports had been received at frequent intervals giving position data on elements of the Japanese navy attack force and the invasion force. At 6:30 a.m., a PBY reported two battleships 225 miles from Midway. A few minutes later, Lieutenant (jg) Norman Brady of VP-23 followed oil slicks leading into an adjoining sector. The slicks led him to two capitol ships (heavy cruisers or battleships); both were damaged. The Marines of VMSB 241 took off at 7:00 a.m. with six SBDs and six SB2Us. They followed the slick to the target and carried out an attack. Direct hits still eluded the bomber forces from Midway, and the two damaged targets continued on course. One bomber with pilot and radio technician were lost to antiaircraft fire.

That morning, breakfast on Eastern Island was in the open air with a row of tables serving the chow line. It was surprisingly good, considering the circumstances. There were portable water tanks for drinking water.

By 8:00 a.m., the reasons for the failure of the expected bombardment and invasion by landing forces were becoming more apparent. Four of the carriers of a striking force were known to have been burning fiercely, and some of them were presumably sunk by then. One battleship had been reported to be hit. Three U.S. carriers were in the area and had scored direct hits on the four enemy carriers with 500-pound and 1,000-pound bombs.

It was assumed that the Intelligence data that had allowed the U.S. task force to intercept the enemy fleet was supplied by submarines. There were reports that one submarine had attacked the carrier force and some of the screening ships. Although the invasion could not be ruled out at this point, it did appear that the odds of an invasion were beginning to turn against the IJN forces.

Pappy Cole's crew of 44-P-10 did not expect the flight on 5 June to be routine. It was not. Their course took them through the area where heavy fighting had occurred the day before, where burning carriers had been seen.

On the outgoing leg of the patrol, a raft with survivors was sighted, but to land would have violated all orders. Their job was to thoroughly search the patrol sector. Ralph Donaldson carefully plotted the raft position, and M. R. Ubben sent out the data by radio. The course brought into the plane's view a long, widely spaced line of rafts with survivors. The last in the line was a small raft with a single man on board.

Arcia Turner and Jack Bohner were operating the two .50-calibers, and Bill Harmon was manning the tunnel .30-caliber gun. Tommy Thompson was in the tower. Suddenly, Turner's voice came over the intercom advising that aircraft were closing in but that they looked friendly. "Shall I shoot?"

"If they attack," said Cole. A large aircraft carrier then came into view. The carrier was signaling the identification challenge code for the day with a signal lamp. Quickly, Jack Bohner grabbed the Aldis lamp and sent the proper reply to the challenge. "Thanks and good luck," the carrier signaled back.

At 8:30, work for the day had just started. Before reaching the end of the search sector, four enemy ships were sighted, two pairs of line ships (ships capable of undertaking battle, as opposed to cargo or transport ships) traveling together. Thompson and Turner both spotted a Japanese float plane, but apparently they were unseen by this threat. After maneuvering to position, Cole dropped down to near-surface and made a run at the ships for identification. They picked up heavy antiaircraft fire and identified the ships as unfriendly. The day had been busy for all hands, especially for Ubben and Donaldson. Navigation kept Donaldson working hard, and Ubben had handled an unusual amount of vital radio traffic that day.

Into the return leg, Cole asked Donaldson to give the course to the last survivor they had sighted, the one most distant from Midway. In a magnificent feat of navigation, the lonely little raft appeared dead ahead. This spot, a tiny speck in a vast expanse of ocean, was located after hours of flight from the original sighting and after several hundreds of miles had been traveled. Cole polled the crew for agreement to land and pick up the survivor.

Knowing the risks involved, every man nevertheless favored the rescue immediately.

With Roy Robinson in the copilot seat, Cole carefully lined up for the landing and set down. The tips of the wings lowered to act as flotation gear. The ship handled beautifully but had some buckling, popped rivets, and strut deformation. Great care had to be taken to keep the survivor from hitting the float part of the wing. A line was thrown over the raft, but the man was unable to pull himself in. Robinson went to the wing tip and climbed down to the float. Laboriously and carefully, Cole put the float near enough to the raft for Robinson to attach a small line. Robinson then climbed back up to the wing and back to the waist hatch and pulled the line in.

The survivor was identified as Ensign G. H. Gay of the Douglas TBD Devastator Torpedo Squadron VT-8, plane number T-14, from the U.S. carrier *Hornet*. Ensign Gay was the sole survivor of VT-8 consisting of 16 torpedo bombers and 32 men. He had passed over the Japanese carrier *Soyru* while trying to drop his torpedo. Twenty-one Zero fighters had hit the squadron; 15 planes had been destroyed by the fighters before they had reached the target. ARM2c B. K. Huntington, radio gunner with Gay, had been killed. Gay's plane had cartwheeled into the ocean after crossing over the carrier, but he had miraculously cleared the plane and extracted the small raft. Gay had been the only man to witness the destruction of all four of the Japanese aircraft carriers in the invasion fleet. He would go on to become an American hero and deserved recognition. It is ironic, however, that the skill, perseverance, and daring of those who rescued him, particularly Navigator Ensign Ralph Donaldson and Pilot Lieutenant (jg) Shelby Cole, went relatively unnoticed and unrecognized.

The rescue, completed to this point, was only part of the problem for the crew. With some damage to the plane and with the seas that were running, the takeoff could be hazardous. Cole judged that they would have to dump some gasoline and, once airborne, return directly to Midway. They had previously sent in position reports on all rafts they had sighted that day.

Dumping the gasoline proved to be a problem. The plane was designed to dump fuel when airborne but not while on the surface. First, the dump valves opened. Next, one man was stationed at the port wing tip, one at the center of the wing, and one at the starboard wing tip. On command, the center man and the man at the starboard wing tip ran one-half the distance of the wing to port.

A few gallons of fuel slowly drained out with the rock of the plane. The two men then at the port wing tip and the one at the center of the wing ran one-half the distance of the wing toward the starboard. Again, more gasoline drained as the ship rocked to starboard. After some 30 minutes of rocking, enough fuel was released for takeoff.

Traffic on the Eastern Island airstrip around 11:00 a.m. consisted primarily of B-17s. As information continued to become available to personnel on the line, it appeared that a significant naval battle had occurred on 4 June and that the outcome favored the U.S. forces. Three U.S. carriers positioned to the northeast — the *Enterprise, Hornet,* and *Yorktown* — had intercepted the Imperial Japanese Navy attack force. Four of the IJN attacking carriers were destroyed, some of the screening ships were damaged, and possibly one battleship was sunk. Some of the news was saddening: the *Yorktown* was badly damaged and many lives had been lost.

The names of men and squadrons who had performed heroically were mentioned among the flight line personnel. Prominent among them was Major Lofton H. Henderson, USMC, who had led the attack of VMSB 241. Reportedly, when he saw that his bullet-riddled plane would not reach the carrier that was his objective, he aimed his SBD bomber for the center of a battleship. A radio gunner died in the plane with Henderson. Also named were Lieutenant Langdon Feiberling and Ensign Albert Ernest, whom we had seen land, of VT-8, and Captain James Collins, who had led the raid of the B-26 Marauder bombers.

Also mentioned were aviation squadrons that were not familiar to the men on Midway. Lieutenant Commander J. C. Waldron did a superb job of leading Torpedo Squadron VT-8 to the IJN fleet. The early torpedo attacks by U.S. carrier-based

planes had met the same fate as those launched from Midway — many men were killed.

Dive-bombers from the *Yorktown* and *Enterprise* were credited with the successful ambush of the four enemy carriers. Commander C. W. McClusky leading the VB-6 bombers and VS-6 scouting planes from the *Enterprise,* was credited with good judgment, perseverance, and determination in the initial sighting and subsequent successful attack on two carriers. Lieutenant Commander M. F. Leslie of VB-3 from the *Yorktown,* with 17 dive-bombers was credited with killing a third carrier.

During the afternoon, a second force of 25 dive-bombers from the *Enterprise,* led by Lieutenant Earl Gallaher, had located and killed the last of four carriers in the Japanese armada, the *Hiryu.*

The *Hornet* had formed a flight of 16 dive-bombers to attack the same target. However, the carrier was burning when they arrived, so they elected to attack a heavy cruiser, the *Tone.*

Around 2:00 p.m., the PBYs started returning from patrol flights, and additional information became available at the airstrip. Pappy Cole's plane, 44-P-10, landed, and an ambulance pulled up immediately. One man, who appeared to be a pilot, was lifted from the aircraft. Very soon, word on this pilot — Ensign G. H. Gay of Torpedo Squadron VT-8 of the *Hornet* — and his squadron became available.

Raids carried out by the B-17 Flying Fortresses continued. Unaware that their targeted aircraft carrier had been sunk, they found a destroyer to attack. One plane dropped its bomb-bay fuel tank and failed to return. Another ran out of fuel and ditched. On this occasion, the bombers had counted one near-miss for a fragment that had hit a gun mount, killing six of the enemy. There were six new arrivals in the B-17 ranks, and one squadron of 12 refueled and left for Oahu. Their departure relieved some of the congestion on the airstrip.

Near sunset and through the twilight, a lonely figure sat on top of the Marine bunkers at the eastern end of the airstrips, silent and unmoving, gazing out to sea. There was a white bandage on the back of his neck. It was Ensign Bert Ernest. He and his radio operator, RM3c Harry Ferrier, were the sole survivors of the TBF-1 six-plane raid on the IJN carrier task force in the early morning hours of 4 June.

No one approached the bunker or tried to console Ernest in his grief. Everyone understood that he needed time alone with that vision of the sea and of his friends passing before him. Who on the island would ever forget the sight of the wonderful young men in the torpedo planes as they took off on the morning of 4 June?

That evening, a sadness touched the hearts of those people on Eastern Island. Many had lost good friends and shipmates. All hands felt a sadness for the loss of hundreds of fellow compatriots who perished in the battle at sea and on the atoll. There had undoubtedly been a great loss of life from the damage to the *Yorktown*.

Yet there was a strange feeling of joy, a feeling that perhaps Pearl Harbor was partially avenged, that perhaps a major naval victory had been achieved. There was a feeling of relief that the likelihood of the expected invasion had been greatly diminished.

The sound of the breakers crashing on the reef along the southern shore seemed less threatening that night, and some slept soundly.

6 June 1942 — Rescue Work

With the dawn came the realization that the enemy fleet was in full retreat and soon to be out of range. The priorities shifted to rescue and survey of the floating wreckage from the battle.

Early in the day on 6 June, PBYs rescued a crew from the carrier *Enterprise*. Another plane picked up Captain Dick Blain and his radio gunner Private First Class Gordon McFreely of VMSB 241. These fellows received a warm welcome on the island from their buddies in the Marine Corps.

Ensign Richard V. Umphrey and his crew, formerly of 44-P-7 but then in 44-P-9, with another PBY from VP-24 located VP-24 plane 24-P-11 commanded by Ensign Gaylord D. Propst, missing from the night torpedo attack on the invasion fleet on 3 June. Propst and his crew, along with 24-P-7, 24-P-12, and 51-P-5, had taken off in the evening to attack. En route to Laysan — one of the westernmost of the Hawaiian Islands where the other three

planes had landed — Propst ran out of fuel and had to land on the open sea. They had drifted in the ocean since the morning of 4 June.

The crew of 24-P-11 loaded into Richard Umphrey's plane and then sank their own. Umphrey then ordered everything movable and loose to be jettisoned. In spite of the hazardous seas, gasoline load, and the extra weight, Ensign Humphrey coaxed 44-P-9 into the air and toward Midway.

The two crews of 44-P-9, its own and that of 24-P-11, landed on Eastern Island in the early afternoon. The craft showed the evidence of the severe effort with rippled skin and popped rivets. It was the second plane of the squadron that rendered superior service for Umphrey and his crew during the battle. The first, 44-P-7, had served its crew well in the battle with the Mitsubishis and had been so damaged that it was being returned to Ford Island.

And there was more rejoicing at the rescue efforts to come. Lieutenant (jg) Norman Brady of VP-23 had located the survivors of Robert Whitman's ill-fated 44-P-12. Brady and his crew had spent much of the previous day shadowing the heavy cruisers *Mikuma* and *Mogami* of the invasion fleet. They had provided valuable position data for several attacks made upon the cruisers that day. When they took off on a rescue mission on 6 June, they were tired. Even so, they considered that mission one of their most important.

They were a part of a search organized to locate any possible survivors of 44-P-12. Aviation Pilot Strohmair, navigating for Brady, studied water currents, weather conditions, and position reports and carefully made projections of possible locations for any survivors. During the outbound leg of the flight, he again used every means available to navigators to track flight position. Having searched the assigned sector at 350 miles without results, Brady, using Strohmair's data, extended the search, and 100 miles away, they spotted a raft with four occupants.

It would not be possible to adequately describe the joy felt by the survivors on the raft when they saw the PBY as it started its slow circle toward them. Saved from a tragic death at sea was Ensign Lee C. McCleary, AOM2c Philip L. Fulghum,

Japanese prisoners of war on the USS *Ballard* (AVD-10), Midway, June 1942. (National Archives)

Later, given his choice of duty, he requested naval aviation flight school. During the flight school training, he was killed in a plane crash off Pensacola Naval Air Station.

Ensign McCleary later described the technique used to signal to Lieutenant Brady's PBY. While facing the aircraft, he held his left hand up at arm's length, directly toward the plane. Then, holding a mirror in his right hand, near his eye, he moved it until the light was shining on his other hand. Then by removing his sighting hand, the reflected light was shining toward the plane. He kept repeating this aiming procedure from the time the men on the raft saw the plane until it turned and headed toward them. Today, McCleary has the mirror sealed in an enclosed glass display case.

That evening of 6 June, the lonely figure of Ensign Bert Ernest could again be seen on the Marine bunkers maintaining his watch over the lonely ocean.

7-9 June 1942 — Aftershock and Departure

Routine flights were being made regularly, not to locate the enemy but to find shipmates who had been downed during the battle. VP-44 was engaged in these searches, but there were plenty of reinforcements. Detachments from VP-12 and VP-91 of Patrol Wing One sent out search patrols every day, and detachments from Patrol Wing Two included VP-23, VP-24, and VP-51. The seas were searched thoroughly in the areas of the battle wreckage.

The crews who had flown the long search missions before and during the battle could then relax,

AMM2c John C. Weeks, and AMM1c Virgil R. Marsh. Ensign Jack H. Camp was seriously wounded and died the next morning on Midway.

Philip Fulghum was awarded the Navy Cross for his part in the 4 June fight with the *Chitose*. He had destroyed one of the attacking float planes with his .50-caliber machine gun. And before 44-P-12 crashed into the sea, and on his own initiative, he had gone forward and released the two 500-pound bombs. He had retrieved the raft from the burning plane and helped save the wounded crew members.

but they found that the past few days were becoming a blur. Those in the second flight crews, whose duties had been limited to support on the flight line, also found the recent experience becoming a blur at times. With the added patrol crews, there was an opportunity for both groups to sit in the shade of the giant wings of their planes to visit, talk of home, and rest with the pressure now off.

The saddening news arrived that the *Yorktown* had sunk during the morning hours, reminding everyone, again, that they were fortunate to be alive.

The days and hours seemed to blend into one. A group sat in a circle one afternoon underneath the wing of a plane. An albatross, a "gooney bird," had joined the circle and seemed content to stand and look at the speakers as the conversation ebbed and flowed. Archie "Whitey" Lippens had a small amount of "torpedo juice" — alcohol — and he gave the bird a bit of it. The albatross seemed very surprised at first and then gave the appearance of being appreciative. In a few minutes, he decided to fly and turned away from the group, running to get up flying speed. The takeoff by the birds was always an experience to see. This one was special. Going at full speed toward the airstrip, he would tilt to port, then starboard, and then he would tip over. After three tries to take off into flight, he decided that he couldn't make it and waddled back over to his place in the circle by Whitey. As is often the case after a small drink, the bird appeared to become sleepy. His eyelids closed and his head drooped. The moment his beak touched the coral, he would open his eyes, jerk his head erect, then look around at the group as if to see whether he was being watched.

The next morning, everyone went to see if the bird was all right. He was in good shape and seemed especially friendly toward Whitey. Had the squadron remained on the island, the bird would doubtless have become a drunkard.

Another flight of Army Air Forces planes had landed on Eastern Island on 7 June — four B-24 Liberator bombers. We learned that they had arrived to conduct a bombing mission against Wake Island. They took off late in the evening. None of

the planes found their target, and one of them, bearing Major General Clarence L. Tinker, did not return from the mission.

On the evening of 8 June, plans for VP-44's departure from Midway were announced. The news of the transfer was welcome. The saddening aspect of the return trip was the casualties sustained by VP-44 during the assignment:

Four aircraft damaged in actions with twin-engine land-based medium patrol bombers
One aircraft shot down by carrier float planes
George W. Grove Sea2c, wounded in action
Francis E. Ford AMM3c, wounded in action
Lyonal J. Orgeron AOM3c, killed in action
Lieutenant (jg) Robert S. Whitman, killed in action
Ensign Walter H. Mosley, killed in action
James W. Adams ACRM, killed in action
Clarence J. Norby, Jr. AMM3c, killed in action
William H. O'Farrell RM3c, killed in action
Ensign Jack H. Camp, mortally wounded in action
John C. Weeks AMM2c, wounded in action
Ensign Lee C. McCleary, wounded in action

At 8:30 a.m. on 9 June, the ten remaining planes and their crews took on a few squadron passengers and departed for Ford Island. The rest of the squadron personnel boarded an R4D-1 twin-engine transport. About nine hours later, the entire squadron was back on Ford Island. More than one crew member kissed the side of the old Catalina when they climbed out of her that afternoon.

Shortly thereafter, an announcement was made that was well received: all hands would prepare for temporary shore duty. The officers and men were to report to the Ala Moana and the Royal Hawaiian hotels on Waikiki Beach for duty at the beach.

Chapter 6

The Royal Hawaiian

THE Ala Moana and Royal Hawaiian hotels will always be special to VP-44. The hotels and Waikiki Beach made a perfect combination to help heal the spirit and put the events of the past few weeks in perspective. The opportunity to rest in such luxury and beautiful surroundings came as a complete but welcome surprise.

Registration and check-in at the Royal Hawaiian were on a first-come, first-served basis when our special bus arrived at the hotel on 9 June 1942. AP2c Bill Beck, ACRM Cesare Cavadini, and I shared a room, which had three large beds and was the most lavish quarters we sailors had occupied. Few of the personnel went on liberty in Honolulu that evening; most turned in early. Before drifting off to sleep, Cavadini wondered aloud if the room we were sleeping in was the one that movie actress Myrna Loy had when she had visited the Hawaiian Islands.

Service at breakfast was a special treat, for in the large dining room was a buffet the likes of which few of the sailors had ever seen. In addition to well-prepared and standard breakfast dishes, the spacious serving area had every kind of delicious fruit available in the islands and on the mainland. An ice cream bar, serving every imaginable ice cream dish, was open 24 hours every day.

The hotel lobby made an excellent place to sit, visit, rest, and talk about home, family, and things far removed from the war and recent experiences.

On one day, much to my surprise, AP1c Armido Mancini was wearing an undress (working) white seaman first class uniform. I asked Armido about it. "You might be surprised at the difference in prices in Honolulu between seaman and petty officer ratings," he replied. Apparently, businesses charged less if you wore a seaman's uniform.

At that time, the grounds of the pink rambling hotel structure extended hundreds of feet in every direction. The tall palms, shrubs, and flower gardens made an idyllic setting for the center of paradise. The large veranda faced the ocean and provided a view past the Ala Moana and the large banyan tree near it, along Waikiki Beach, and out to Diamond Head. The long beaches curved around the blue water with its gentle swells and surf. Tall, slender coconut palms leaned out toward the ocean as if they were trying to determine whether to touch the coral blue waters or the azure blue skies.

The days of rest and relaxation at Waikiki were the most peaceful that most of the men had known. Many did not leave the hotel grounds and beach. Several members of the Fleet Air Wing school group established a routine of eating a late breakfast and swimming all morning, broken by long periods of rest under the banyan tree. We showered, had lunch, and rested on the veranda during early afternoon. Another swim and shower before dinner closed out the day's exercise. During the evenings there was more good conversation and a visit to the ice cream bar before going to bed.

Many of the submarine sailors from the work at Midway were also staying at the hotel. Beck and I were invited to one of their rooms one evening for "torpedo juice." Submarine sailors have a reputation for expert conversion of denatured alcohol into good, drinkable juice. We accepted. After a few drinks, the conversation unintentionally drifted toward the differences in the submarine and aviation Navies. Submariners have no use for Airedales, as we fliers were known to them. They claim, and

rightly so, that fliers can't tell the difference between friend and foe submarines. Just before the situation became too heated, I picked Beck up, threw him over my shoulder, and carried him to his room.

One morning while resting under the banyan tree, our talk turned to the blind poet Don Blanding, who had written his work under the banyan. Cliff Troland, Reid Wilson, and I agreed that we would buy Blanding's two books, *Vagabond's House* and *Drifter's Gold*. From that time on, the rest periods under the banyan tree became reading periods. Few people with sight have been able to describe Hawaii as well as the blind poet. For one of our group, *Vagabond's House* became a favorite and served as the inspiration to build a house in the spirit of the poem.

On 16 June, Squadron VP-44 returned to duty flying patrols from Ford Island. Some of the privileges of the Royal Hawaiian were retained. Three days were spent on duty, and shore leave at the hotel was granted on the fourth day. Through July, the FAW school group continued to enjoy the beach at Waikiki and those lazy mornings under the banyan tree with the afternoons on the veranda.

Changes came for VP-44 with a transfer to NAS Kaneohe Bay. By that time, the scars had begun to heal and the squadron was ready to go back to work.

Chapter 7

NAS Kaneohe Bay

August 1942

THE squadron started training in earnest with the move to NAS Kaneohe Bay on Oahu. Guarding the approaches to the Hawaiian Islands was required by regular patrols. These patrols provided surveillance and flight training for the less experienced flight crews being formed. Advanced base duty at Johnston Island, about 500 miles south-southwest from Kaneohe Bay, extended the area under surveillance.

The large Kaneohe Naval Air Station had excellent living conditions as well as a base for operations and training. The bay, with its beautiful, many-colored coral formations, made a sheltered seaplane base to the west of the land-based airfield. The runways of the airfield were wide and long, and the prevailing trade winds were favorable for takeoff and landing. The air station personnel housing, industrial buildings, grounds, and other developed facilities were lovely.

The station was situated on the easternmost tip of a prominence, Mokapu Point, on the windward side of Oahu. To the west and beyond the multicolored waters of the bay was the city of Kaneohe, located on a gentle upward slope to the distant cliffs and mountains of volcanic origin. About 20 miles west of the air station, Pali Pass appeared as a small cleft in the rugged mountain range of the backbone of Oahu. It provided the only passage across the island; all other roads went around the island.

Liberty was available on weekends. The long trip over or around the mountains precluded frequent trips to Honolulu, although a monthly shopping trip or a return to Waikiki Beach for an afternoon made a pleasant excursion. Some of the squadron old-timers and their families lived in Kaneohe. As for the FAW school group, many took up tennis. Both the Bachelor Officer's Quarters and the ships' service areas had excellent courts.

At the end of June 1942, the squadron personnel strength had been at 397: 47 officers, 19 chief petty officers, 9 naval aviation pilots, 180 petty officers, 132 seamen, and 10 mess attendants.

The Pacific Fleet Aviation Wings were undergoing changes in support for the patrol squadrons. Several four-stacker destroyers had been converted to two stacks and modified to provide tender service — providing quarters, a mess hall, fuel, and other services for seaplane squadrons — augmenting the larger tenders such as the USS *Curtis* (AV-4). The modified destroyers included the USS *Thorton* (AVD-11) and USS *Ballard* (AVD-10). Newer ships had been designed and built specifically for tending the Navy seaplanes. One example was the USS *Coos Bay* (AVP-25).

Accordingly, the Fleet Air Wing squadrons in the combat areas were converting from a full ship's company complement of personnel to flight crews with a command staff and key maintenance personnel. Patrol Aircraft Service Units (PATSUs), with their own command staff, were formed for the purpose of providing ground and maintenance service. The PATSUs were supported by the seaplane tenders as well as the aviation squadrons.

In line with these operational changes, the staffing of VP-44 reduced to provide the command staff, key maintenance personnel, and flight crews. Lieutenant Commander R. C. Brixner; Lieutenant W. L. Richards, executive officer; Lieutenant Donald G. Gumz; Lieutenant John Simpson, personnel officer; Lieutenant R. L. Summers; and Kenneth H. McCardle ACMM, squadron leading chief, formed the command staff. Key maintenance personnel included C. C. Vandergrift, Stephen Leflar, John Griffith, Archie Lippens, Robert Barnes, and Smith E. S. Boyer, all with ratings in machinist, ordnance, or radio. Lieutenant C. E. Olson, flight officer, formed the squadron into 18 flight crews — three sections, called A, B, and C, with six crews in each section.

There were other changes. Many of the older, more experienced squadron personnel who had trained the young sailors transferred to other squadrons. They would again take untrained and inexperienced crews and pilots and help build an efficient patrol squadron.

The Fleet Air Wings were forming several squadrons of new Lockheed twin-engine land-based patrol bombers called Vega Venturas, designated PV-1. Vinton Pease and Cesare Cavadini transferred to one of the new squadrons. In the coming weeks, the radio crew of VP-44 were saddened to learn that Chief Vinton Pease had died in a PV-1 crash at sea.

Classes in ship and aircraft identification were conducted daily for all personnel. Gunnery classes and aerial gunnery practice were conducted on rigorous schedules.

September 1942

The Navy's utility plane by Vought Sikorsky, designated J2F-6 and affectionately called the Ugly Duck, was used extensively for in-flight gunnery practice. The powerful R-1820 Pratt and Whitney engine gave it plenty of maneuverability. The biwing craft, with a deep hull for flotation that extended below and out in front of the engine, had two open cockpits, forward and aft. Sturdy landing gear and a tail wheel made it amphibious and ideal for both a tow target carrier and gunnery practice ship. The planes were flown by aviation pilots for all gunnery exercises.

An ordnance man and I finished a gunnery practice run in the J2F just before lunch on 23 September 1942. Our pilot brought the plane into the final approach for landing. Just as the plane was ready to touch the end of the runway, it lurched violently, and the port landing gear flew up between the wing and tail section. The pilot skillfully held the aircraft upright on the starboard landing gear as it steered slowly to starboard and began to lose speed.

Several hundred sailors were sitting underneath the wings of their Vought Sikorsky OS2U observation scouting float planes parked on the apron in front of the hangars. The parking apron was adjacent to the edge of the landing strip. In the next instant, a sea of white hats fled toward the hangars as the J2F steered in their direction. The pilot slowly lowered the port wing of the plane, and the hull touched the concrete strip. A stream of sparks and showers of debris made a long plume behind the aircraft. I thought the ordnance man, who was down in the flotation hull, must surely be losing his legs. The plane made a loop in the center of the airfield with a brilliant display of fireworks. At the end of the first loop, I jumped out, and on the second, the pilot and ordnance mate did likewise. The pilot hit the concrete, then jumped up to the after cockpit

Lieutenant (jg) R. L. Summers, host, VP-44 picnic, Kaneohe, Hawaii, December 1942. (Robert L. Hayden)

screaming, "Where are my passengers, where are my passengers?" He smiled when both of us shook hands with him and congratulated him on an excellent landing. The hundreds of sailors who had scrambled for the hangars then encircled the plane. The fire truck with lights flashing and siren screaming came streaking toward the crippled aircraft and the crowd around it.

The next morning, Arthur Arsenault, Patrick Mahon, and I walked out to the end of the landing field to see what had happened during the landing. At the scene of the impact was a concrete conical landing field light base split down the middle. It

was about 18 inches in diameter at the base and in height. The executive officer, safety officer, and other air station personnel were there, preparing a report of the accident. My respect for the station's ship's company and the Navy safety programs continued to grow. On the following morning, we revisited the end of the runway and found that all runway lights were already mounted in a concrete base, flush with the surface of the runway.

October 1942

In early October 1942, a prominent American and World War I air ace, U.S. Army Air Forces

Admiral Chester W. Nimitz (right) and party, NAS Kaneohe Bay, 7 November 1942. (James F. Scott)

Awards Ceremony, NAS Kaneohe Bay, 7 November 1942. From left to right: Lieutenant Donald B. Gumz, Distinguished Flying Cross; Lieutenant Commander William L. Richards, Silver Star Medal; Ensign Richard V. Umphrey, Air Medal; Ensign H. C. Smathers, Distinguished Flying Cross; Philip LeRoy Fulghum, Aviation Ordnance Man First Class, Navy Cross; Lieutenant William E. Chase, Air Medal; Ensign Theodore S. Thueson, Distinguished Flying Cross; Lieutenant (jg) John E. White, Air Medal; and J. I. Foster, Chief Aviation Pilot, Distinguished Flying Cross.

Captain Edward V. "Eddie" Rickenbacker, who was on a mission for Secretary of War Henry Stimson, had been reported missing, his B-17 apparently down at sea in the southwestern Pacific. A number of the FAW squadron aircraft were detached to Johnston Island and organized for a rescue search mission.

There were some storms in the area when the crew of VP-44's C Section, crew number 15, took off in the early morning hours of 6 October from Johnston Island. They were a part of a large search and rescue mission that extended to the South Pacific Ocean. The crew consisted of PPC Lieutenant (jg) Harry D. Metke; Lieutenant (jg) H. A. Sorenson, copilot; Ensign Genuit; Ensign Lewis; Conrad E. Smith AMM2c, plane captain; Thomas F. Reeder AMM2c; James O. Pearson AMM2c; W. Reid Wilson ARM2c; Clifford V. Troland ARM3c; and John C. Stark AOM3c.

Before takeoff, the plane's radio direction finder was not operating properly, and with the limited resources on the island, the unit could not be repaired. The decision was made to go ahead with the mission without the RDF equipment. A box search pattern would be used to locate Johnston Island upon returning in the afternoon, if navigation was in error.

The flight was uneventful, but the crew could not find the island on their return. As fuel supplies dwindled, Harry Metke advised Reid Wilson that he would put down on the water with sufficient fuel for Wilson to operate the radio all night. By morning, Johnston Island, Palmyra atoll, and Canton Island had located radio fixes on the downed PBY. However, Patrol Plane Commander Ensign "Jack" Jewell H. Reid of crew number 1, Section A, had his own radio position report on the plane, and his crew was dispatched by the commanding officer of Johnston Island for the PBY's rescue. Crew members included Ensign Thomas G. Monahan, copilot; Ensign R. L. Summerell; Furman P. Jackson AP2c, fourth pilot; Wilford M. De La Mare AMM2c, plane captain; James Roskowick AMM3c; Walter L. Possage AMM3c; John W. Griffith ARM1c; Edward P. Harty ARM3c; and Robert K. Barnes AOM1c.

Luck had changed for Lieutenant Metke's crew number 15, for the black storm clouds low on the horizon had not reached them when Jack Reid's

rescue plane arrived. Metke's plane, with the white parachute draped over the high tail section, was clearly visible.

However, an open-ocean landing is never without its risks. The seas are seldom calm. Ensign Reid landed successfully with only a few popped rivets in the hull, and those below the waterline were quickly plugged with sharpened pencils. He had wisely refused to bring filled containers of gasoline — which could leak with altitude changes, creating an extreme fire hazard — and instead had brought along empty five-gallon cans and a sump pump.

Because high seas were running 20 feet to the crest, it was necessary to keep the two planes widely separated. Reid's crew members, with lines tied to them, went out on the wing and used the small hand-operated sump pump to draw out fuel from their aircraft's tanks to fill the five-gallon cans. The cans were lowered to a waiting life raft from the other plane, and two men rowed the raft to the waiting aircraft. The process was reversed on the downed plane to get the fuel into the fuel tanks. Three times the trip was made to get enough fuel into Metke's PBY to get back to base. The seas were running so high that the small rubber life raft was only visible from the planes when both plane and raft were on top of a crest of the waves.

The mission was successful. The aircraft and crew had been saved.

November 1942

When awards were presented to naval personnel at NAS Kaneohe Bay on 7 November 1942, Admiral Chester W. Nimitz, commander in chief of the U.S. Pacific Fleet, made the following remarks:

Officers and Men of the Pacific Fleet:

Just 11 months ago this morning the Japanese began their march through the Pacific by treacherous assault on this very spot. The instant courage shown by Kaneohe's defenders on December 7 has since consistently been matched by Kaneohe flight crews in almost every combat operation of our patrol squadrons from Java Sea to Midway and the Solomons.

Our air personnel have won an enviable position in the van of our hard hitting team.

It is a genuine pleasure to see here Ensign Jewell H. Reid. Reid was the first man to sight the Japanese fleet nearly 800 miles from Midway at noon last June 3. I assure you that Reid's thrill when he sighted the enemy through a rift in the clouds was no greater than my own when his dispatch reached me.

His courage and tenacity in tracking the enemy for nearly three hours, despite enemy aircraft patrols in his immediate vicinity, with utter disregard for his personal safety, is certainly in keeping with the highest traditions of the Navy.

Also being honored is Lieutenant William L. Richards and several members of his group which successfully located the enemy that midnight, hundreds of miles west of Midway, and attacked with torpedoes from close range. This surprise attack, first of its kind, contributed greatly to the ultimate success of our forces in the action.

Time is to[o] short for me to read the citations of all who are being honored here today, but I do want to mention Aviation Ordnance man Phillip Fulgham [*sic*]. His patrol plane was attacked by several enemy off Midway and he shot one down before his plane was set afire and crashed into the sea. He braved fire from the burning wreckage to transfer his wounded comrades to the rubber life raft.

Since Midway, personnel of the patrol squadrons in the Solomons have performed with extraordinary devotion their task of seeking out the enemy over vast and often storm-swept regions. Neither the dangers of distance and weather, nor enemy assault have deterred them from their duty. Their devotion is typical of the Army, Navy, Marines and Coast Guard forces who are fighting side-by-side in the Solomons.

Changes in Squadron VP-44 were being made regularly, and a new deployment seemed likely. Lieutenant Commander R. A. "Rosy" Rosasco relieved Lieutenant Commander R. C. Brixner as commanding officer. The PBY-5a amphibian seaplanes that the squadron had flown since receiving them at NAS Alameda were exchanged for the PBY-5 seaplanes. Squadron operations shifted from the airfield to the seaplane base and seaplane ramps.

There were other changes. The squadron's size was trimmed from 18 to 14 flight crews. The squadron strength was then at 144 officers and crew: 46 officers, 10 aviation pilots, 4 chief petty officers, 83 petty officers, and 1 seaman second class. Of the original FAW school group, only nine members remained in the squadron: John J. Klopp AMM2c, Patrick J. Mahon AMM2c, George W. Newcombe AOM2c, Willard H. Nicks AMM2c, Edwin L. Olsen ARM2c, Clifford V. Troland ARM3c, W. Reid Wilson ARM2c, Lloyd D. Wood AMM2c, and I, rated ARM2c. In December, Clifford Troland joined the growing numbers of men whose applications for flight training had been approved and who were enrolling in flight school.

December 1942

A change in duty for the squadron was anticipated with the change in command. By early December, all training courses for personnel had been completed and patrol flight duties had been shifted to other PBY squadrons. On 18 December, Chief Kenneth H. McCardle announced a squadron party sponsored by Lieutenant R. L. Summers at the Cook estate, the home of a prominent Hawaiian family.

The party was a good mixer. Officers and enlisted men became better acquainted with the new skipper, Rosy Rosasco. Excellent food was served during the afternoon. One of the highlights of the day was organized by Whitey Lippens: the crew tossed the skipper into the swimming pool.

After the CO had changed into a dry uniform, Chief McCardle called a muster and all hands to attention. Lieutenant Commander Rosasco read the squadrons orders. We would prepare to depart NAS Kaneohe Bay and pack personal gear to include only one set of undress white uniforms, work uniforms, skivvies, and shoes. All other clothing would be placed in storage or sent home. The squadron personnel and aircraft would deploy to

Some of the crew of 44-P-1. Left to right: Lieutenant (jg) R. C. Donaldson, James R. Bunch, George W. Newcombe, John F. Gammell, Theodore L. Beck, Melvin R. Ubben, and Lieutenant Donald G. Gumz. (Loren G. Judas)

"Old Hands." Left to right: Gordon Crawford, Archie "Whitey" Lippens, and Kenneth McCardle. (Loren G. Judas)

Some of the crew of 44-P-9 and others (unidentified). Back row, far right: Arthur Arsenault. Center row: William O'Daniel, James Mills, and Patrick Mahon. Front left: Lieutenant (jg) Leonard D. Sullivan. (Loren G. Judas)

Crew of 44-P-2. Standing, left to right: Lieutenant (jg) John N. Andregg, Eldon Algood, Earl Bryant, John Gadway, and John Albers. Sitting: Wallace Petrie, Edward McLaughlin, Frank P. "Pappy" Neufeld, and George Hitchcock. (Loren G. Judas)

Left to right: John W. Griffith, George W. Blatherwick, Robert B. Ford, John H. Albers, Lieutenant (jg) Clarence E. Olson, unidentified, Lieutenant (jg) Pettiet, and Ensign R. E. McCallister. (Loren G. Judas)

Water landing. Tony Holden is one of the tossers; from left to right: Harry L. Gerkin, George Newcombe, Bill Harmon, Willard Nicks, and Robert Ford. (Loren G. Judas)

New Hebrides, Espiritu Santo, and undertake patrol and other duties as directed.

The squadron personnel enjoyed a pleasant Christmas day and dinner at the air station. Life had been agreeable on this beautiful Navy base. The planes of Squadron VP-44, 44-P-1 through 44-P-14, were refurbished and ready. The crews were rested, had received additional training for combat,

and were ready to take up new duties in the South Pacific theater of operations.

As 1942 came near its close, the empire of Japan was at its peak. The circle bounding that empire ran from the outer islands of the Aleutian chain to Wake Island, the Solomons, New Guinea, Netherlands East Indies, Burma, the coastal China mainland, and Manchuria. The expansion, however, had been

The skipper, Lieutenant Commander R. A. Rosasco, welcomed by VP-44. Tosser with hands in air is Tony Holden. (Loren G. Judas)

Smiles after the dunking. Left to right: Harry Sorenson, Harry Metke, and Lieutenant Commander R. A. Rosasco. Far right: William "Swede" Lundberg. (Harry D. Metke)

slowed. The Imperial Japanese Navy had suffered a decisive defeat in the Battle of Midway in June. And although in May we had lost the carrier USS *Lexington* in the Coral Sea battle, the Japanese attempt to take Port Moresby had been repulsed. On 7 August, the Marines, under the command of Major General Alexander A. Vandegrift, had landed on Guadalcanal in the Solomon Islands.

On the European continent, bitter fighting had raged between the Soviet and German troops on the Russian front. The loss of life on both sides was the greatest ever recorded in any war. The United States had declared war on Bulgaria, Hungary, and Romania.

In Africa, the German army had seized Tobruk but was halted at El Alamein by the British in July. On 23 October, the British had begun their offensive thrust at El Alamein. Allied forces had landed in North Africa in November.

Chapter 8

Destination Segond Channel

AT 8:00 a.m. on 26 December 1942, the crews of the second section of two seven-plane sections — 44-P-8 through 44-P-14 — stood by on the seaplane ramps at NAS Kaneohe Bay, ready to board their planes. Each aircraft was scheduled to take the crew, extra passengers, and personal gear. By 8:30 a.m., all planes lifted off the bay and set a course of 195.7 degrees to the Palmyra atoll, 1,118 miles away.

The Palmyra atoll consisted of small islets connected by coral strips, forming a U-shaped pattern along the north, east, and south sides. Three lagoons were located inside the "U." A coral barrier reef surrounded the islet, and during low tides, parts of the reef were exposed. The largest of the little islands was called Coopers Island and was six feet above sea level. The west lagoon bordered Coopers Island and provided a sheltered landing area and buoys to tie up the aircraft. Navy Construction Battalions (Seabees) had built a pier, quarters for crews of transient aircraft, and living and administrative areas for station personnel.

On the following morning, the planes took off for Canton Island on a heading of 228.1 degrees for a relatively short flight of 893 miles. The island consisted of a lagoon surrounded by narrow strips of coral sand and coral reefs a few feet offshore. A small natural entrance to the lagoon from the ocean was located on the western side. Near the entrance, and inside the lagoon, the coral was dredged to a suitable depth for a seaplane landing area.

Both Canton and Palmyra Islands are tiny specks in a vast ocean. They are so small that the strategic value of these stepping stones to the South Pacific may not be immediately clear. But for our navigators, they were a perfect pathway from the Hawaiian Islands in the North Pacific to the Solomon Islands in the South Pacific.

Suva Fiji was an 8.7-hour flight from Canton at a heading of 213 degrees and 1,252 miles. The landing in Suva Harbor, at the island of Viti Levu, gave the flight crews a strange feeling of returning to civilization, albeit a very different civilization. With few exceptions, this was the first opportunity for the crews to visit a country other than their own or one of its possessions or territories. The busy harbor, wharf, and streets with heavy traffic controlled by the island's Melanesian police wearing high headdresses and broad-leaf skirts made a colorful spectacle. Most of the businesses were operated by immigrants from India or by their descendants. As our planes lifted off the next morning, each one of us carried a few souvenirs of Fiji.

The delight we had felt with a visit to a new civilization was heightened at New Caledonia. The latitude of 25 degrees below the equator made an ideal climate, with crisp, cool air and bright sunshine. The Grande Rade Harbor formed by Ile Nou and Presqu'ile Ducos led to the sparkling city of Nouméa. Nouvelle Caledonia, a Free French Possession, appeared to be orderly and well developed with a beautiful countryside of farms and mountains. Nouméa would rival any of the small cities of France. The official language of the island was French, most of the people being French immigrants and their descendants. A few were native Melanesian peoples.

Commander South Pacific (COMSOPAC) Fleet Headquarters was located aboard the USS *Argonne* in Grande Rade Harbor. Admiral William F. Halsey had replaced Admiral Robert L. Ghormley as commander in October.

PBY squadrons in the South Pacific Ocean reported to COMSOPAC through the chain of command from Fleet Air Wing One. Several squadrons rotated for duty in the Solomons area, including VP-12, VP-23, VP-24, VP-44, VP-51, VP-52, VP-72, and VP-91. Very early operations in the South Pacific were provided by VP-11, which had transferred to the South Pacific shortly after the Battle of Midway and which operated out of Fiji and New Caledonia.

A seaplane repair center on Ile Nou was equipped with a seaplane ramp to beach the planes and several buoys offshore. There were tents for transient aircraft crews, a mess hall, and Bachelor Officer's Quarters.

A few of the fortunate crews would remain over one day at the U.S. Navy Seaplane Base on Ile Nou to remove the anti-icing equipment from the aircraft wings. The others would leave the next morning. The route taken thus far had led south by south-

west. The New Hebrides lay on a northward course of 6.5 degrees back toward the equator, at a distance of 465 miles.

The crew of 44-P-9 lifted off the Grande Rade Harbor in the afternoon of 31 December 1942. Lieutenant (jg) Robert A. Swan, patrol plane commander, had elected to take off late in the day since it was only a short flight to the New Hebrides. With Swan was the crew who had flown with him for the past several weeks and, with few exceptions, would fly together during the entire tour in the Pacific: Lieutenant (jg) Leonard D. "Harry" Sullivan, copilot; Ensign Howard E. Rumrey, navigator; William C. O'Daniel AMM1c, plane captain; Patrick J. Mahon AMM2c; James J. Roskowick AMM3c; Joseph A. Kammerer ARM3c; Arthur J. Arsenault, Jr. AOM3c; and I, rated ARM2c.

As the plane circled in salute to the base personnel, we could see the harbor and city with the green mountains and farmlands in the background. We thought that we would be fortunate to visit this island again.

Clear skies gave way to gray as the plane approached the Hebrides. The island group came into view as a green strip of jungle low on the horizon. Beyond the islands to the north and west were towering storm clouds, adding to the gloomy and foreboding appearance of the area.

I stood on the catwalk, looking out the plane between the pilots and across the bow, observing the islands as they came closer. Sully and Swan were discussing the possibilities of being assigned quarters on the USS *Curtis*, the USS *Tangier*, or the USS *Mackinac*. Sully favored the *Tangier*.

As they talked about living conditions on the ships, I recalled stories of the early Dutch traders in this area and of the aboriginal peoples of the islands, whom the Dutch had called the Big Numbers and Little Numbers. Cannibalism had been practiced here until the early 1900s. I fervently hoped to see these people during the time in the Pacific.

The waters below began to take on a dark color, losing all the blue. As Aore Island — which also lay on Segond Channel, across from Espiritu Santo — and Ile Toutouba slipped past, Swan turned to port and pointed ahead and below. There, lying at anchor, was a mighty fleet of ships in a line along

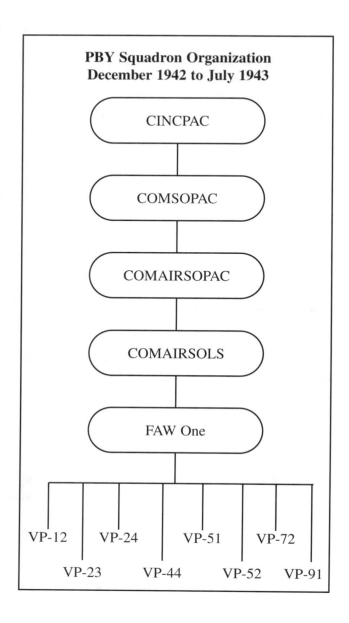

**PBY Squadron Organization
December 1942 to July 1943**

CINCPAC

COMSOPAC

COMAIRSOPAC

COMAIRSOLS

FAW One

| VP-12 | VP-24 | VP-51 | VP-72 |
| VP-23 | VP-44 | VP-52 | VP-91 |

of the crew boarded the boat and left for the ship while the remainder stayed to gas the plane. After taking on fuel, it was nightfall. Because a watch on the aircraft was needed, Patrick Mahon and I volunteered to stay aboard. We had not particularly cared to go aboard the USS *Curtis*, as the ship's personnel seemed to dislike fliers. Perhaps they resented providing services to others. The officers and men of VP-44 were of the same mind; in fact, several men of other crews had also stayed aboard the planes. The caustic comments of some of the sailors revealed their poor attitudes. We simply did not want to tolerate unwarranted comments from the ship's company and felt that we might have some trouble with them.

Most of the planes and crews of VP-44 spent New Year's Eve 1942 on the Segond Channel of Espiritu Santo, New Hebrides. Early arrivals had already assumed patrol duties. Two planes of our squadron were expected from Nouméa on the next day.

Officers and enlisted men of the squadron had been mindful of the progress of the worldwide war during the summer and fall of 1942, primarily through the one-page news briefs of the Public Affairs Office of NAS Kaneohe Bay. But the level of detail possible in the publications could never convey a realistic understanding of the fighting and conditions under which the fighting occurred on the islands of the Solomons and the waters around them. We knew little of the overall battle situations, tactics, victories, or losses on either side of the battle lines, ashore or afloat. As 1942 drew to a close, what were the conditions under which men were fighting and what was the status of the Battle of Guadalcanal and control of the Solomons?

Admiral Ghormley, who had been in general command, did little of the planning or execution of the invasion of Guadalcanal on 7 August 1942 because he had been busy moving his headquarters from Auckland, New Zealand, to Nouméa, New Caledonia. The expeditionary force commanded by Admiral Frank J. Fletcher had been made up of three groups around the aircraft carriers *Enterprise*, *Wasp*, and *Saratoga*. An amphibious force had been commanded by Rear Admiral Richmond Kelly Turner.

Major General Alexander A. Vandegrift had

the eastern half of the length of the channel: two light cruisers, several destroyers, liberty ships, victory ships, seaplane tenders, and a large white hospital ship with a red cross on an upper deck. Of the crew, only Swan, who had tracked the Japanese fleet at Midway, had ever seen such a concentration of ships.

The seaplane tender USS *Curtis* was recognizable by its large crane on the stern and afterdeck for seaplanes. Swan flew to the west and came in on the landing approach to the east. The hulls of ships flashed past the PBY as we landed.

A boat from the *Curtis* standing off a buoy signaled, and we taxied up and tied to the buoy. Most

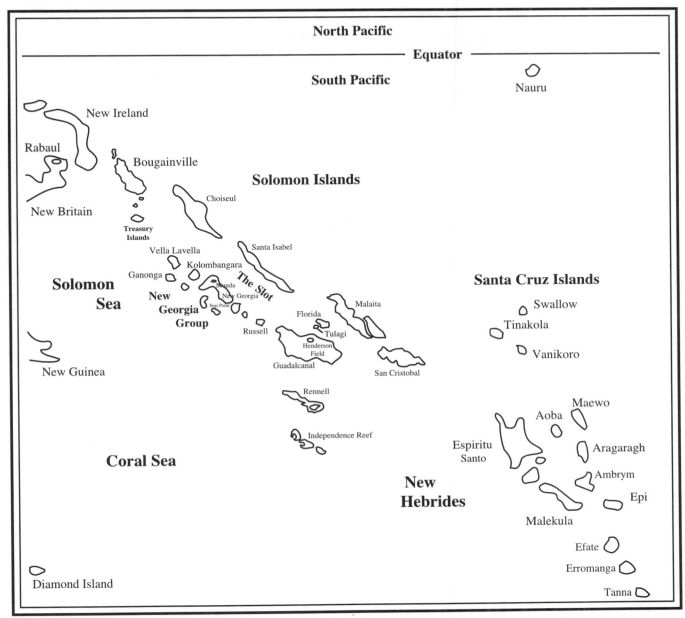

North Pacific

Equator

South Pacific

Nauru

New Ireland

Rabaul

Bougainville

New Britain

Solomon Islands

Choiseul

Treasury Islands

Vella Lavella

Santa Isabel

Solomon Sea

Ganonga

Kolombangara

Munda

New Georgia Group

Segi Point

New Georgia

The Slot

Santa Cruz Islands

Swallow

Tinakola

Vanikoro

Florida

Malaita

Russell

Tulagi

Henderson Field

New Guinea

Guadalcanal

San Cristobal

Rennell

Maewo

Aoba

Independence Reef

Espiritu Santo

Aragaragh

Ambrym

Coral Sea

New Hebrides

Epi

Malekula

Efate

Diamond Island

Erromanga

Tanna

South Pacific Ocean.

landed 10,000 Marines on Guadalcanal and 6,000 on Tulagi and Gavatu. That afternoon, 7 August, the forces were struck by enemy aircraft from Rabaul, New Britain. There was a heavy loss of life, but the attackers were beaten off by the carrier group's air cover.

The Japanese made up a force of 50,000 men under Lieutenant General Gunichi Mikawa with orders to drive the Marines into the sea. From Rabaul, they had sent a task force made up of five heavy cruisers, two light cruisers, and a destroyer toward the slot, a channel with islands of the Solomons on either side. At high speed, they had come upon the U.S. forces in the Savo Sound off of Guadalcanal. We had been completely unprepared for them. Admiral Fletcher had retired out of harm's way and was refueling. In 30 minutes, the Japanese cruiser force sank four cruisers, three American and one Australian, and damaged another, handing the U.S. Navy its worst defeat. Turner's

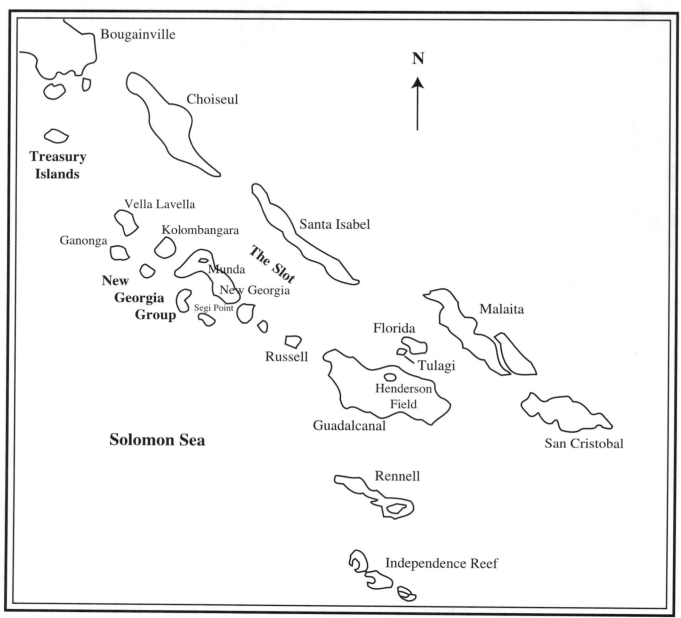

Solomon Islands.

amphibious forces retreated with a few Marines still on board and most of the supplies for the landing forces.

What followed then was a valiant fight by the Marines to take the area around the Guadalcanal airstrip under some of the most horrible conditions of climate, terrain, and disease while on starvation rations and without medical supplies. But they did it. They took the field and named it Henderson Field after one of their own who had died at Midway. Ground, air, and naval battles continued for months around the airfield. The fighting was conducted under most inhumane conditions for both the defenders and the attackers.

The combined Japanese fleet under the command of Vice Admiral Nobukate Kondo, made up of the carriers *Shokaku* and *Zuihaku*, the seaplane carrier *Chitose*, the light carrier *Ryujo*, and two

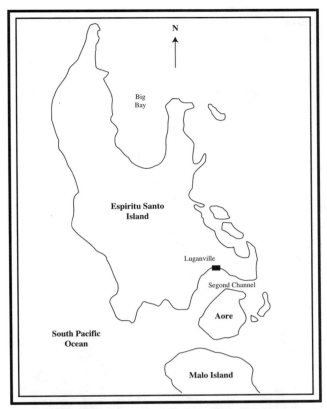

Segond Channel — Espiritu Santo, New Hebrides.

battleships, several cruisers, destroyers, and transports with reinforcements, steamed down toward the slot to retake the Guadalcanal airfield.

The forces of Henderson Field and aircraft from the *Enterprise* and *Saratoga* engaged Kondo's forces on 24 August. The carrier *Ryujo* was sunk and the *Enterprise* severely damaged. Lieutenant (jg) Robert S. Whitman and his crew of 44-P-12 were partially avenged when the seaplane carrier *Chitose* was damaged by planes from the *Saratoga*. The battle was inconclusive with both sides taking losses.

The "Tokyo Express" had continued to send ships down the slot to resupply, reinforce, and make ship-to-shore bombardments of the American positions.

In October, Admiral William F. Halsey had replaced Admiral Ghormley as COMSOPAC, and Rear Admiral Thomas C. Kinkaid took over for Admiral Frank J. Fletcher as commander of carrier operations.

A massive land assault had been launched in late October against Henderson Field. Naval forces under Admiral Chuichi Nagumo were stationed northeast of the Santa Cruz Islands. The forces of Admiral Kinkaid, including Task Force 61 around the *Enterprise* (back from repairs and in service again), Task Force 17 around the *Hornet* (with Admiral George Murray), and Task Force 64 around the battleship *Washington*, were closing to take up the challenge. The *Enterprise's* SBD bombers hit the carrier *Zuiho* and the *Hornet's* aircraft hit the carrier *Shokaku*, putting both enemy ships out of action. The cruiser *Chikuma* was damaged.

On the American side, the *Hornet* was sunk. The battleship *South Dakota* and cruiser *San Juan* were slightly damaged. The battle of Santa Cruz ended with losses to both sides.

Ground reinforcements for the Japanese continued to pour onto Guadalcanal at Cape Esperance, and air raids from Rabaul continued to hit the island. A force of two battleships, the *Hiei* and *Kirishima*, came down the slot. A force of U.S. cruisers escorting troop transports put up a good fight, but two were sunk, though they did damage the *Hiei*. Planes from Henderson Field and the *Enterprise* sank the *Kirishima*. The next day, Marine and Navy aircraft sank six transports that were still trying to land troop reinforcements.

The failed Japanese attempt to land reinforcements on 14 November was their last effort to send in more troops on Guadalcanal. The forces already there stayed locked in combat with Henderson Field's defenders. The Japanese received no support, supplies, or medicine. Lacking these, their plight was worse than the Americans', which was bad enough.

As the year ended, the battle perimeter around Henderson Field continued to see heavy fighting, and many lives were lost. The Japanese forces had lost more than 890 aircraft and 2,300 naval airmen.

There were still more naval encounters to come, but the U.S. forces controlled the waters around Guadalcanal.

USS *Curtis* (AV-4). (National Archives)

USS *Tangier* (AV-8). (National Archives)

USS *Mackinac* (AVP-13), Mare Island Navy Yard, 13 September 1943. (National Archives)

Chapter 9

Espiritu Santo

THE Navy base at Segond Channel in the New Hebrides allowed surveillance by the long-range PBY Catalina seaplanes over a 700-mile arc to the west, around to the northwest across the Solomon Islands, and to the north.

The Japanese base on Nauru Island, 1,036 miles to the north at a heading of five degrees, was well fortified. It provided a center of operations for the enemy surveillance aircraft to the Solomon area and seas south of Nauru toward the New Hebrides. Vanikoro, located 264 miles north of the Hebrides, lay on a heading of 354 degrees. By stationing seaplane tenders at Vanikoro and operating from there, the island of Nauru lay only 100 miles beyond the turning point of the PBY flight radius.

Henderson Field on Guadalcanal and the nearby seaplane base at Tulagi in the Florida Islands were 642 miles away from Segond Channel on a heading of 316 degrees. Farther on, at New Britain, the IJN forces at Rabaul were 1,285 miles away. All of the

Solomons were well within bombing range of the enemy at Rabaul.

By using an advanced base fueling station, long-range Japanese bombers could reach all of the U.S. bases in the theater, including the New Hebrides. Rennell Island, south of Guadalcanal, was 530 miles from Espiritu Santo at a bearing of 300 degrees. Moresby, New Guinea, and Cook Town, Australia, were both about 1,400 miles west across the Coral Sea at headings of 289 and 258 degrees, respectively. South of the Solomon Sea, and farther south across the Louisiade Arch, the Coral Sea extended south to Australia. That part of the Coral Sea to the west of New Hebrides, to a radius of 700 miles, lay within the range of the watchful eyes of VP-44 on Espiritu Santo.

PBY-5a planes (from other squadrons) operating off Henderson Field and the PBY-5 seaplanes operating from the Tulagi seaplane base in the Florida Islands could easily range over parts of New

Active volcano Tinakula erupts on Tamini Island in a patrol sector south of Nauru Island. (Navy photographer, USS *Curtis*; courtesy Allen Thompson)

Guinea. They could also provide surveillance around New Britain and the Rabaul base and New Ireland to the west.

Our primary mission was to provide surveillance for the seas within our range. We would soon learn that this would carry a higher priority than any other activity the squadron commander or his people might wish. To conserve aircraft and provide essential surveillance, we were prohibited from taking offensive action.

The Fleet Air Wing Commander did not want to consider any mission other than the primary one and so risk the loss of a patrol plane for the patrol work. Our job was vital but was without the glory of being locked in daily combat, as were the Marine Corps and Navy fighter pilots on Henderson. That did not mean that the days to follow would be without risks to men and planes. Deadly encounters with the Japanese patrol planes, hundreds of ocean miles from base, would soon become commonplace.

A secondary mission assigned to the squadron offered more risk and danger than the primary one. One or two planes and crews were assigned to the Tulagi seaplane base. The purposes of the Tulagi detachment were to provide air-sea rescue (termed Dumbo missions) for airmen downed at sea and for coast-watcher supply and transportation. These missions would involve flying far behind enemy lines and bases. Rescue missions frequently required open-sea landings, sometimes within range of enemy shore-based artillery.

The gods of radio silence and secrecy of operations ruled. Plane crews would seldom know what the other crews were doing, which limited the perspective of all personnel on the squadron's operations. A crew might have orders to make a long flight to a distant point, hold position at that point, and then return to base without knowing why. But secrecy of operations was not the only factor that limited the knowledge of the plane crews. We were busy during the entire tour — flights were frequent

The crew of 44-P-6 at Vanikoro Island, March 1943. Left to right: Frank Michalek, Charles Marsh, George Johnson, Edward McKissick, Samuel Minervino, Arthur Carson, and William Junck. (Edward McKissick)

and long — so there was little time to visit with close buddies in other crews. Good friends were more apt to have a chance encounter at an advanced base than at the home base of Espiritu.

The facilities for aircraft maintenance in the harbor at Espiritu Santo were good, but we worked in the open and in the oppressive heat. At the far west end of the string of buoys for the planes was a little cove on the Espiritu side of Segond Channel. The PATSU detachment had built a small shed there to protect tools. There was a steel mat ramp and mat-covered parking area for up to two planes. Whenever possible, the maintenance work was done on the parking mat. The planes' equipment included work stands that hung from the engine nacelles — enclosed shelters for the engines — when in use. A screen came with the stands to catch parts and tools that accidentally fell or dropped. No one wanted to try to retrieve fallen tools or parts in these waters. Sharks came up frequently to investigate the commotion when tying up to a buoy.

Within 100 yards from the cove was a small pier made of coconut logs tied together with a coconut tree fiber. Huge piles of coconuts were just beyond the pier. Every day, three or four people worked on the coconuts, apparently taking out the meat to dry for "copra," as the source of coconut oil.

From the pier, a small rocky roadway led along the shore to the east. On the eastern side of the island were large tracts of coconut palms. There was a rumor that the Palmolive Peet Company owned the palms. The story circulated that the company charged $200 for each tree cut during construction of a large airfield.

Because the buoys where the planes tied up paralleled the roadway, we had a good view of any traffic on the road and of the houses along it. There was a shed near the small pier and three large houses that probably belonged to planters or plantation owners. There was also one large house that seemed to be the only official or government building on the island. A Free French flag flew near it.

Two distinctive types of people occasionally walked along the roadway. Both men and women of one group wore large, fitting black pants and long black jackets that hung down to the hips. They were of small stature and wore large conical hats of palm leaves. The clothing design allowed the flow of

The crew of 44-P-1 aboard the USS *Curtis* at Segond Channel, *circa* May 1943. Standing, left to right: F. O. Scofield, M. R. Ubben, G. W. Newcombe, R. Bunch, S. Schwartz, T. L. Beck, and Chief Aviation Pilot J. F. Gammell. Sitting: Ensign Waite Bolden, Lieutenant (jg) R. C. Donaldson, Lieutenant Commander R. A. Rosasco, and unidentified. (G. W. Newcombe)

cooling air. They walked in pairs, and the women always walked several feet behind the men. We learned later that they were Cantonese from Canton, China. The second group was French Indo-Chinese. During the entire tour, no one would see the European-born settlers who occupied the planters' homes.

The squadron lost no time in taking up patrol duties. The skipper, Lieutenant Commander R. A. Rosasco, set the pace for patrol schedules and special flights. His crew on 44-P-1 was made up of himself, Lieutenant (jg) Ralph C. Donaldson, Ensign Waite Bolden, John F. Gammell AP1c (NAP), F. O. Scofield AMM1c, Stanley Schwartz AMM2c, Theodore "Red" Beck AMM2c, Melvin R. Ubben ARM1c, Richard "Dick" Bunch ARM3c, and George W. Newcombe AOM2c.

It was a safe bet that whatever assignment a flight crew received or wherever one of our planes touched down, the skipper had been there first. His crew put in over 112 hours' flight time in January, most of it on patrol duty. Ten hours was spent searching for a B-17 crew down at sea and eight hours on a round trip to Rennell Island to pick up

Marine coast watchers. Lieutenant Donald G. Gumz, the squadron "exec," usually alternated with Rosasco as PPC on flights.

We of 44-P-9 flew 89 hours in January. The first flight was a 13-hour patrol to a point north of the Solomons and back to Vanikoro on 6 January. The seaplane tender was tied up to a buoy. A "Higgins boat" — a small utility boat used by the tender — served as a fuel barge, and motor whaleboats provided transportation to and from the ship. The tender served good meals for flight crews as well as lunches for outbound patrol flights. Sleeping quarters were spotlessly clean and comfortable.

Patrick Mahon and I again volunteered to sleep aboard the aircraft for the night watch. We had not yet been aboard a tender except at Vanikoro for meals. During the one-day layover, the crew cleaned the aircraft and checked all inboard equipment. These activities provided a relief from boredom and helped keep the ship spotless. On the morning of 8 January, we departed for a 12-hour patrol flight terminating at "Buttons," the code word for Segond Channel.

As our plane neared the Hebrides, we saw the

islands lying like a green belt on the dark sea; storm clouds towered beyond. In minutes, PPC Bob Swan was turning over the jungle on the final leg, and as we approached the water, we saw the long line of ships' hulls and anchor chains off the starboard beam. Swan settled the aircraft down gently in a stall landing on the smooth channel waters.

Several days later, on 19 January, Lieutenant (jg) Harry Sullivan came out to the plane to see Pat and me. His feeling was that we had lived on the plane long enough, nearly three weeks, so we agreed to move aboard ship.

The shower late that afternoon was welcome, and the special soap designed for use in saltwater worked well. The ship's chow was good, but to our surprise, the squadron personnel were sleeping on the afterdeck in sleeping bags. However, rest came quickly and completely when we climbed into the bags at darkness.

We awoke to the sight of the fiery red ball of the sun just at the skyline of Ile Toutouba east of Segond Channel. It was lying in the mists, and water vapor gave it the burning red color and made it appear larger than normal. The sun signaled another hot and sultry day. It had rained overnight, and there were small puddles of water scattered among the sleeping bags.

During the month, there were two Vanikoro trips, one to Tikopia Island, a one-day search (along with the skipper's crew) for the downed B-17 crew, and two local patrols. We had not had an encounter with the enemy, but that would change very soon.

Minor changes were made in crew assignments. Frank P. "Pappy" Neufeld replaced William C. O'Daniel, who went to another crew.

February 1943

Action for VP-44 came on 1 February. Lieutenant John N. "Andy" Andregg and his crew in 44-P-2 — Ensign Hutchinson, Loren G. H. Judas AMM1c, John H. Albers AMM3c, Edward C. McLaughlin AMM3c, Earl F. Bryant ARM3c, and John M. Gadway AOM2c — were assigned an outgoing patrol with a scheduled return to Vanikoro. They sighted a small surface vessel at five degrees south latitude and 163 degrees east longitude. They were carrying four depth charges. Andregg made a gliding run on the target from 500 yards, dropping

the charges in two salvos of two each. The hydrostatic fuses were set for a depth of 50 feet. The objective was to inflict damage from the bottom up. The port waist .50-caliber strafed the target during the bomb run, but the crew was not able to observe any damage to the vessel.

Lieutenant (jg) Henry S. "Hank" Noon and his crew in 44-P-5 — Ensign R. L. Summerell, T. J. Watkins CAP (NAP), A. C. Jocius AMM1c, Thomas F. Reeder AMM3c, James F. Scott AMM3c, Norman E. Bauer ARM1c, Orval W. Davis ARM3c, and James F. Sewell AOM2c — encountered a Kawanishi 97 flying boat on 2 February in the same area that Andy Andregg had located the surface vessel on the previous day. The Kawanishi came upon the port quarter and started firing at about 1,100 yards. The aircraft made turning runs on each other, but the Kawanishi was slightly faster and could pull away when the pilot wished. The PBY used the waist hatch .50-caliber guns. The aircraft exchanged short bursts for about five minutes, then Noon purged the unprotected fuel tank of all but about 200 gallons and filled it with CO_2, which prevented explosive gas fumes from filling the empty portion of the tank.

The second attack also lasted about five minutes. Fifty-caliber tracers appeared to enter the bow of the enemy boat and in the area of the 20-mm cannon. All rounds fired by the Kawanishi were low and behind the Catalina.

Noon's crew experienced some difficulty with the armament. After about 80 rounds with the port waist hatch .50-caliber, the gun jammed. Later, the jam cleared and started firing again. Both of the .30-caliber guns in the bow jammed after one round each, and one gun remained out of action due to a broken bolt group. The bow guns failed to operate on several occasions when the target was within range and good position. In the end, the fight was a draw, for the Kawanishi pulled away.

During the quiet morning hours of 3 February, our crew of 44-P-9 was on a routine patrol flight out of Segond Channel. Bob Swan was scanning the horizon with binoculars from the cockpit, and Copilot Harry Sullivan touched the trim tabs occasionally to keep altitude and course. Pappy Neufeld was enjoying the view from the tower. In about an hour, he would be relieved and prepare lunch for

The crew of 44-P-5 at Segond Channel, April 1943. Standing, left to right: Orval Davis, James Sewell, Ryan, Thomas Reeder, Norman Bauer, Alexander Jocius. Sitting: Lieutenant Robert Hayden, Lieutenant Henry Noon, and Chief Aviation Pilot Frye. (Charles D. Davis)

the crew. Howard Rumrey was busy over his maps at the navigation table. At the radio position, I always monitored the interphone system on one side of the headset and the radio search frequency on the other and checked the radar screen two or three times per minute. We always operated under conditions of radio silence except when in contact with the enemy. Changes in orders or other communications came to us from the base radio control station of Commander Fleet Air Wing One (COM-FAIRWING One), whose headquarters were on the USS *Curtis* at Espiritu Santo.

Normally there was little communications traffic on the radio circuit, and thus the sound of a very strong signal tuning up on frequency came as a surprise. After a series of dots and dashes, the radio station then called our base control and gave a message using the call sign of one of the VP-44 patrol planes. The message was in the same form we used in all communications, but the signal was much stronger than any I had heard and the rhythm and precision of the operator were better than any of our operators, including me. The body of the message

was in plain language, and that was also unusual. It gave the heading, speed, and location of a Japanese force of two battleships, six cruisers, eight destroyers, and troop transports. The base acknowledged the transmission.

I typed the message out as I heard it and then went over it with Howard Rumrey. I explained that I did not believe it was from one of our planes, that none of our operators were as good as the one sending the message. Howard went over it with Swan and then gave me the following message to send to base: "We do not believe the previous message was from VP-44 patrol craft; it appears to be a fake." I encoded the message and sent it off. Shortly, base radio came back with the response, "Stay on course."

Later, on 7 February, we were staying overnight at Vanikoro. I discussed the incident with Norman Bauer, radio technician of 44-P-5. He too had heard the message and also a weak signal from a PBY denying that they sent the message. On 9 February we were off duty and aboard the *Curtis*. I learned from the small news bulletin issued on the ship that the enemy forces had used a decoy force and a destroyer force to rescue 12,000 troops from Guadalcanal.

Also on 3 February, Lieutenant Andy Andregg and his crew in 44-P-2 continued to set the pace with enemy contacts. After their attempt to sink the small surface vessel on 1 February, they had returned to Vanikoro for two nights and one day. During the return leg of the patrol to Segond Channel, a Kawanishi 97 flying boat pulled up abeam the port side. The two planes exchanged gunfire for several minutes. Andregg's plane took several hits in the bow section from 7.7-mm shells and several in the waist and tunnel section. One of the shells in the waist area was from a 20-mm cannon.

AOM2c John M. Gadway, bow gunner, was hit by the smaller caliber gun. Andy had him put in one of the bunks and rubbed some of the new sulfa drug, an antibiotic, into the bullet holes in the calf of his leg. He happened to have a flask in his kit, from which he gave Gadway several stiff drinks. From that point, Gadway felt no pain. The crew said that he sang all the way back to Buttons.

A motor whaleboat was making way from the beach maintenance area toward the *Curtis* when 44-P-2 landed. As the plane made for a buoy, the motor whaleboat received a signal to go directly to the plane. The vertical stabilizer — the vertical portion of the tail — had a large cannon hole in it. On closer inspection, several smaller holes in the waist area and tunnel section were discovered.

A stretcher bearing Gadway emerged from the waist blister and was placed in the boat. "There is a lucky man," said the boat coxswain (Cox). "He'll go to the hospital ship from the *Curtis* and from there to the States." Any person on the boat would have gladly traded places with Gadway.

Hank Noon and Andy Andregg seemed to be getting all the action. On 4 February, Hank Noon encountered a Kawanishi north of the Solomons. The enemy approached from the rear firing the large- and small-caliber guns. The planes crossed over paths as the Kawanishi climbed to the PBY's altitude. The PBY used all gun positions, firing 400 rounds of .30- and .50-caliber ammunition. The range was about 400 yards at crossover. The enemy plane eventually broke off and left, but the PBY was pretty well shot up.

The enemy had abandoned attempts to reinforce troops on Guadalcanal in November 1942; then they gave up on trying to retake Henderson Field with ground forces in early February 1943. The IJN forces instead expanded and operated Munda airstrip and nearby Villa strip, both on New Georgia.

VP-44's Lieutenant G. W. Hanthorn and Lieutenant R. L. Summers, with their respective crews and aircraft, landed on 11 February at the seaplane base at Halavo Beach on Tulagi Island, which was part of the Florida Islands, for Dumbo and coastwatcher supply operations. What followed was an intensive and challenging series of missions, most behind enemy lines in areas where enemy aircraft operated and many times in weather normally considered impossible to fly in.

Fighter protection from Henderson Field usually accompanied the PBY Dumbo flights. The fighter escorts joined up with Dumbo at a prearranged point and provided cover during most of the flight. Escort aircraft included 6 to 20 fighters.

Lieutenant Hanthorn's mission on 12 February was to fly to Boy Boy Bay, Choiseul Islands, which was in the northern Solomons. En route, he and his crew were to inspect the tip of Santa Isabel Island for a possible landing area in Hero Passage. They picked up seven F4F Wildcat fighters at Henderson, and two hours later eight Bell P-39 Airacobras joined them. Hanthorn and crew successfully delivered supplies to the coast watcher and picked up three U.S. Navy fliers who had survived aircraft crashes. On the return leg of the flight, they found two enemy barges loaded with supplies and made strafing runs on them. When the fighter pilots saw the action, they joined in and soon made burning hulks of the barges. The rescued aviators were returned to Guadalcanal at Lunga Point, and Dumbo returned to Halavo Beach.

Lieutenant Summers's mission on the same day took him and his crew of 44-P-13 to Sandfly Bay at Vella Lavella Island, about 30 miles beyond the Japanese Munda and Villa airfields. An Australian coast watcher accompanied them on the flight.

They picked up an escort of seven F4U Corsairs

The crew of 44-P-9 aboard the USS *Curtis* at Espiritu Santo, April 1943. Standing, left to right: Joe Kammerer, Patrick Mahon, Arthur Arsenault, James Roskowick, Frank Neufeld, and James Mills. Sitting: Ensign Howard Rumrey, Lieutenant Robert Swan, and Chief Aviation Pilot Samuel Wideberg. (James C. Mills)

and proceeded to Sandfly Bay. They landed in open sea and then taxied to the shoreline. Natives in canoes met them to pick up the Australian coast-watcher supplies and delivered two Marine Corps fliers from Unit 1060 of Squadron VMS 112. Summers and crew learned that a Kawanishi 97 flying boat had landed and taxied to the shoreline that morning; it had had a fighter escort of eight Mitsubishi Zeros. During the return trip, one of the F4U escorts had aircraft trouble, and the pilot bailed out. The PBY landed in open sea to pick up the escort pilot.

On 13 February, Hanthorn and his crew flew another mission to locate a downed flier at the eastern tip of New Georgia Island. They searched the area and extended it to Baraker Island. Finding no one, they landed near the island. One officer and two enlisted men went ashore in the rubber life boat. They located one .45-caliber pistol in a holster, one empty holster, a khaki shirt with the name "Rathsol" over the left pocket, one dungaree shirt, and a pair of Army coveralls. Four hundred feet

from the clothing they found a life raft paddle with a life jacket hanging on it but no survivors.

On the 14th, Lieutenant Summers flew to Hero Point at Hero Passage with an escort of eight F4F Wildcats and unloaded supplies to natives. The coast watcher was not present.

The 15th was Lieutenant Hanthorn's duty day. He took off with supplies and a radio for the coast watcher in the Russell Islands, a few miles west of Guadalcanal, and to locate a squadron leader of the Royal Australian Air Force, named Widdy, and his party. He landed between Lona Island and Talina Island, where there was a native village. The natives took the supplies and explained that there were officers on Banika Island. Hanthorn and crew taxied about two miles to another beach and found Colonel Long and Lieutenant Colonel Gibson of the Army and Second Lieutenant Mulvey of the U.S. Army Air Forces, who had landed his P-38 Lightning when he had run out of fuel. The party of fliers was taken aboard. Flying in a northwesterly direction, Hanthorn then located canoes with

The crew of 44-P-10 aboard the USS *Curtis* at Espiritu Santo, April 1943. Standing, left to right: O. E. Evans, J. W. Ward, J. J. Finn, A. E. Downer, G. B. Johnson, and D. G. Grimwood. Sitting: Lieutenant (jg) Thomas G. Monahan, Lieutenant C. G. Conrad, and Ensign E. D. Brchan. (Thomas G. Monahan)

squadron leader Widdy and his party, who also boarded Hanthorn's plane.

The rescued officers directed Hanthorn to the northeastern side of Pavuvu Island. There they picked up another party that had been saved by coast watchers. That afternoon, Hanthorn and crew landed at Lunga Point on Guadalcanal with Colonel Long, Lieutenant Colonel Gibson, Second Lieutenant Mulvey, Squadron Leader Widdy, and First Lieutenant Holt of the Royal Australian Navy.

Hanthorn's next mission was on 17 February. He and his crew went to Lunga Point to pick up a Colonel Pashel and a major of the Marine Corps. They then took off as directed, flew the party to the Russell Islands, and returned to Halavo Beach. The

fighter escort for the mission was four F4U fighter aircraft.

On 19 February, Hanthorn and crew took Lieutenant Train and Chief Petty Officer Schroeder of the Royal Australian Navy to an island in the Ontong Java group and returned on the following day. The trip was made without fighter escort. When they arrived back at Tulagi, they found that Lieutenant Andy Andregg and crew in 44-P-2 had arrived from Espiritu Santo.

On 21 February, Hanthorn's crew was ordered out to locate and rescue a lone swimmer. Four P-40 Warhawks proceeded with the Catalina to the point near Baraker Island and sighted the man. They landed and picked up the grateful swimmer and took him to Lunga Point. That night, the Tulagi seaplane base at Halavo Beach was raided by a single enemy plane. One man — Clifford A. Olin of VP-44 — was killed and three officers were wounded: Ensign J. K. Hutchinson and Ensign R. C. Trejo of VP-44 and Ensign Norris of VP-24.

Meanwhile, patrol work continued unabated at Espiritu Santo. On 12 February, Lieutenant (jg) Bob Swan and our crew on 44-P-9 sighted a Kawanishi 97 flying boat on the port quarter and well out of range of gunfire. Our PBY turned slowly to port to close the distance, but the enemy turned likewise to keep the space between us. Again, Swan turned slowly, and the Japanese flying boat headed for a cloud. It began to appear that the Kawanishis had learned a lesson. Our guess was that they wanted no part of the .50-caliber machine guns in the waist of the PBY.

Lieutenant R. L. Summers and his crew in plane 44-P-13 were the first to contact a Mitsubishi twin-engine medium T-96 bomber. On 28 February, they sighted the bomber five miles off their starboard quarter. The enemy closed rapidly and began firing what they estimated to be a 20-mm cannon. At close range, he opened up with the small-caliber guns. They exchanged fire for about three minutes with the PBY using 75 rounds of .50-caliber ammunition.

Lieutenant C. G. Conrad and his crew in 44-P-10 also hit a Mitsubishi T-96 on 28 February. The crew included Lieutenant (jg) Thomas G. "Tom" Monahan, P. R. Barker AP1c (NAP), Ensign E. D. Brchan, "Danny" G. Grimwood AMM1c, J. W. Ward AMM3c, O. E. Evans AMM3c, George B. Johnson ARM2c, James J. Finn ARM3c, and A. E. Downer AOM3c.

There was a wild exchange of gunfire as both planes maneuvered in turns and altitude. All of Conrad's guns had a good workout. They did an inside turn to within 200 yards of the T-96, and the bow gunner got off over 200 rounds of ammunition. Several bursts showed tracers entering the lower part of the enemy's fuselage. The waist gunners both fired 50 rounds. The T-96 pulled out of range and circled. He then took off on a bearing of 345 degrees. When the bomber was out of sight, the navigator, P. R. Barker, gave Conrad a corrected heading, and they continued on patrol.

The baptism of fire for us in 44-P-9 also came on 28 February. There is nothing in the world that gets your attention in a PBY as well as the Klaxon calling battle stations.

I had been on radio watch during the morning. It was possible that several kinds of battle reports would require transmission that day, and I had encoded the most likely reports in advance so that the message could be sent out faster if needed. Pappy Neufeld and Patrick Mahon were on lookout in the waist hatches, Neufeld to starboard and Mahon to port. James Roskowick was in the tower, and Arthur Arsenault was resting in the bow turret. Bob Swan and Harry Sullivan were in the cockpit while Howard Rumrey poured over his navigation charts. With no lookout needed, I lay down on one of the bunks until time to shift positions.

The Klaxon sounded. I hit the deck just as Neufeld and Mahon lifted the hatch covers. The wind in the hatch area immediately pulled toilet paper from the roll hanging on the bulkhead. The air filled with swirling paper. I was suddenly and inexplicably embarrassed at what the aviators in the enemy plane might think of the lack of organization on our part. Hastily, I grabbed all the tissue and threw it out the starboard hatch. This may have mystified the pilot of the brown and gray twin-engine bomber out about 1,500 yards on the starboard quarter. Ducking into the tunnel area, I opened the bottom hatch and locked it up. Next, I swung the .30-caliber gun into place and locked it. A round pumped into the chamber and it was ready to go.

Curiosity got the better of me. Pappy Neufeld's gun was not firing. The enemy was just off our starboard quarter, and Pappy was fussing with a jammed gun. Both of the enemy pilots' faces were in full view. I knew that when they realized Pappy's gun was stuck, they would close fast with all guns blazing. Quickly, I grabbed the .30-caliber, put it on safe, and laid the barrel on the edge of the waist hatch. The purpose was to replace the jammed .50 or, as a last resort, fire it from a free position. At that instant, Pappy waved me off, slammed the breech cover in place, and started firing. Rumrey climbed into the waist and said, "Mills, you can't hit anything with a free gun."

"I know it," I said, "you know it, the Navy knows it, but the Japs don't know it."

Next, I locked the .30 back in place, and then what followed seemed to be a series of great aerobatic maneuvers.

We went into a dive and I became airborne. We pulled out sharply, and I held on desperately with my hands as my head and shoulders went out the tunnel hatch. There was an excellent view of miles and miles of ocean. Below us were puffs of black smoke from a 20-mm cannon. Howard pulled me back into the tunnel and asked if I was all right. "Yes, but dammit, I lost my hat," I said.

Pat Mahon's .50 was pumping slugs, and the music and rhythm of that gun sounded beautiful. When he stopped, Art Arsenault started singing with the twin .30-calibers in the bow. They were delivering bursts of 300 rounds per minute.

Pat told me that after the bomber pulled away, it had gone above us and dropped two bombs. He saw them fall about ten feet from our fuselage between the wing and tail section. I went into the radio compartment and Joseph Kammerer was all smiles. He had successfully sent out his first radio dispatch in the heat of battle, the coded message for "attack by twin-engine bomber," and the base had acknowledged.

A good supply of sharpened pencils was ready for use, and I gave them to Pappy. He then started looking for holes below the waterline and plugging them with the pencils. I took over the radio watch, and Kammerer went to the waist for lookout duty as we continued on patrol. Pat took over the tower while Pappy Neufeld and James Roskowick did a damage assessment. When he finished with the plane inspection, Pappy cooked and served a big lunch for everyone. Judging from the smile on his face as he served the meal, Pappy was happy with pilots and crew.

We went over the plane in detail on the maintenance ramp the following morning. There were holes in the wing fuel tanks, but the bullets had not penetrated the protective rubberized tank. Holes were in the fabric, hull, auxiliary power plant, and radar antenna. Identify Friend or Foe radar (IFF) antennas were broken. One hole was in the fuselage just below the waist hatch blister. There should have been an exit hole for the bullet, but I could not find it. Archie "Whitey" Lippens of the maintenance crew was working with me. When I pointed

out the hole to him, Whitey stepped out on the ladder, examined the hole, came back into the plane, and looked at it again. He looked around the waist hatch area and then pointed to the yellow life raft. We took the raft out of the plane and unrolled it, and there in the center of the floor of the raft was a 7.7-mm slug.

"Whitey, why don't you keep that slug as a souvenir — show it to your grandchildren someday and tell them the story of 44-P-9," I said.

March 1943

A small contingent of officers and enlisted personnel arrived at Espiritu Santo in March to reinforce the patrol and maintenance effort. The new men were quickly integrated into the flight and maintenance crews. The Tulagi detachment was necessary, but it did drain the resources to keep up the required patrol schedules.

Lieutenant (jg) Harry Sullivan was transferred on 3 March from 44-P-9 to another crew, where his services were needed. Everyone in our crew felt the loss, for Harry was highly respected. I particularly missed him because he and I had enjoyed some competitive crap games in the plane at night during stopovers at Vanikoro. Aviation Pilot Samuel R. Wideberg, then Ensign Wideberg, replaced Sully. Sam was liked by everyone, and we had flown with him frequently for nearly two years.

When returning from long patrols, one of the small pleasures we enjoyed was flights over the Swallow Islands, which were approximately 200 miles north-northwest of Segond Channel. Occasionally the natives would wave to us as we passed over. The Swallow Islands were low coral atolls around a deep blue lagoon. They were covered with palms, and those near the shorelines leaned across the white coral sand beaches and out over the water. Both in topography and in origin, the Swallows differed from the volcanic islands in the area. They differed also in terms of inhabitants. The people of the coral atoll did not have the high, bushy hair of the Melanesians; they were instead fairer of skin and graceful in movement.

On 11 March our crew received orders for a spe-

The crew of 44-P-8 at Segond Channel, Espiritu Santo, April 1943. Standing, left to right: unidentified, Robert Shafer, Clifford Studdard, William Burns, Jr., Albert Allen, Zygmunt Zydak, Dale Brown, and Chief Aviation Pilot Roy Robinson. Sitting: unidentified, Lieutenant (jg) J. J. Lyons, and Lieutenant (jg) Thorn. (Dale E. Brown)

cial flight. We were surprised because we had just returned the day before from a three-day patrol on the Vanikoro route. Another surprise came when we rendezvoused off the tip of Ile Toutouba with a J2F "Ugly Duck" utility aircraft and set course for the Swallow Islands.

As we approached the atoll, the J2F broke out to lead over its intended landing place, and our PBY followed. We made a turn to port and came in low over the landing area and witnessed one of the most spectacular events in the Pacific during those times.

Midway between the shoreline and landing area, 30 long outrigger canoes were headed in our direction. Each was manned by ten persons paddling in unison with a tall man at the stern calling cadence. It was a scene no Hollywood set could reproduce.

The bronzed bodies of the paddlers were decked out in flowers and leis.

Lieutenant Bob Swan called for launching a smoke bomb to provide wind direction for the landing J2F. I went to the tunnel, inserted one in the launcher, and called, "Smoke bomb away." I watched through the tunnel hatch until the bomb splashed and smoke started lifting. It had landed about 100 yards in front of the path of the canoes. Quickly closing the hatch, I went into the waist to enjoy the spectacle below. There to our starboard quarter were the 30 canoes paddling full speed back toward the shoreline. They had reversed course instantly by jumping up and turning around in the canoe seats. Apparently, they were fearful of the smoke bomb.

The PATSU crew and 44-P-8 on the beach near the seaplane base at Tulagi, Solomon Islands, *circa* March 1943. (Thomas G. Monahan)

Circling, we came back over the area and all canoes had gathered about the J2F. We watched as a man and several boxes of gear came out of the side hatch and into the lead canoe. We felt privileged to have this limited contact with the people of the Swallow Islands. There was also a feeling of remorse and sadness, for we knew that the opportunity to land and visit the area was unlikely to occur.

On 14 March, a detachment of two planes and crews from VP-44, one from VP-24, and a detachment of PATSU 1-4 maintenance personnel arrived at Halavo Beach in the Florida Islands to relieve the contingent on station there, which included Lieutenant William Scarborough and Lieutenant Robert W. Weber of VP-91, Lieutenant Douglas of VP-72, and a PATSU contingent. They then departed for Buttons. The arrivals made camp that evening and settled in for the night:

44-P-7
Lieutenant Clarence E. Olson
Lieutenant (jg) Harry A. Sorenson
C. E. Frye AP1c (NAP)
Gordon H. Crawford ACM
John H. Albers AMM2c
Robert B. Ford AMM2c
Edwin L. Olsen ARM2c
Robert Bowman ARM2c
George W. Blatherwick AOM2c

44-P-8
Lieutenant (jg) J. J. "Jiggs" Lyons
Lieutenant (jg) Thorn
Roy H. Robinson AP1c (NAP)
Zygmunt F. Zydak AMM1c
Albert D. Allen AMM2c
Clifford L. Studdard AMM3c
Dale E. Brown ARM1c
Robert L. Shafer ARM2c
William W. Burns, Jr. AOM2c

Coast watcher and crew approach the crew of 44-P-8 in the Solomon Islands, March 1943. (Dale E. Brown)

VP-24
Lieutenant Norris
Lieutenant (jg) Pearck
Foster CAP (NAP)
Kline AMM1c
Voss AMM2c
Anderson ARM1c
Peck ARM3c
Dorosz, Air Bomber

PATSU 1-4
Romine AM1c
Alexander AMM2c
Scott AMM3c
Miner ARM3c
Coon AOM3c

The Tulagi detachment flew nine missions from 14 March through 23 March. Several required fighter cover; one included 16 fighters. They deliv-

ered more than 2,000 pounds of coast-watcher supplies, made one rescue mission, ferried military personnel on special assignments, and did two searches for life rafts.

On 24 March, the crews of 44-P-7 and 44-P-8 readied their PBYs for takeoff and return to Segond Channel. Jiggs Lyons took off first while Clarence Olson stood by. Lyons gained some altitude, then dove on the Tulagi base in salute. Roy Robinson believed he was trying to blow down the miserable tent in which they had been living. Lyons pulled up at high speed at the end of the dive, and both engines died. The port wing hit the water first and broke off. The plane then cartwheeled, and the starboard wing broke off and the plane sank.

Olson purged his gas tanks in 44-P-7 before attempting takeoff in order to remove any water in them, then he and the VP-24 crew departed for Buttons.

Lyons and his crew and the PATSU crew remained behind to begin salvage operations on 44-P-8 immediately. The nearby USS *Butternut* located the plane, then moved it to shallow water near Halavo Beach. Salvage operations commenced after lunch that day. On the following day, Lieutenant Hank Noon and his crew landed at Halavo Beach flying in Olson's 44-P-7.

April 1943

Bob Felmuth and his crew — Ensign Chadron Hunter, Ensign R. L. Summerell, Gordon M. Merrow AP1c (NAP), Vernon T. Holden AMM1c, John J. Klopp AMM2c, Richard G. Watson AMM2c, Julius G. "Red" White ARM2c, and Henry F. Saliger AOM2c — made contact with the enemy on 7 April in 44-P-12. The Mitsubishi T-96 came up on their port quarter and made crossing runs from port to starboard and back. The PBY had a firing range of 400 yards for both .50-calibers in the waist and the .30-caliber in the tunnel hatch as they climbed toward cloud cover. The bomber appeared to use the top turret cannon and all for-

Crew of 44-P-3 and PATSU crew display captured Japanese flag, *circa* March 1943. Sitting, front row center: Lieutenant (jg) Leonard D. Sullivan and Lieutenant Robert B. Hays (second from right). (Dale E. Brown)

ward machine guns. The Catalina was hit in the cockpit, port wing, and tail section.

Two plane crews made contact on the following day. Patrol Plane Commander Lieutenant W. E. Roy and Copilot Harry Sorenson encountered the enemy at 9:45 a.m. local time. The crew fired 150 rounds of .30- and .50-caliber ammunition. Patrol Plane Commander Lieutenant (jg) R. C. Donaldson and Copilot Ensign T. J. Atkins made contact at 12:25 p.m. Their PBY dropped from 600 feet altitude to 150 feet. The Mitsubishi bomber dropped to about 50 feet altitude and fired a cannon at a range of about 800 yards. When the Catalina opened fire with the .50-caliber, the enemy pulled away. The engagement lasted five minutes.

Lieutenant Commander R. A. Rosasco, in a let-ter to CINCPAC, COMAIRPAC, COMAIRSO-PAC, and COMFAIRWING One dated 16 April 1943, commented on these and other engagements:

Enemy tactics . . . again emphasize the reluctance of Japanese medium bombers to close to effective gun range even though possessing superior speed and maneuver-ability over the PBY. It has repeatedly been observed that the enemy will not close if fire is opened by the PBY, and will close immediately if he observes or believes the waist guns in the PBY to be out of com-mission. Standard doctrine in PBYs on search missions in the South Pacific is to avoid combat whenever possible. For this

Lieutenant (jg) Leonard D. Sullivan (left) and Lieutenant Robert B. Hays on Tulagi, Solomon Islands, *circa* March 1943. (Thomas G. Monahan)

furnished a fighter escort and originated at the seaplane base at Tulagi. But in this case, the flight was originating hundreds of miles away at Espiritu.

While in the Bougainville area, a flight of P-38 Lightnings were sighted. They were flying at low altitude, as was the PBY. Although the PBY was monitoring the fighter radio frequency, neither the Catalina nor the fighters broke radio silence. The plane delivered the supplies for the coast-watcher station and picked up a downed airman the natives had rescued.

All hands aboard were monitoring the fighter frequency and listened to a battle in progress, involving the P-38s. A dogfight ensued, and several planes were shot down. When word came over the radio that his mission was accomplished, Metke made a wide, sweeping turn to head back to base.

reason, fire is opened by PBYs at extreme range in an effort to discourage the attack. Additional defensive armament is urgently required in the PBY.

On 18 April an unusual mission was assigned to Lieutenant (jg) Harry Metke and crew of 44-P-6 — Frank Michalek AP1c (NAP), Arthur T. Carson AMM1c, Edward J. McKissick AMM2c, Charles M. Marsh AMM3c, Samuel A. Minervino ARM2c, George B. Johnson, Jr. ARM3c, and William C. Junck AOM2c. They took on supplies for a coast-watcher station on Bougainville Island. The location of the station was well behind the enemy forces on the New Georgia group of islands. Dumbo flights into the New Georgia group were always

A P-38 fighter pilot then came on frequency and reported that his plane was shot up. The pilot pulled up alongside the PBY. Charles Marsh was on watch in the starboard blister and was able to get a close look at the fighter plane. One engine was out, and oil appeared along the nacelle of the damaged engine. Metke asked if the pilot was all right. If he wanted to bail out, Metke assured him, he could pick him up very easily. The pilot thought he could make it and would try for Guadalcanal. He asked for that particular course, which Metke gave to him. The Catalina followed the same course for some time, watching for a downed plane, before heading for Espiritu Santo. The round trip flight was logged as 9.9 hours.

The next day, the news flashed across the harbor

Crew of 44-P-3 in the New Hebrides, *circa* April 1943. Standing, left to right: Virgil Hobart, unidentified, Keith Wilkason, Harold Blair, Patrick Fitzpatrick, and Loren Judas. Sitting: unidentified, Lieutenant Robert Hays, and Chief Aviation Pilot Clifford Adams. (Patrick Fitzpatrick)

Crew of 44-P-12 at Espiritu Santo, April 1943. Standing, left to right: Henry Saliger, Louie Lundgren, Richard Watson, Vernon T. Holden, John Klopp, and Julius White. Sitting: Lieutenant (jg) Chadron Hunter, Lieutenant R. B. Felmuth, and Gordon Merrow. (Richard Watson)

Lieutenant (jg) W. E. Roy's crew at Espiritu Santo, April 1943. Standing, left to right: Willard Nicks, Hillis Coker, Lloyd Wood, Robert Kallam, Richard Miller, and Robert Barr. Sitting: unidentified, Lieutenant (jg) W. E. Roy, unidentified, and Chief Aviation Pilot Armido Mancini. (Robert Barr)

that Japanese Admiral Yamamoto and his party had been intercepted and shot down by U.S. forces. Were Metke and his crew a part of the mission to provide Dumbo service for those forces? If they were a part of the operation, they would have been the last to know, thanks to radio silence and secrecy.

As time passed, the attitude of the USS *Curtis's* personnel toward Squadron VP-44 did not improve. The overnight stops at Vanikoro provided an opportunity to visit with the other crew also stopping over, usually during the evening mess hour. One crew member from 44-P-3 mentioned that conditions with the ship's company were in fact getting worse.

We had been at Vanikoro over one day and were going out on the following morning and back to Buttons that night. We arrived at Espiritu the next afternoon. I had forgotten the comment about the *Curtis's* company. After a shower and good food that evening, it took only a few minutes standing by the ship's rail, as it grew dark, to become sleepy and ready to turn in. I undressed, put my clothes in the locker, and stretched out on the upper bunk.

It was 30 minutes to lights out, but I knew I would go to sleep long before that. Several other fellows had already turned in, and the quarters were quiet and peaceful. At that moment, from the hatchway, someone shouted obscenities about the Airedales.

Looking up, I saw a bosun mate looking in. "OK," I shouted, "you've been asking for it for a long time; now come and get it." He answered the challenge in an instant. By the time I swung from the top bunk to the deck, he was there. It was a fast and furious slugging match. Fortunately, he fell to the deck exhausted. In a few more seconds, I would have collapsed. Four of the other fellows picked him up by each hand and foot, carried him up the ladder, and tossed him out the hatch.

On the following morning, there were no incidents, nor in the days to follow. When the particular bosun mate came out on deck that morning, he spoke to me in a civil tone. I had been warned that fighting aboard ship was against regulations. When Lieutenant (jg) Bob Swan and Howard Rumrey made a rare appearance on the afterdeck, I was apprehensive, feeling that I might have a problem. But Swan said, approvingly, "Mills, I just wanted to

The crew of 44-P-6 at Espiritu Santo, April 1943. Standing, left to right: unidentified, William Junck, Samuel Minervino, Edward McKissick, Arthur Carson, Charles Marsh, and Frank Michalek. Sitting: unidentified, Lieutenant (jg) William Cullin, Lieutenant (jg) Harry Metke, and Ensign Johnson. (Edward McKissick)

let you know that I always thought the squadron could take care of itself." To my knowledge, there were no more disparaging remarks directed toward Squadron VP-44 by ship's company during the remainder of the tour.

May 1943

At some point in time, perhaps May or June, the officers and crew of VP-44 received a one-step promotion in rank or rate. The original Fleet Air Wing school group were all promoted to petty officer rating of first class.

The end of April had also brought another welcome change. Several of the squadron personnel moved aboard the USS *Mackinac*. There, we were treated as valued guests. We believed that we were privileged to be staying on the ship and considered every one of the ship's company a respected host. The quarters were semiprivate with nice showers, and the food was excellent. One disadvantage of the move was that our crew of 44-P-9 was then quartered on three different ships: the *Curtis*, *Tangier*, and *Mackinac*. But we all seemed to arrive at the plane for patrols at the same time, and the disad-

vantage was one that those of us on the *Mackinac* were willing to endure.

Ship's company cooks (SCs) took great pride in their work. Pappy Neufeld, by then rated ACMM, found a wonderful surprise in the box of provisions for our first day's flight from the good ship *Mac*. A note in the box read, "If you want pies on your next flight, bring the pie plates back." The pies were a great hit. The cooks were then supplying lunches for the entire squadron of planes, and there was never one instance of a lost pie plate.

Contacts continued unabated with the Mitsubishi twin-engine medium bombers. On 9 May, Lieutenant H. T. Skelley and Lieutenant (jg) R. L. Hayden with their crew flushed one out. The tactics used by the enemy were by then predictable. The PBY, at about 500 feet altitude, maintained course while the enemy bomber pulled up on an after quarter. If the waist gunner on the PBY fired, the enemy would attempt to cross under and try the other waist gun. If it fired, he pulled away.

From 100 to 200 rounds of ammunition were normally used in each engagement. The Catalina crews by then felt confident; they and the planes had proven themselves. But every encounter was treated as potentially tragic. The excitement never failed to build. Our crews respected the enemy crews, and it was obvious that our slow, lumbering seaplanes and their crews had earned the respect of the enemy.

On 11 May, we had engine trouble and returned to base at Segond Channel after logging about one hour of flight. On landing, 44-P-9 pulled up on the ramp and was parked alongside 44-P-6, which also had problems.

At midafternoon, our plane was ready for checkout. I started to climb out the waist hatch to escape the noise; Pratt and Whitney engines make a terrible racket as the RPM reaches a peak. Just as I raised my right leg to turn and step on the ladder, my eyes suddenly locked upon an unexpected sight.

There, standing on a log, just beyond the metal toolshed and to the left of it, were four huge native islanders from the Big Numbers tribe, judging from their size. They were looking intently at the activity on the seaplane ramp. I was astounded and felt privileged to see them. They had survived — they had maintained their native dress and weapons and appeared to be untouched by the white man's customs. Each man was armed: one carried a bow and a roll of arrows slung to his back; one carried a spear; and one carried a hatchet. All wore one long decoration hanging from one ear and had high, bushy hair. All carried a pouch at their side suspended by a dark leather shoulder strap. A small leather-looking piece covered them at the crotch. Each had a bone or stick in the nose, and one had a necklace of boar tooth tusks. They were tall, muscular, and well built and were proud men.

Afraid that they would leave, I approached them with my hand held up as a greeting. As I walked toward them, they watched me and then ducked and vanished. The engine on 44-P-9 was revved up at full speed. Even the coconut trees seemed to tremble at the noise. The humid air formed a funnel at the surface of the ground, and condensed water vapor streamed into the jungle behind the PBY. These special camp visitors could not be blamed for being fearful of the noise the plane made. For the first time on this tour, I deeply resented the regulation preventing personnel from having camera equipment.

The next visit ashore would also hold an unexpected and most pleasant surprise. Chief "Frenchy" Alman of PATSU 1-4 had visited the French Embassy building on shore several times. He spoke excellent French and had come to know the French Indo-Chinese representatives of the Free French government. One evening he invited me to go with him to visit the embassy on the following day.

After lunch, we took the motor launch from the *Mackinac* to the repair area and walked along a path to the pier where coconuts were processed. Two Cantonese men were at work on the coconuts, and as we passed, they looked up and smiled and waved. We returned the greeting. Frenchy, sensing my shock and dismay, which I was trying to conceal, said, "Betel nut — it contains a mild narcotic and they chew it daily." Rather than two rows of white teeth, each man's smile displayed two black rims caused by the betel nut.

The walk along the roadway was pleasant. It was the first time I had had an opportunity to see our plane from the shoreline with the ships anchored in the background. At the gate to the embassy, Alman called out, and in a short while, our hosts came out and escorted us to the doorway. They were two French Indo-Chinese who spoke excellent English when they greeted me. My high school French courses did not serve me very well, for I understood none of the conversation.

Though I was not trained in air conditioning, I recognized that the building was designed for maximum cooling in a hot climate. The west side of the large room was built with screen louver panels. It was not a two-story house as it appeared from our plane but rather had high ceilings for cooling effects. We were seated on rattan couches, which were placed on both sides of the room with a table between them. Beyond our sitting space, the floor level was raised, and farther beyond was a kitchen. On the adjoining raised area was a ping-pong table.

As we were seated, we were joined by two handsome women. They wore neat shorts, built along the sarong style, and matching trim blouses. The long black hair, flashing black eyes, and lovely bronze skin were set off by gold bangles worn in each of the ears. The men and women had a lively conversation with Alman and seemed pleased that we came to visit them. The women then decided to

The crew of 44-P-4 aboard the USS *Curtis* at Espiritu Santo, April 1943. Standing, left to right: Alfred Mullikin, Richard Ball, Allen Thompson, P. J. Hubbard, C. E. Harmon, Charles Cox, and Chief Aviation Pilot M. L. Stitt. Sitting: Lieutenant Lindsey Guehery, Lieutenant Russel Neil, and Ensign Thomas. (Allen J. Thompson)

The crew of 44-P-11 aboard the USS *Curtis* at Segond Channel, April 1943. Standing, left to right: Elmer Conrad, Harry Gerkin, Louie Lowinski, Luther Pinner, Ward, and Paul Barker. Sitting: Ensign Charles Pacey, Lieutenant S. Greene, and unidentified. (Louie Lowinski)

Crew of 44-P-14 aboard the USS *Curtis*, April 1943. Standing, left to right: George Frankiewich, J. Downer, John Stark, Carl Lutton, James Pearson, and Reid Wilson. Sitting: Lieutenant (jg) Pettiet, Lieutenant (jg) P. W. Vannoy, and Chief Aviation Pilot Thomas Watkins. (Reid Wilson)

play ping-pong, and soon the ball was clicking from one end of the table to the other. I did my best to pretend an interest in the conversation between our two male hosts and Alman, but my effort must be classed an utter failure. I understood not one word of the conversation to my right and could not take my eyes off the sights to my left.

The little white ball sped from one set of flashing smiles, golden bangles, and swaying hips to another sight of equal beauty. Left right, left right, left right! They seemed to enjoy the game and the audience. After two games, one of the men spoke to the women, and they vanished. It was time to leave, and we expressed our thanks for the visit. As we walked along the path toward the coconut pile, Alman mentioned that the women were normally dispatched to the bushes behind the house when foreign visitors arrived. On this occasion, they had been allowed to stay and visit with us. Alman felt

complimented and believed that the event spoke well of the confidence our hosts had in us.

That evening, the crew of 44-P-9 was ordered to pack all personal gear and prepare for departure to Tulagi for advanced base duty. Up until that point in time, I did not know that any of the squadron flight crews had been based at Tulagi, which shows that flight crews knew little of the activities of other crews. Later that evening, two of us were standing at the *Mackinac's* rail watching darkness fall on the harbor, and I mentioned the assignment. My friend replied, "Be careful at Tulagi; that's where the fighting is. Also," he continued, "don't count on the P-40 escorts they give you. They'll run out on you."

"How do you know these things?" I asked.

"We were there for two weeks," he replied. "That's where Olin was killed."

Until then I had heard nothing of Cliff Olin's death.

Chapter 10

Tulagi

LIEUTENANT (jg) Bob Swan with our crew in 44-P-9 departed 1 June 1943 for Halavo Beach, Tulagi, Florida Islands, in the Solomons. It was a short flight of 5.3 hours. When we arrived, sights along the beach, shoreline, and waters off the beach confirmed heavy fighting in the past.

In a partial clearing were some tents, and in front of those were work stands, a tower constructed of palm logs and lumber, and a steel mat that ran down into the water for launching seaplanes. Several palms and other trees were only tall, jagged stumps, the tops having been blown off. Scattered throughout the area were broken and twisted tree trunks. A pier of palm logs and planks ran about 50 feet out into the water.

The water in these islands was even darker than it was in Segond Channel. Not far offshore was the stern end of the hull of a small utility ship that had sunk bow-down. As Swan taxied up to one of the several buoys offshore, Pat Mahon dropped a sea anchor, and Pappy Neufeld hooked a buoy ring and

tied up the plane. A small motor launch set out from the pier to pick up the crew. One pleasant surprise was the sight of PBY number 44-P-7 tied up at a nearby buoy.

We all loaded onto the motor launch with our personal gear and made for the pier. On the way, the coxswain pointed out the officers' tent and one for the crew. The crew tent was located west of the main cluster of tents, just across a small creek with running water that flowed down from the jungle-covered hills behind the tents. The small rectangular building with a tent roof was the cook house. Food was served from the enclosed building through a sliding net window over a wooden shelf. The mess hall was an eight-man tent with two rows of tables. We checked out sleeping cots and bedding and then began setting up quarters for an extended stay. As we were doing so, 44-P-9 — our plane — took off with the crew whom we had relieved. We would be flying 44-P-7.

The crew tent had plenty of room for eight

people. The flaps were pulled taut in line with the roof to allow circulating air from all four sides. Mosquito netting covered the walls, and smooth planks covered the raised floor. It was as comfortable as possible in the hot, humid climate of the Solomon Islands.

The first advice we received suggested that we build a good slit trench. After we set up quarters, we investigated the immediate area and found a small clearing with several coconut palm logs already laid out parallel on the ground. At the time, the logs seemed to offer good slit-trench protection and had obviously been used for that purpose.

The control tower at the beach was inoperative because the ladder was missing and part of the roof and walls of the shed at the top had been blown away. One of the ship's company at the Tulagi seaplane base told us that the tower had been bombed so many times that they simply quit repairing it. The station air-raid siren was hung on one of the remaining upright supports. Near our tent, two small radios hung suspended from a palm tree trunk. One was tuned to the coast-watcher radio frequency and the other to the fighter radio frequency used by the aircraft at Henderson Field.

A mean surprise came with the evening meal, which consisted of only chipped beef cooked in a gravy and spread over two pieces of toast and two pieces of fried Spam. We discovered what others before us had learned: the cook shack was totally enclosed to prevent the customers in the chow line from getting their hands on the cooks.

That night we learned that a new movie was shown every evening, rain or shine. There were enough downed or leaning trees so that one could find a spot to see the show in relative comfort. Everyone on the tiny base came out to see the evening movies. There were about 75 people in the crowd.

When it grew dark, lights went on and the movie started. In terms of title and list of the cast, it promised to be a good one. None of our crew had seen a movie since the pleasant days at Kaneohe Bay. There were about 30 soldiers in the audience, and all of them carried ponchos and used them as seat cushions. But just as the movie started, the lights went out, the movie stopped, and the air-raid siren sounded.

Our crew kept close to each other, and we groped our way back across the little creek and located the clearing with the logs for protective cover. No sooner had I laid down between two logs than bombs started exploding, or so I thought. They made brilliant flashes. The palm fronds overhead, the clusters of small green coconuts, and the bark of the trees were lighted with flashes that silhouetted them against the black sky. Suddenly, I remembered that this was the place where Olin was killed. The two frail coconut logs beside me seemed to offer poor protection.

The flashes with accompanying explosions continued, but a pattern was emerging. Four explosions occurred in succession followed by a pause, and then they repeated. During pauses was the sound of a multiple-engine aircraft. The pilot, "Washing Machine Charlie," was regularly desynchronizing the engines — varying the engines' speed to change their sound, which helped avoid being tracked by the sound detector of the Army's antiaircraft batteries. The large enemy bomber was sent out over the U.S. positions to keep our personnel awake by dropping a few bombs.

We learned that we were located not too far from 90- and 120-mm antiaircraft batteries, which accounted for the soldiers we had seen at the movies. The morning after the air raid, we scouted the area and found the antiaircraft cannon emplacements as well as some 40-mm cannon emplacements.

Another mean surprise came with breakfast. The food placed on the tray and pushed out the window consisted of two pancakes, sweetened water for syrup, and a butter substitute that resembled colored sawdust. There was a large puddle of orange marmalade with the stuff. This was the usual breakfast fare. The exception was reconstituted eggs that had been dehydrated, Spam, and orange marmalade.

The lunches provided for us to take on flights were better. The box of food the cooks gave to Neufeld for flight rations was good. All the food was canned. It included stew, yams, potatoes, green beans, and fruit. The fruit cocktail was especially good, and we considered it a treat.

On our second evening at Tulagi, we gathered with the rest of the station personnel and soldiers for the evening movie. During the day we had obtained ponchos from the small stores hut. Raindrops started splattering the palms before the show started, and soon it began coming down in torrents. Amazingly, the rain did not deter the audience. They simply moved from under any shelter so that the cooling rain would keep the temperature under the steamy poncho to a more tolerable level.

The show, appropriately titled *And the Rains Came* with Myrna Loy, started despite the noise of the rainfall and reduced visibility. It provided an escape from the reality of the present to a place and time of beautiful memories.

One of our crew knew how to play contract bridge, and he taught three more of us, to make up a foursome. Within two days we began to understand the game. The flight missions were infrequent, so the bridge sessions were a real help in relieving boredom in the tent.

The heat and humidity were oppressive around the clock; from midmorning to late afternoon it was terrible. No one in the tiny compound moved outside his tent during that period unless it was necessary.

One afternoon, six natives came out of the hills and walked along the little creek beside our tent and on toward the shoreline; they then turned westward. They looked neither left nor right as they passed through the area. It was as if our settlement did not exist in their minds. I felt a great sorrow for them, as they appeared to be ill. All had large sores on their legs. One young woman had a terribly disfigured breast, distended and enlarged at the end, swinging from side to side as she walked.

Our first flight from Halavo Beach came on the morning of 6 June. Lieutenant Donald G. Gumz met our crew on the pier that morning and took charge of the flight. Until then, we did not know he was on the island and in charge of the detachment there. The Dumbo mission was to the island of Ganonga, one of the western islands of the New Georgia group. It lay to the southwest of Kolombangara.

We picked up a fighter escort of F4Us from

Henderson for the flight, which would take two or more hours, and landed offshore without incident. Supplies were loaded into waiting canoes, and an Army Air Forces pilot who had survived a plane crash came on board. He was taken to Lunga Point, Guadalcanal, and our 44-P-7 then pointed toward Halavo Beach. Lieutenant (jg) Bob Swan commanded the next mission to Malaita, west-northwest of Guadalcanal, where we left coast-watcher supplies; we then returned to base.

A secret and dangerous mission was in the making on 12 June. Don Gumz received a message to go to Segi Point on the eastern tip of New Georgia and from there proceed as directed to the Rennell Islands, consisting of the main land mass, called Rennell, and several smaller land masses. The message came directly from Admiral Marc A. Mitscher, the commander of aircraft in the Solomon Islands (COMAIRSOLS). Gumz radioed back for additional information but was advised that he would receive further instructions en route.

Early the next morning, 13 June, Gumz met our crew on the pier for a pre-mission briefing. An officer of the Royal Australian Army coast watchers was also present. Gumz gave us what little information he had. "It will be a dangerous mission; keep all guns ready at all times; be alert every minute for enemy forces," he asserted.

We were to pick up a fighter escort of 18 P-40 Warhawk fighters on the southern shore of Guadalcanal. My heart sank at the mention of P-40 escorts because of the warning I had received at Espiritu Santo. "Now you know as much about this mission as I do," said Gumz as we boarded the motor launch. We took off with a reduced crew, in order to have room to take on several passengers, we later found out, at about 7:30 p.m. Pat Mahon operated the tower, Art Arsenault took the bow guns, Pappy Neufeld was on the port .50-caliber, and I was on the starboard .50. The pilot's voice-radio transmitter and receiver were set to the fighter frequency used at Henderson Field.

Gumz steered the ship across Guadalcanal to the shoreline and turned westward. "Keep a lookout for a squadron of P-40s," Gumz voice cautioned over the interphone. "Don't shoot at them." Looking back across the island, I could see a swarm of what looked like insects across the horizon. When they came close enough, I verified that they were P-40s and announced the arrival and gave their position.

The Australian coast watcher making the trip with us chose the starboard waist as an observation point. He and I watched together as one of the escorts drew alongside. The squadron leader checked in with Gumz and announced their intentions to check out for the flight. The voice on the radio had a definite Australian accent. One by one, the planes dove at the water, squeezed off a few rounds of machine-gun fire, and announced a problem with the aircraft; they then peeled off to withdraw and return to base. As the last Warhawk turned around, I looked at the Australian and shook my head in disbelief. He likewise looked down and shook his head. They did not intend to go with us. Perhaps they feared going into enemy territory.

We kept low over the water while flying along the coast. Passing Vangunu Island, Gumz steered northward into Segi Point on New Georgia and made a neat open-sea landing offshore. He pulled in close to shore near some large trees and turned into takeoff position. He then ordered a sea anchor out. He kept the engines running at idle, and the anchors held us close to position. A native canoe came up to the starboard waist bearing a coast watcher. We did not find out until much later that this coast watcher was Donald Kennedy, the courageous man whose voice we listened to daily on the coast-watcher frequency, which was broadcast from Segi Point. He was a good friend of the Australian officer with us, and they shook hands as only good friends do. The watcher with us took several items from his pack and passed them to Kennedy in the canoe as they talked and furtively watched the skies. Included in the items was a bottle of gin, mail, and other supplies. Pappy tapped my shoulder and pointed toward the beach. A native was standing there under the canopy of large trees with a camera pointed in our direction. He may have been taking pictures for Kennedy, who, it turned out, had a small army of natives sympathetic to his cause and the Americans' cause in the Solomon Islands. However, farther north on New Georgia, many of the natives were sympathetic to the Japanese. In almost all of the Solomons, the natives were wise enough to help the side they thought was going to win. The coast

watcher's canoe shoved off in about five minutes, Neufeld pulled in the sea anchor, and we moved out at full power from that point. The Australian went forward to provide directions for the pilots.

We flew for only a few minutes at low altitude in a southwesterly direction around the shoreline and then turned inland. In front of us appeared a broad river flowing from the hills. Gumz lowered the plane until we were at tree-top level with the canopy of large, broad-leafed trees whose limbs grew out and down to the water. We were flying between two walls of a green canyon over a smooth river, which was curving westward. We were in a circular landing path. Gumz cut the engines and the plane sat down. We taxied slowly to port toward the brilliant green foliage, and then we picked up some ground fire. Both Neufeld and Arsenault had sensed the direction of fire and had their machine guns aimed at the source. "Hold your fire," said Gumz. We taxied on for a few minutes, which seemed like an eternity. Just before the port wing touched the green wall of foliage, both engines were cut.

As the propellers stopped, four outrigger canoes darted out of the foliage and pulled up to the starboard blister. Mahon came out of the tower to the waist to help take passengers aboard. As he stepped into the waist hatch area he looked upward, then pointed; about 1,000 feet above us flew three formations of enemy bombers. They apparently did not detect us. Holding the gun at ready, I stood watch as Neufeld, Mahon, and the coast watcher took a litter from the natives in the first canoe. A beautiful woman lay on the litter, and nestled next to her was a newborn baby. The men carefully took the litter forward and placed it on the lower starboard bunk. Next, another native woman came aboard; she was attending the girl on the litter. Two bags of personal belongings were handed up. Then came two chicken coops. They came as quite a surprise. The chickens were clucking loudly and apparently anxious about the trip they were taking on a U.S. Navy man-of-war. The last to board were four native scouts.

As soon as they boarded, the canoes pulled back immediately and rounded the bow of the ship. At that moment the starter engaged the engines, and we were pulling back into the center of the river. We had landed in a turn and would have to take off in a turn. It looked tricky, but Gumz used both rudder and lowered starboard wing float to keep it in the turn as we gained flying speed. By rocking the plane up on the step it broke free of the smooth water and climbed out of the walls of green foliage.

The flight to Rennell was on a southeasterly heading and would take less than three hours' flight time. We were soon clear of the dangerous areas around the Munda airfield where squadrons of Japanese fighters operated. The machine guns were stowed and latched. We were able to relax for the first time on the flight. There was then the opportunity to observe the cargo and our passengers.

As the chicken coops were passed on board earlier, I noticed that they appeared to be of excellent design and construction. I took care to examine one in detail. It was made of long, thin limbs of constant diameter woven in intricate patterns. On the bottom was a pad of woven palm leaves so that nothing could soil the plane. The sides and top were attached by delicate threading of coconut palm fiber. The doorway was framed of carved wood with wooden hinge points that fit precisely into the doorway jamb. It represented the finest craftsmanship I had ever seen. As I raised my eyes from the chicken coop, I saw the lovely, fair-skinned Polynesian passenger — the new mother — watching me as I examined and admired the coops. We exchanged smiles, for she was aware that I respected the workmanship the coops represented.

The four scouts with us wore neat tan shorts and shirts of Australian design. Around the waist they wore a belt and bayonet in a scabbard. They were proud men, muscular, and the type you wanted on your side in a fight to the death. Each of them had several souvenirs taken from Japanese soldiers who had engaged them in such fights.

Rennell was soon in sight. As the plane flew over Kanggava Bay at Kanggava, a fully opened white silk parachute held by many people was seen on a small spit of land that curved out into the harbor. They were lifting it up so that it billowed out and floated down, then they lifted it again.

Our plane landed in Kanggava Bay and taxied near the shoreline. Arsenault dropped the bow anchor on command, and no sooner had Gumz cut the engines than a wide semicircle of outrigger canoes pulled up to the starboard blister. The chief's canoe was nearest the plane. It took only a moment to scan the crowd of canoes and pick him out. He was older than any of the others, probably 35 or 40 years of age.

He barked out a command, and one of the canoes pulled up to the waist hatch. We passed the young Polynesian girl and baby out the waist hatch, and the litter was carefully placed on the side struts of the outrigger. The girl's companion was helped out into another canoe, which followed the first one to the shoreline. Next, the chicken coops and baggage came out, followed by the four scouts. Our officers exited next with Gumz into the chief's canoe, followed by Bob Swan, Howard Rumrey, Sam Wideberg, and our coast-watcher passenger. All went ashore in separate outriggers.

The remaining canoes closed in on the ship. Eager and smiling, the natives beamed when we invited them all to come aboard. Their joy could hardly be contained as they streamed on the plane. We took them in groups of five or so and walked them through the entire ship, from the tunnel hatch to the pilots' compartment, through the hatch and up on the wings. They were respectful of all equipment and took great pleasure in lightly touching everything. At one point there were 80 people up on the wing.

As we filed back through the hatch and out of the plane, we gave them everything we did not need or knew we could replace. They invited each of us into separate canoes, and we went ashore in style. When we touched the beach, a lovely young woman and a young man took me by the hand to walk me around the area to show me where they lived. They were both dressed in a sarong cloth of Australian manufacture and wore flowers around their necks and in their smooth, black hair.

The girl was beautiful with bronze skin; flowing, flower-bedecked hair; and a smile that showed perfect white teeth. It was difficult to talk, for neither of us could understand a single word the other said. Furthermore, it was not possible to use sign language, for the young man and woman each kept a firm grasp on my hands. The man was pleasant and respectful, but I could hardly take my eyes off the beautiful woman on my right.

There were many children in the crowd, and all

of them wanted to touch us. But something was different, and I had trouble sensing what it was at first. Then it came suddenly: there were no old people on the island. The chief was the oldest inhabitant, and he was relatively young by our standards. On a signal, everyone walked to the shore, and a canoe took each of us back to the plane.

During our trip to Segi Point on New Georgia and to Rennell, 45 enemy bombers from Rabaul, supported by as many fighters from Munda, raided Henderson Field. The fighting over the channel at Lunga was fierce, and both sides suffered heavy casualties. The bombers were those that had passed directly overhead while we were on the river in New Georgia.

The day had been one of tension, then new sights and an adventure on Rennell that we would not soon forget. As we prepared to leave the 44-P-7 after landing, Neufeld found a bottle of bourbon in a spot where there had been none when we left that morning on the flight. It must have been placed there for us. Before the meal of chipped beef, we all had a drink. It had such a good effect that everyone seemed to enjoy the stale bread and beef.

For the first time since arriving at Tulagi, we had a good time at the evening mess. Gumz came by the mess hall to join in the fun. He asked if we had any of the bourbon left. The answer was yes, and we all went to our tent. We passed the bottle around until it was empty. Gumz was normally strictly Navy, but he enjoyed getting drunk with the rest of us. We had had nothing to drink for months, and that, coupled with the hot, humid climate, had a devastating effect. The next day we had terrible hangovers.

It was a long time before we found out that Admiral Marc Mitscher had not ordered Lieutenant Donald Gumz and crew to take a beautiful female civilian passenger aboard a U.S. Navy man-of-war and transport her to Rennell Islands. He had merely ordered assistance for the highly respected Royal Australian Army coast watchers as required by them. And it was obvious that whoever she was, the lovely Polynesian and her baby were very important to the chief, whose help, in turn, was important to the coast watchers — and to us. Lieutenant Gumz had not quoted Navy regulations — which prohibit civilians from boarding military planes — when his passengers boarded; he had been watch-

ing for enemy attackers and did not see his passengers until he arrived at Rennell.

At 11:00 a.m. on the morning of 16 June, the radio set to the coast-watcher frequency crackled with activity. The reports indicated large numbers of formations of planes headed for Guadalcanal. Later, the radio on the U.S. fighter frequency became busy. The Henderson Field fighter groups were airborne, and the air armadas had engaged each other. Early on in the battle, it was difficult to discern the nature of the action from the radio.

The planes were at high altitude and out over the channel, which made it difficult to spot them with the naked eye, but those hit and falling in a downward spiral were easy to see. As the battle progressed, it became less difficult to follow the pilots' chatter and correlate it with the actions observed from the beach. They were quick to warn each other of the enemy fighters — the Zekes, their direction of approach, and when they got a hit. "I'll get him," said one. "Got him." And a burning plane started falling from the sky. There was a report that an F4U pilot had to jump when his plane was hit and that his parachute had failed to open, but he survived the fall to the ocean and was later rescued.

The raid was the last of the major Japanese air attacks from Rabaul and Munda against the Henderson Field forces. The enemy lost about 100 planes against U.S. losses of only four Marine Corps fighter planes. It marked, as much as any other single action, the turning point of a defensive war within the Solomons against the Japanese forces attempting to retake or strike back at Guadalcanal.

Spirits were high on the evening of 17 June on the *Curtis, Tangier,* and *Mackinac* when the crews of the VP-44 learned that the squadron had orders for a night bombing attack. The planes had been fueled to 500 gallons. They were equipped that day with three MK-12 500-pound bombs for heavy explosive work, a demolition bomb with daisy-cutter extension, which caused the bomb to explode slightly above the earth, and one MK-4 incendiary cluster, used to start fires, in the tail to be dropped from the tunnel hatch. At long last, the squadron was given a mission to carry offensive action to the enemy. The bombing that many of the crew members had endured at Midway was to be avenged.

Under orders from COMFAIRWING One, two three-plane sections of PBYs took off at 8:30 a.m., 18 June, under the command of Lieutenant Commander R. A. Rosasco to conduct a night attack on the bivouac and revetment areas of Nauru Island. Our planes landed at Vanikoro Island at 10:45 a.m. and were fueled to capacity (1,450 gallons).

With all planes flying in a "V" formation, departure from Vanikoro was taken at 9:37 p.m. Average altitude was 800 feet. Frontal weather and cloud cover occurred at 1,200 feet, but the flight remained below cloud cover. The six planes kept up contact, and the formation was maintained throughout the flight. At 75 miles out, the weather cleared to scattered broken cover at 1,200 feet. Formation lights were used by the two section leaders to 100 miles out from the target to assist wing planes in keeping formation.

At the 100-mile point from the target, the two sections began the climb to 7,500 feet and 8,000 feet, respectively. Conditions appeared favorable for a level bombing attack. At 545 miles from the Vanikoro departure point, Glenn Bacher in the commander's plane, 44-P-1, picked up the target on radar dead ahead at 11:06 p.m. He reported that the island and installations made a "hot radar target." Glenn was a lead radar technician in PATSU 1-4 and had been asked by the commander to join his crew for the attack. The crew with the skipper's plane included Lieutenant (jg) R. C. Donaldson, John F. Gammell AP1c (NAP), F. O. Scofield AMM1c, Stanley Schwartz AMM2c, Theodore Beck AMM2c, Melvin R. Ubben ARM1c, Richard Bunch ARM3c, and George W. Newcombe AOM2c.

The other planes and crews in the formation included Lieutenant G. W. Hanthorn and crew in 44-P-13; Lieutenant (jg) Hank Noon and crew of Lieutenant (jg) Robert L. Hayden, C. E. Frye AP1c (NAP), A. C. Jocius AMM1c, Thomas F. Reeder AMM3c, James F. Scott AMM3c, Norman E. Bauer ARM1c, Orval W. Davis ARM3c, and James F. Sewell AOM2c in 44-P-5; Lieutenant E. A. Conrad and crew; Lieutenant H. T. Skelley and crew; and Lieutenant R. L. Summers and crew.

Sight contact was made at 11:27 p.m. through a rift in the clouds at a distance of ten miles. All planes made independent attacks when signaled by the flight commander, who proceeded to attack immediately. After his attack, he retired out at ten miles south to observe the results. Rosasco dropped his bombs at 200-foot intervals. Two hit the bivouac area and one hit an oil tank. The fire emitted a dense black smoke and was visible to 60 miles out. The bombs in the bivouac area started small fires that extinguished quickly. The first incendiary cluster dropped within the shoreline without apparent effect. The second cluster landed in the vicinity of the oil fire, increasing its intensity.

Lieutenant Hanthorn's plane dropped all bombs and incendiaries in a straight line from 7,500 feet altitude at a spacing of 300 feet. Only two flashes were observed, indicating one was a dud. An incendiary cluster landed on the island's runway, illuminating the entire operating area.

Hank Noon, in 44-P-5, attacked at 1,200 feet from a glide diving run. The bombs hit between the wharf and number two phosphate plant. A single machine-gun bullet entered the plane's cockpit, hit the controls, and then ricocheted into Hank's face. Bob Hayden took over the controls and retired safely to the south.

Lieutenant R. L. Summers released all bombs at 3,000 feet on a glide bombing run from 8,300 feet at 250-foot intervals. All ordnance exploded.

Lieutenant E. A. Conrad dropped his ordnance at 1,100 feet in 200-foot intervals from an 8,000-foot glide pattern. Bombs exploded in the revetment and building area with small fires resulting. The plane received 26 holes from small-caliber machine guns or rifle fire, but no one was injured.

Lieutenant H. T. Skelley released bombs at 2,500 feet from a 7,000-foot glide at 300-foot intervals. One bomb and one incendiary landed offshore, one bomb landed on the runway, and the rest of the bombs hit the housing area at the southern end of the runway.

All ordnance operated satisfactorily except for one possible dud of the 18 bombs dropped. The bombsights functioned properly. The enemy did not use searchlights or heavy-caliber antiaircraft fire; they apparently were not forewarned of the attack, indicating an absence of radar. Two of the PBYs were hit with light-caliber antiaircraft fire, and one man was wounded. No airborne aircraft were encountered.

All squadron planes set a course for Vanikoro. There, Hank Noon was taken aboard the USS *Chincoteague* and treated by the ship's doctor while the planes were refueled to 500 gallons. All hands had a good meal and an opportunity to rest a few minutes before departing for Espiritu.

The month of June produced two other engagements between planes on patrol with the twin-engine bombers of the Mitsubishi T-96 class. The clash on 3 June 1943 had provided the Japanese with a lucky hit by a 20-mm cannon in the bunk area of a PBY. It started a fire, and four of the crew were injured. That evening the four were treated by Commander A. D. James MC-V(S) USNR aboard the good ship *Tangier*. Lieutenant (jg) J. J. Lyons and AMM2c Albert Denver Allen were treated and placed on the sick list. Ensign William John Hubbach, Jr., and ARM3 Craig Allen Johnson were treated and released to duty.

The detachment on Halavo Beach, Tulagi, received welcome orders to return to Espiritu Santo on 21 June 1943. A happy group of men, Bob Swan's crew and eight men of the PATSU team loaded aboard 44-P-7 and set course for Segond Channel. When we arrived that afternoon, there was information to exchange with friends in the squadron on the Dumbo experience at Tulagi, the raid on Nauru, and the patrol engagements during the month.

The greatest news was held until last. The squadron was scheduled to return to the States for a 30-day leave for all hands. It was a chance to see families and friends back in the hometowns, cities, or farm communities scattered across America. The news was the best that any officer or man in the squadron could have received. The men of the FAW school group could barely contain their joy; we had not seen our families since May of 1941.

We started readying the aircraft that very day for the trip home. The USS *Curtis* also received orders to return to the Mare Island Navy Yard in San Francisco Bay for a well-deserved leave for all

hands. Maintenance crews and the PATSU unit would return on the *Curtis*. During preparations for the return, news came down the line that the *Chincoteague* at Vanikoro had been bombed and suffered severe damage. "Washing Machine Charlie" had a single lucky hit with one bomb. A revenge attack for the raid on Nauru met with great success.

As we prepared the planes and our personal gear and eagerly adjusted psychologically to the trip home, thoughts and questions remained concerning recent events in New Georgia. The mystery of the beautiful young Polynesian woman and baby who flew with us to Rennell Island remained with us. And at that time we still did not know whose voice came to us on the coast-watcher frequency that we listened to every day. How did these events and actions tie together? During the period of duty at Tulagi, we witnessed the last of the significant actions against the forces on Guadalcanal. What did the future hold for the forces remaining there?

The PBY crews who flew the patrol and Dumbo missions were busy. They seldom were aware of the actions of other crews in their squadron. They could not possibly know or have a full view of the part played by those they helped in the terrible and tragic, yet successful, Solomons campaign. It would take time to learn of the role played by others in the effort. It would take time for historians to assemble and present the data.

Many individuals in a host of organizations worked together, sometimes in mysterious ways, to change from a defensive to offensive stance in the Solomons, which started in July 1943. According to Walter Lord's *Lonely Vigil*, Admiral Halsey and his staff were planning and scouting the New Georgia group of islands for an offensive push to take or bypass islands, whichever was most cost-effective, as early as March 1943. On 3 March, Lieutenant William P. Coultas, Naval Intelligence on Halsey's staff, and party had landed behind enemy lines at Segi Point. With Coultas were Captain Clay Boyd of the 1st Marine Raiders, Sergeant Frank Guidone, Marine Gunner Jim James, and Corporal Robert C. Laverty. The party had gone to Segi by a PBY and were met at the landing by Donald Kennedy, coast watcher, whom we later discovered we had also met at Segi Point on 13 June.

Kennedy had worked with the scouts all day,

briefing them on the area and enemy positions. That evening, he had invited them to his home. Although the Japanese base of Viru was only a few miles away, they were entertained royally, beginning with Scotch served on the veranda by houseboys in white jackets.

The scouting party had been amazed at the extent of the monitoring network, facilities, trails, native scouts, communication and signaling systems, and logistics that Kennedy had established and operated. His network extended many miles beyond his headquarters.

Using Kennedy's network and his scouts, the party was able to go to the outskirts of the Munda airfield, which they observed along with Rendova Harbor. They were able to see and observe the detail of all activity and actions of every individual on the airstrip. While there, they were able to sketch out a landing plan at Zanana, five miles from Munda. Members of the party made detailed sketches of Viru, just 1,200 feet across the harbor from the Japanese camp.

The scouting parties had reassembled at Segi on 16 March 1943, and by 20 March they were back at Nouméa to report personally on their findings. Scouting data was hammered into a final plan, prepared by Admiral Kelly Turner's staff, to take Munda. It called for landings at Zanana near Rendova, Wickham Anchorage, Viru, and Segi. An airstrip would be built on Segi to support the advance. On 20 June 1943, ten days earlier than planned, Colonel Michael Currin and 400 4th Marine Raiders raced toward Segi to defend and build a

fighter strip on the point. The next day, Commander Wilfred L. Painter and party landed. Painter had boasted that he would build the airfield in ten days. When bulldozers and graders arrived on 30 June, he promised to build the airfield from scratch and call in the fighters on the morning of 11 July. He kept his promise.

As VP-44 was on the last leg of the flight to Kaneohe, 30 June 1943, Commander Painter's bulldozers were landing at Segi Point. Coast watcher Donald Kennedy knew that an attack on his organization and facilities was imminent. He evacuated his dependents seven days before the action at Segi started.

Our crew of 44-P-9 carried the memories of the mysterious and lovely Polynesian girl and her baby for many years. For some of us, it would also be years before learning the name of the coast-watcher extraordinaire, Donald Kennedy. His voice broadcast many of the accounts on Munda. His broadcasts and those of his staff were invaluable to the forces on Guadalcanal.

As the crews of VP-44 were winging their way home and the offensive in the Pacific began, the outcome of the war in Europe and Africa was weighing in favor of the Allied forces. On 2 February 1943, the last Germans at Stalingrad had surrendered to the Russian army. On 7 May, Tunis and Bizerte had fallen to the Allies, and on 12 May, all resistance to the Allies in Africa had ended.

As Bob Swan and our crew of 44-P-9 were making our last flight together in June of 1943, the invasion of Sicily was scheduled to start in ten days.

Chapter 11

Homeward Bound

ON 27 June 1943, Bob Swan and our crew with five other planes in the section set out for Suva Fiji on the first leg of the trip home. After the flight from Suva, one night at Canton Island, one night on Palmyra, and an eight-hour flight, we were circling for a landing on the beautiful multi-colored coral bay at NAS Kaneohe Bay, Oahu, Territory of Hawaii. The beach crew was ready for the flight as the planes were pulled one by one up on the seaplane ramp. Not a man in any of the crews failed to pat the side of the grand old ship that brought them back. More than one kissed the side of the ship at the waist hatch ladder, and several kissed the seaplane ramp. Many who landed that afternoon had felt their chances of returning to U.S. soil were not good. The same drama was replayed on the following day as the last flight of Squadron VP-44 planes landed and were pulled up on the ramp.

For most of the crews, this was the first time we had had an opportunity to take a freshwater shower since leaving Kaneohe over six months before. The evening meal offered treats of fresh fruit and vegetables served at the Bachelor Officer's Quarters and mess hall. Kaneohe had always served excellent food, and then it tasted better than ever. There was little time for liberty in Honolulu; we had uniforms to buy and small stores and personal gear to prepare for the trip home.

On Friday, 3 July 1943, Chief Kenneth McCardle held a muster of all hands. There were many pleasant surprises that morning. Several old friends were wearing the uniform of chief petty officer. Every man of the old FAW school group was wearing the stripes of petty officer first class. I looked slowly and carefully at everyone at muster that morning. Each man was a friend and buddy; many were close friends. Among them were ten of us who had worked, traveled, and sweated together since boot camp. Most of those assembled had mustered together many hundreds of times under Chief McCardle. Along with the joy I felt at the

Lieutenant John Simpson, Personnel Officer, and Kenneth McCardle, Squadron VP-44 Leading Chief, aboard the USS *Curtis*, Segond Channel, Espiritu Santo, May 1943. (George W. Newcombe)

prospects of going home, a great sadness filled me, for I knew that this was likely the last muster we would stand together. McCardle announced that on Sunday morning we would assemble and board buses for Pearl Harbor. The squadron had a berth on the USS *Long Island* for a trip back to San Diego, California.

Time passed quickly. We soon boarded the *Long Island* and rounded the point of land called Diamond Head. The yellowish color of our skin, caused by the Atabrine pills we had taken daily to prevent malaria, began to disappear. The recent memories of the saltwater showers, contacts with the enemy patrol planes, stifling humid heat, mud, and jungles were fading. On our second day out, the squadron assembled in the hangar for the ship's photographer.

After morning chow, a number of us congregated near the starboard bow. We were due to sight land at 0900 hours and scheduled to dock at the pier on North Island that morning. Soon a speck of land appeared on the horizon — San Clemente Island. A school of porpoise joined us. "That's a good sign," said Whitey Lippens. "Picking up a school of porpoise on the way into a harbor is always a sign of good luck." We watched them as they sped through the wake of the prow and shot out in front of the ship. They played at the bow as the shoreline of

Pilots of VP-44 aboard the USS *Curtis*, Espiritu Santo, April 1943. (George W. Newcombe)

VP-44 flight crews aboard the USS *Long Island* (CVE-1), 16 July 1943. (Thomas G. Monahan)

At the Grant Hotel, San Diego, California, July 1943. Left to right: Bob Sivertsen, Reid Wilson, Lloyd Wood, John Klopp, R. D. Scott, Jim Roskowick, and Jim Mills. (James C. Mills)

America came into view and until we reached the vicinity of Point Loma.

We were ready for the Naval Air Station and San Diego, and they were ready for us. All hands agreed that we would take enough time to have tailored uniforms made and a liberty in San Diego before going on leave. Ship's service and the Officers Club assisted in many ways on preparations for our leave. Yeomen at the air station operated travel and reservation centers; they made reservations and purchased tickets for the entire squadron. They also helped in refurbishing the full complement of uniforms and in providing information on tailors in San Diego for uniforms. Ship's service had a list of squadron personnel authorized to purchase and wear the campaign ribbons and new Combat Air Crew wings.

Fortunately, a few of the FAW school group and other good shipmates met in the lounge of the Grant Hotel during our last night on shore in San Diego before going on leave. The faces of these men are etched into my memory, as are those of the rest of the officers and crew of the squadron. I seem to be able to hear the sounds of their voices exactly as they were on the interphone system of 44-P-9. I can hear them as we talked by the rail of the *Mackinac*, watching darkness capture Segond Channel and the fleet anchored there. I shall forever remember Edwin Olsen's prayer that he offered as the coral sand beneath us heaved and pitched with the blasts of the bombs during the 4 June 1942 raid on Eastern Island, Midway atoll.

In the veritable avalanche of memories and recollections of events, times, places, and sounds of long ago emerges a pure thread of thought. It is of the men and machines of VP-44 and the many other PBY squadrons who performed equal or even greater feats. It is of the heroic actions, which at the time seemed mundane and even routine, they took in emergencies. In a special place in my memory are the mental pictures of those who were so full of life and courage who did not come back with us. To Lieutenant (jg) Robert S. Whitman, Ensign Walter H. Mosley, AMM3c Clarence J. Norby, RM3c William H. O'Farrell, ACRM James W. Adams, Ensign Jack H. Camp, AOM3c Lyonal J. Orgeron, and AOM1c Clifford A. Olin, I raise my hand in salute to you. My presentations of the events in this story are in fact a salute to them, to the men of VP-44, and to all the men who flew the PBY Blue Catalinas, Dumbos, and — later — Black Cats all over the world during World War II.

Pencil sketch of ACRM James C. Mills by Clayton Braun, 1945.

As the group parted that evening at the hotel — and for several, it was a final parting — we wished each other well and prepared to go our separate ways. The collection of memories was to continue to grow for each of us.

With my Union Pacific Railway ticket I set out the following morning for my beloved family, friends, and relatives. Many of my relatives had scheduled a trip to our home to see me.

My ticket read: Los Angeles, El Paso, and Little Rock, Arkansas. The thoughtful men at the ship's service had also included a bus ticket that read: Little Rock to Waldron, Arkansas.

Epilogue

IN late 1943, after a well-earned rest, VP-44 Squadron re-grouped in San Diego. A few of the old hands remained to provide a core of experienced personnel. Most went on to provide training for new squadrons being formed. Lieutenant Commander Donald G. Gumz, with Dale E. Brown, Patrick Mahon, and others, formed a new squadron using the PB4Y Privateer, a variant of Consolidated's B-24 heavy bomber, a new addition to the Fleet. Lieutenant Thomas G. Monahan and John Klopp went to the staff of the commander of Tarawa Island. Lieutenant Gerald Hardeman became flight officer for a "Baby Flattop," a small aircraft carrier. Reid Wilson went to VP-71 where he earned the Distinguished Flying Cross and two Air Medals. C. E. "Bill" Harmon and I went to Admiral William F. Halsey's staff of the Commander South Pacific (which later became Commander 3rd Fleet). There Bill served as plane captain and I as radioman on the admiral's converted Consolidated PB4Y-1 Privateer. Some went to

the new PBM Mariner squadrons. Several members of the squadron went on to flight school, obtained their commissions, and rendered a great service in the Navy and Marine Corps as pilots.

In the same pattern followed by VP-44, all Fleet units expanded and multiplied and the Navy grew stronger. As it did so, the Japanese forces did not keep pace. They began losing men and materiel faster than they could be replaced.

The re-grouped VPB-44 left San Diego in late 1943 to go back to the South Pacific and continued to add to a distinguished service record (bombing had become part of the patrol squadron's mission, changing the designation from VP to VPB).

Under the command of Lieutenant Commander Gerald S. Bogart, the Black Cat Squadron — so called because many of the Blue Catalinas had been painted black in late 1943 to serve as night raiders — went to Espiritu Santo. They trained and operated with high-power searchlights used in conjunction with PT boats and Marine bombers.

The squadron went on to Green Island. There the mission was to keep the bypassed Japanese forces of Rabaul, Bougainville, and other islands bottled up. As the war progressed, VPB-44 stretched its reach from Green Island to New Guinea, the Philippines, Palau, and Fiji.

On 12 April 1945, with the Cats of 44 finally reassembled on Green Island, the battle-weary sailors and battered and weatherbeaten planes lifted off the runway for the last time. VP-44, tour two, returned again to San Diego for another well-earned rest.

The plane that was supposedly obsolete on 7 December 1941, with her crews, had grown stronger and better with time. In August 1945, at the end of the war, the PBY Black Cat was the scourge of the Japanese naval forces and Japanese shipping. She was employed by the U.S. Navy, U.S. Coast Guard, U.S. Army Air Forces, and by Great Britain and Australia.

The VP-44 Association (tour one) held a reunion in 1993. Our conversations easily transported us back to those exciting times in the Pacific. If we could have foreseen our future in 1942 and 1943, we would not have been disappointed. I have met and corresponded with most of the members during the past three years and have come to know them better. Many remained in the Navy and had rewarding military careers. Some did well in federal civil service, industry, business, local government civil service, and agriculture. Others went on to college and earned degrees. From those ranks came doctors, lawyers, engineers, scientists, and teachers.

I am proud of the generation of men who flew the PBYs. They, with thousands of their comrades, went on after the war to work and to produce, and they raised the standard of living in America to the highest level achieved by any nation in the history of the world.

It is my hope that the patriotism, loyalty, and family values of these men will serve as a model for future generations. Currently, it appears to many that the military forces are being sacrificed for political expedience. Some believe the military capability of the United States is surely being destroyed.

It is my hope that a wiser and more responsible generation of young men and women will soon appear who will recognize that America must maintain a working, functional military with high standards and high morale.

The values of the men of the PBYs serve well as a model for that generation.

Appendices

Appendix 1

Muster Roll of the Crew

of the USS PATROL SQUADRON FORTY FOUR (VP-44)
for the quarter ending 31 December 1940

Source: National Archives

Name	Rate	Service No.	Date on Board	Name	Rate	Service No.	Date on Board
Alford, Frank, Jr.	AMM1c	287-12-55	6-24-40	Harris, Conrad G.	AMM1c	265-58-54	9-1-38
Arnold, Phillip A.	Sea2c	342-17-42	3-25-40	Harris, William P.	AMM3c	356-59-99	3-1-40
Asquith, Robert D.	AMM3c	337-14-08	9-25-39	Harstritt, Jerome C.	Sea2c	328-64-64	5-17-40
Barnes, Robert M.	AOM3c	385-74-05	11-05-40	Hawley, Truett S.	Sea1c	287-34-09	6-29-40
Beatty, Paul E.	Sea2c	337-26-34	5-25-40	Haynes, Frank N.	CRM	279-06-37	9-1-38
Beneck, Joe F.	ACMM	267-76-23	2-1-40	Hicks, William W.	Sea1c	261-98-45	11-1-39
Benolkin, Bernard M.	Sea2c	328-25-60	5-5-40	Hines, Gordon L.	AM3c	368-31-88	11-7-39
Bessette, Ward A.	Sea2c	300-00-34	7-25-40	Hodde, Warner W. H.	Sea1c	316-61-92	4-29-40
Brandt, Richard E.	RM3c	243-64-09	5-15-40	Hodges, Sherfy	CY	295-03-19	9-5-38
Brockman, Samuel F.	Sea2c	342-15-95	3-8-40	Hokfle, Ralph R.	AOM3c	359-90-18	9-28-38
Brown, Lon A.	RM2c	381-22-67	9-1-38	Jocius, Alexander C.	Sea1c	243-57-01	9-1-38
Brown, Richard W., Jr.	AMM3c	201-69-32	6-27-40	Johnson, Alfred E.	Y3c	311-15-32	9-28-38
Brown, Roy F.	AOM	271-50-23	7-5-40	Johnston, Goulden W.	Sea1c	356-21-83	6-29-40
Copple, Hal E.	AMM3c	316-15-45	4-8-40	Joyce, John P.	Sea1c	342-19-45	5-17-40
Copple, James H.	AMM2c	316-45-12	5-31-40	Kates, Nathaniel A.	Matt1c	265-88-87	9-1-38
Dalton, Lionel B.	Phm1c	274-11-40	7-16-40	Kay, Glenn B.	AMM1c	385-59-84	11-25-38
Delaney, Richard L.	AMM3c	234-09-52	11-26-40	Kieth, Paul E.	ACMM	295-09-38	10-3-38
Derouin, Raymond J.	Sea1c	300-01-05	7-22-40	Kiner, John M.	ACMM	316-08-48	9-1-38
Dorsey, Henry M.	OS3c	258-14-97	9-7-38	Kirby, Jack F., Jr.	RM3c	342-09-26	10-17-39
Downs, William L.	Sea2c	278-28-45	11-25-40	Kraemer, William F.	Sea2c	380-30-43	?-2-40
Earnest, Harlay G.	Sea2c	321-39-10	5-17-40	LaLonde, Felix A.	ACOM	305-14-97	9-1-38
Eikleman, John L.	Am2c	336-97-04	5-24-40	Lamson, Wilbur V.	AMM1c	201-38-14	9-1-38
Faulkner, French E., Jr.	Sea1c	360-09-45	6-29-40	LaPorte, Thadeus L.	ACMM	261-35-16	9-1-38
Felton, John L.	Sea2c	300-03-18	5-3-40	Lee, William H.	Sea2c	266-01-66	3-11-40
Fisher, Joseph R.	Sea2c	316-16-69	6-29-40	Leone, George R.	Sea1c	393-32-30	6-29-40
Ford, James R.	P2c	279-46-16	7-7-39	Lundberg, John W.	Sea1c	321-33-85	11-13-39
Fornataro, Anthony R.	Sea1c	234-20-96	5-31-40	Marsh, Virgil R.	AMM3c	279-42-81	11-8-39
Forsythe, Joseph E.	Sea2c	295-06-01	7-23-40	Martin, Alcysius N.	Sea1c	328-62-25	4-29-40
Foster, James C.	RM3c	372-01-46	3-19-40	Mason, Donald F.	AMMc	328-39-50	9-1-38
Foulks, Ralph E.	RM1c	355-95-47	10-24-40	Mathews, Edward F.	Sea2c	321-37-79	4-3-40
Frankiewich, George	Sea2c	223-23-16	7-29-40	Maulding, Eugene C.	AMM2c	385-56-81	11-1-38
French, Donald R.	ACMM	291-26-29	10-22-40	McCandless, Guy D.	ACMM	250-07-83	5-2-40
Gammell, John F.	AM3c	380-84-08	4-15-40	McCinty, Joseph J.	AMM2c	375-82-40	9-1-38
Gardiner, William D.	RM3c	346-64-43	9-13-40	McLean, Lorne O.	AMM2c	393-18-41	9-1-38
Gregg, Perry J.	ACMM	311-07-53	9-1-38	Meagher, Joseph E., Jr.	Sea2c	382-19-18	10-31-40
Gregory, Randolph	Sea1c	356-14-04	9-23-39	Medler, Clement D.	RM3c	283-24-59	11-21-38
Griffin, Lloyd E.	Sea1c	321-31-78	5-13-40	Mellinger, Charles D.	RM2c	375-94-28	12-12-40
Gunderson, Knute C.	AMM1c	328-06-07	9-1-38	Melton, Horace P.	Ptr1c	355-72-03	9-15-38
Hackett, Noel L.	AMM2c	375-83-88	7-15-40	Miesse, Harvey W.	Sea2c	382-09-55	9-25-39
Hardy, Clarence B.	AM2c	258-18-2	8-5-40	Minnehan, Burr J.	Sea2c	337-21-59	7-22-40

Name	Rate	Service No.	Date on Board	Name	Rate	Service No.	Date on Board
Montgomery, Bonney	OC1c	143-44-77	10-7-40	Smith, Conrad E.	Sea1c	287-36-89	5-17-40
Moran, Charles L.	AOM2c	316-45-11	12-16-40	Stanford, Donald E.	CRM	392-76-05	9-19-40
Myhan, Charles L.	AMM2c	272-03-17	12-5-40	Stout, Russel L.	AM1c	279-30-55	5-7-40
Nease, Frank	BM1c	261-45-51	9-1-38	Takacs, Alexander A.	AMM3c	223-35-93	9-1-38
Neidert, Charles C.	AMM3c	295-50-67	6-25-40	Thiemer, Ernst A.	Sea1c	225-54-26	5-15-40
Neuneker, Keith E.	Sea1c	299-99-83	12-7-39	Tinley, Oscar E.	Sea2c	258-26-29	4-15-40
O'Daniel, William C.	Sea1c	287-35-29	4-29-40	Tiskie, Peter P.	AMM1c	253-08-38	9-1-38
Oldenurg, Albert C.	Sea2c	321-34-06	11-13-39	Vaughn, Edgar	Sea2c	266-04-00	4-1-40
Pentz, Dallass M.	Sea2c	385-76-70	10-31-41	Watts, Ralph A.	Sea1c	265-76-42	9-1-38
Petersen, Willard L.	RM3c	382-08-89	9-26-39	Welker, Theodore E.	ACMM	279-31-99	5-17-40
Place, Ernest R.	AMM1c	316-22-08	6-17-40	Wellman, Howard A.	Sea2c	311-31-35	5-17-40
Poteet, Raymond C.	AMM1c	341-79-67	10-2-40	Welsh, John P.	AOM2c	328-41-50	6-16-39
Redfield, Vernon L.	RM1c	259-76-26	9-1-38	Whitehouse, Warren M.	RM2c	201-52-41	5-26-40
Reid, Donald E.	SK1c	385-64-51	12-11-40	Williams, James B.	Matt3c	266-04-73	4-15-40
Reid, Jewell H.	AMM1c	267-09-45	9-1-38	Williams, Richard, Jr.	Matt3c	283-30-80	4-15-40
Rich, Edward A.	AM1c	380-64-52	4-15-40	Williams, Warren W.	AOM2c	359-94-90	7-17-40
Riley,Herman C.	AMM1c	256-21-02	9-1-38	Winborne, Lavison	Matt3c	266-04-45	4-14-40
Robinson, Earl H.	ACMM	346-09-70	10-7-40	Wingate, Mathew E.	Matt3c	262-47-20	4-15-40
Rosson, William W.	Sea2c	295-47-90	5-31-40	Worrock, Bryce K.	Sea2c	266-02-99	9-4-40
Schaub, Marion J.	SC1c	320-95-08	5-13-40	Wozniak, Bruce W.	AMM3c	250-26-56	12-14-40
Schmidt, Robert W.	AMM2c	368-28-39	9-1-8	Wrobel, Don F.	Sea2c	316-63-17	5-27-40
Shepard, Bert B.	Sea1c	393-29-36	1-13-40	Zink, Albert J.	AMM3c	243-55-17	9-3-40
Siesser, Maurice A.	Sea2c	368-47-04	7-22-40	Zorbas, George	Sea2c	283-33-29	10-31-40
Simpson, Ernest A.	AMM1c	311-07-53	9-1-38	Zurzanello, George D.	RM2c	223-35-61	11-7-39
Sims, Vinton A.	ACMM	375-36-39	9-1-38	Zydak, Zygmunt F.	Sea2c	385-76-84	10-21-40
Smith, Arthur E.	Sea2c	223-53-40	5-13-40				

116   BLUE CATALINAS OF WORLD WAR II

Appendix 2

Muster Roll of the Crew

of the USS PATROL SQUADRON FORTY FOUR (VP-44)
for the quarter ending 31 December 1941

Original prepared by Lieutenant W. L. Richards, U.S. Navy, Executive Officer
Original approved by Lieutenant Commander R. C. Brixner, U.S. Navy Commanding
Forwarded from Fleet Air Detachment, NAS Alameda, California

Source: Naval Archives

Name	Rate	Service No.	Date on Board
Adams, Clifford A.	ARM1c (NAP)	320-99-40	9-1-41
Adams, James W.	RM1c	320-05-62	12-11-41
Albrecht, Edward J.	CBM	100-33-15	6-10-41
Alford, Louis H.	AMM2c	274-40-22	6-3-41
Allgood, Eldon P.	Sea2c	300-33-57	9-1-41
Arsenault, Arthur J., Jr.	AOM3c	212-57-10	7-11-41
Atchley, Carl D.	Sea2c	356-59-77	12-11-41
Bacher, Glenn L.	Sea2cV3	616-01-61	12-11-41
Ball, Richard J.	Sea2c	320-13-23	10-17-41
Barnes, Robert M.	AOM2c	385-74-05	6-6-41
Barruzo, Buanaventure	OS1c	497-79-11	6-4-41
Bauer, Norman E.	RM3cV6	414-47-03	6-12-41
Beck, Theodore L.	Sea2c	382-49-10	12-11-41
Berke, Dale A.	RM3c V6	411-14-85	6-19-41
Bias, John H.	Sea1c	362-52-06	12-10-41
Black, Leo G.	RM3c	362-40-07	6-3-41
Blackmon, W. G., Jr.	Sea2c	356-45-75	9-11-41
Blatherwick, George W.	AOM3c	243-79-71	7-13-41
Bohner, Jack L. V.	RM3c	321-39-09	6-21-41
Boyer, Smith E. S.	AOM1c	341-94-11	6-3-41
Brandt, Richard E.	AMM2c	243-64-09	6-4-41
Brock, Wendell	RM3c	337-33-38	6-6-41
Bruce, Walter E.	Sea1c	279-77-35	6-6-41
Bryant, Earl F.	ARM3cv3	510-01-21	6-14-41
Buchanan, Charles F.	RM3c	414-48-92	6-24-41
Buckbee, Robert S.	RM3c	414-47-45	6-24-41
Bullard, Lloyd O.	Y2c	337-24-78	6-3-41
Bunch, James R.	Sea2cV3	664-00-88	12-11-41
Burns, William W., Jr.	Sea1c	401-40-04	6-6-41
Callaran, John P.	Sea1c	321-10-88	12-1-41
Campbell, Gordon R.	RM3c	212-49-97	6-24-41
Capps, Damon D.	RM3c	510-01-77	6-22-41
Carson, Arthur T., Jr.	AMM2c	406-17-10	6-3-41
Cavadini, Cesare V.	ACRM	120-94-15	6-22-41

Name	Rate	Service No.	Date on Board
Claunce, Albert D.	Sea2c	356-66-74	11-14-41
Clute, Lawrence H.	AMM2c	320-96-82	6-3-41
Coffin, Charles C.	CRM	383-30-10	12-11-41
Coker, Hillis L.	AMM3c	321-12-50	6-6-41
Cox, Charles R.	Sea2c	386-02-10	12-11-41
Cox, Julius S.	ACMM PA-NAP	330-06-00	10-3-41
Crawford, Gordon H.	AMM1c	261-82-62	8-11-41
Dean, Clifford J.	Sea2c	660-02-20	11-4-41
Degraw, Edwin R.	AMM1c	214-90-53	8-15-41
Dermody, James H., Jr.	Sea2c	274-04-61	12-11-41
Derouin, Raymond J.	AMM2c	300-01-05	6-4-41
Doucet, Chester J.	Sea2c	274-60-66	10-7-41
Doull, Roy D.	AMM2c	223-23-67	6-3-41
Ellis, Harley C.	Sea1c	376-91-22	10-10-41
Faulkner, French E., Jr.	AMM2c	360-09-45	6-6-41
Ferbrache, Dean A.	AMM1c	393-05-77	7-7-41
Fielder, James A.	ARM1c	295-32-98	12-17-41
Ford, Robert B.	Sea1c	632-02-40	12-11-41
Fornataro, Anthony R.	AMM2c	234-29-96	6-16-41
Forsythe, Joseph E.	AMM3c	295-66-03	12-17-41
Frankiewich, George	AMM2c	223-63-15	6-4-41
Freeman, Vernon N.	Sea2c	382-51-96	12-11-41
Frentz, Robert F.	AMM1c	393-22-90	6-3-41
Gadway, John	Sea2c	372-74-90	10-11-41
Gammell, John F.	AP1c	380-84-08	6-3-41
Garner, Edward E.	AMM2c	360-10-57	6-3-41
Gibson, James T.	Sea2c	356-59-61	12-11-41
Goetz, Omer D.	AMM2c	385-84-05	7-14-41
Goovers, George, Jr.	Sea2c	311-70-95	11-10-41
Gould, Norman R.	Sea2c	388-07-02	8-15-41
Gregg, Perry J.	ACMM PA	161-98-04	6-3-41
Griffith, John W.	RM2c	356-05-20	6-18-41
Grove, George W.	Sea2c	327-32-34	6-6-41
Gulch, John B.	Sea2c	311-70-95	11-10-41

Name	Rate	Service No.	Date on Board	Name	Rate	Service No.	Date on Board
Haake, Wallace P.	Sea2c	356-59-50	12-11-41	Morrison, John F.	Sea2c	356-45-39	8-22-41
Hamilton, Herold G.	Sea2c	382-84-19	7-22-41	Mudd, Stephen	AMM3c	287-84-34	7-15-41
Hammerstrand, L. F.	ACMM PA	305-00-27	6 -3-41	Munn, Harold C.	AMM2c	382-13-19	6-6-41
Hanson, R. A.	AMM2c	300-00-25	6-3-41	Musser, Francis G.	RM2c	328-06-89	6-6-41
Hardy, C. B.	AMM2c	250-18-20	6-4-41	Nelson, Monroe	Sea2c	664-00-80	10-27-41
Harmon, Carrel E.	AMM3c	342-18-91	7-14-41	Newcombe, George W.	Sea2c	356-28-59	10-27-41
Harris, Robert E.	AMM3c	355-94-80	6-3-41	Nicks, Willard H.	Sea2c	632-01-13	10-27-41
Harward, Thomas O.	AOM3c	368-61-34	9-18-41	Norvell, Charles E.	Sea2c	356-59-42	12-11-41
Headington, John D.	Sea2c	321-64-18	11-10-41	O'Daniel, William C.	AMM3c	287-35-29	6-4-41
Hester, Clifford F.	RM3c	510-03-88	8-22-41	O'Farrell, William H.	RM3c	336-26-64	6-3-41
Hitchcock, George W.	AOM3C	393-41-51	7-15-41	Olin, Clifford A.	AOM3c	385-81-08	6-3-41
Hobart, Virgil A.	Sea2c	614-00-08	11-10-41	Olsen, Edwin L.	Sea2c	356-57-57	10-27-41
Holden, Vernon T.	AMM3c	311-40-88	7-15-41	Ouellette, Paul F.	Sea2c	201-92-33	10-9-41
Hollister, Oris R.	ARM3c	385-89-87	6-6-41	Owens, Fredrick L.	Sea2c	392-36-26	10-10-41
Holmes, Albert B.	Sea1c	368-66-93	6-27-41	Owings, John T.	Sea2c	360-38-52	11-5-41
Irwin, Harry T.	AMM2c	320-94-30	6-7-41	Paine, Roger D.	Y1c	299-98-03	6-11-41
Isenor, William T.	Sea1c	401-40-08	6-6-41	Panetto, Fredrick S.	AOM1c NAP	321-11-92	6-18-41
James, Jesse	Matt2c	356-20-32	7-4-41	Panter, Wendell J.	AM2c	295-35-32	6-3-41
Janson, Pressley E.	ACMM PA	374-96-21	6-3-41	Parris, Ralph K.	AM2c	295-13-25	6-3-41
Jocius, Alexander C.	AMM3c	243-57-01	6-7-41	Pearson, Jim O.	Sea2c	360-59-39	10-27-41
Johnson, George B., Jr.	Sea2c	356-62-21	12-11-41	Pease, Vinton L.	CRM AA	336-68-39	12-11-41
Johnson, Joe	Matt1c	272-69-82	9-17-41	Petrie,Wallace G.	AMM2c	375-24-22	6-6-41
Jones, Corbett D.	Sea2c	644-00-02	10-3-41	Pickering, Richard W.	Sea2c	664-01-93	9-18-41
Jones, Horace, Jr.	Sea2c	382-49-04	12-11-41	Pierson, William H.	AMM1c	320-92-11	7-7-41
Judas, Loren G. H.	AMM2c	321-38-88	7-14-41	Price, James C.	Sea2c	311-64-41	7-15-41
Kallam, Robert F.	AOM3c	325-57-07	6-3-41	Prickett, Patton M.	ACOM PA	272-79-36	6-3-41
Karls, Raymond	AMM3c	355-86-22	6-3-41	Reid, Jewell H.	AMM1c NAP	287-09-45	6-3-41
Kauffman, Ralph	Sea2c	372-32-51	10-3-41	Rhuss, Frederick S.	Sea2c	337-52-32	7-15-41
Kendra, Frank	AMM3c	300-44-89	11-10-41	Rigsby, Vernon W.	Sea2c	356-50-16	12-11-41
Kiner, John N.	ACMM PA	316-08-48	6-3-41	Roark, Edward C.	Sea2c	356-50-38	12-11-41
Klopp, John J., Jr.	Sea2c	283-53-67	11-10-41	Robinson, Earl H.	ACM PA	341-09-70	6-6-41
Kozak, Leon	Sea2c	382-89-39	12-11-41	Robinson, Roy H., Jr.	AMM2c NAP	322-01-79	9-12-41
Lamson, Wilbur V.	AMM1c	201-38-13	8-3-41	Ronning, Albert A.	AMM2c NAP	225-75-67	12-4-41
Landers, Dewey L.	Sea2c	372-22-34	10-3-41	Rose, Allan J.	Sea2c	391-55-26	10-27-41
Leflar, Stephen L.	ACMM PA	375-22-34	6-3-41	Rose, Angus W.	RM1c	368-15-29	10-11-41
Lippens, Archie	AMm1c	310-86-45	6-3-41	Rosson, William W.	AM2c	295-47-90	6-4-41
Loesch, Jack L.	Sea2c	620-00-23	11-10-41	Russell, Charlie A.	RM2c	262-03-12	6-20-41
Lowry, James R.	AMM2c	385-89-45	7-14-41	Ryan, John J.	Sea2c	291-18-55	7-16-41
Ludwig, Monroe C.	Sea2c	360-41-76	10-11-41	Saliger, Henry F., Jr.	Sea2c	382-51-76	12-11-41
Lundberg, William E.	AMM3c	385-86-36	10-3-41	Savage, Clifford J. R.	Sea2c	3?3-54-71	12-6-41
Lux, Robert A.	AMM3c	381-30-47	6-10-41	Scott, James F., Jr.	AM3c	360-33-58	12-8-41
Mahon, Patrick J.	Sea2c	337-60-35	10-27-41	Scott, Richard D.	Sea2c	628-00-29	12-6-41
Mancini, Armido	AM2c NAP	250-45-57	6-3-41	Sewell, James F. D.	AOM3c	410-00-49	12-27-41
Marsh, Charles M.	Sea2c	662-00-69	12-11-41	Shakour, Richard	Sea2c	624-03-22	9-25-41
Marsh, Virgil R.	AMM2c	668-42-21	6-4-41	Shartts, Sherman L.	Sea2c	376-34-01	12-6-41
McCardle, Kenneth H.	ACMM PA	367-83-54	6-3-41	Shers, Robert W.	Sea2c	372-36-66	12-3-41
McGraw, Jay P.	Sea2c	346-94-10	12-11-41	Shimek, Carl L.	Sea2c	360-39-41	12-6-41
McKinzie, James H.	Sea2c	356-64-15	12-11-41	Siesser, Maurice A.	AMM3c	368-47-04	6-11-41
Meagher, Joseph E.	AMM3c	382-19-18	6-3-41	Silver, Nathan	Sea2c	322-52-01	12-11-41
Mersch, Clyde	Sea2c	320-77-58	7-7-41	Simms, Thomas	Sea2c	624-05-29	11-21-41
Miller, Charles E.	Sea2c	660-00-23	10-27-41	Sivertsen, Robert C.	Sea2c	662-00-73	12-6-41
Miller, Ernest N.	AM1c	291-27-25	6-8-41	Skidmore, Ellis D.	RM3c	393-35-07	6-3-41
Miller, Henry Charles	Sea2c	328-86-11	7-14-41	Sletten, Hiegler	Sea2c	372-34-65	11-21-41
Miller, Richard G.	Sea2c	654-01-57	12-11-41	Sloman, Ernest E.	Sea2c	401-41-57	10-29-41
Mills, James C.	Sea2c	346-93-25	10-27-41	Smith, Conrad E.	AMM3c	287-36-89	6-3-41
Mitchell, Walter E.	Sea2c	356-38-58	10-27-41	Smith, James F.	Sea2c	476-37-36	9-10-41
Moore, Sherman J.	Sea2c	376-32-92	10-27-41	Spencer, Larry M.	Sea2c	270-75-93	6-4-41

Name	Rate	Service No.	Date on Board
Stanley, Parker L.	Sea2c	201-86-36	7-18-41
Stark, John C., Jr.	Sea2c	360-28-95	7-18-41
Stephens, Wallace C.	AM3c	346-77-27	6-3-41
Stewart, Lowell A.	AM3c	296-57-92	6-3-41
Stoval, Joel C.	RM1c	375-37-87	6-17-41
Swinnford, Rex S.	Sea2c	356-57-64	10-27-41
Taylor, Tatum B.	Sea2c	360-39-29	10-27-41
Thompson, Allen J.	AMM3c	365-44-29	6-4-41
Tinc, Charles	AM2c	223-64-00	6-3-41
Toler, Edgar R.	Sea2c	370-35-73	10-11-41
Totten, Robert L.	Sea2c	393-55-27	10-27-41
Toves, Jesus C.	Matt1c	421-05-29	6-3-41
Troland, Clifford V.	Sea2c	664-02-12	12-12-41
Turner, Arcia O.	AOM1c	268-03-67	6-3-41
Ubben, Melvin R.	RM2c	316-63-21	6-20-41
Ulrich, Karl A.	AMM1c	320-82-01	12-3-41
Umphrey, Richard V.	AMM1c NAP	393-16-22	6-3-41
Vandergrift, Clarence C.	ACMM PA	242-23-29	6-3-41
Van Ness, Harland A.	Sea2c	376-23-90	12-11-41
Wade, Robert L., Jr.	Sea2c	360-53-34	9-26-41
Wagner, Dale L.	Sea2c	243-89-73	10-9-41
Warren, Jerome M.	Sea2c	356-63-95	11-26 41
Watson, Frank H.	ACOMM PA	374-87-37	6-3-41
Watts, John T.	Sea2c	654-00-31	10-27-41
Webber, Lee	Sea2c	662-03-82	11-10-41
Weber, John D.	AS	321-69-47	11-12-41
Weeks, John C.	AMM3c	381-31-37	7-15-41
Welch, Forest D.	AS	648-01-69	11-18-41
Weldy, George R.	ACM PA	275-04-69	6-3-41
Wells, Glen E.	AS	668-04-08	11-18-41
Wentschenn, Nelber M.	AS	321-89-69	11-18-41
Wertz, Harry H.	Sea2c	662-05-28	10-24-41
Wey, Raymond W.	AS	300-57-77	11-18-41
Whitaker, Edward R., Jr.	AS	337-07-05	11-18-41
White, Julius G.	Sea1c	385-97-63	9-18-41
Whitmeyer, F. D.	Sea2c	311-65-98	11-10-41
Whitney, Desil E.	Sea2c	376-37-66	11-26-41
Wideberg, Samuel R.	RM2c NAP	367-37-67	9-17-41
Wilkason, Keith K.	Sea2c	337-60-65	11-5-41
Williams, James E.	AS	342-52-72	11-14-41
Williams, Ralph F.	ACM PA	227-93-99	12-9-41
Williams, Richard	Matt2c	283-30-80	10-5-41
Williams, William W.	Sea2c	311-31-40	6-3-41
Wilson, Harry E.	Sea2c	370-35-02	6-26-41
Wilson, Richard A.	AS	342-52-22	11-15-41
Wilson, Sheldon W.	Sea2c	376-24-53	10-12-41
Wilson, Wilbur Reid	Sea2c	668-00-31	10-27-41
Wolfe, Gerhardt O.	AMM1c	341-26-31	6-10-41
Wood, Lloyd D.	Sea2c	663-00-30	10-27-41
Wozniak, Bruce W.	AMM3c	250-26-?6	6-6-41
Zmak, Joseph H.	Sea2c	662-01-90	10-24-41
Zydak, Zygmunt	AM3c	385-76-84	6-6-41

Appendix 3

Deck Log
USS *St. Louis*, Friday, 22 May 1942

Original signed by Captain G. A. Rood, U.S. Navy, Commanding
Examined by Lieutenant Commander J. E. Florance

UNITED STATES SHIP
St Louis Friday 22 May, 1942
(B. K Vickrey/National Archives)
Zone Description + 9 1/2

REMARKS

0 to 4

Moored in berth C-4, Pearl Harbor, T. H. with 15 fathoms of port anchor chain to bouy C-4-N and one wire line aft to Bouy 4-S. MEDUSA moored alongside to starboard with 6 manila and 2 wire lines. Boiler No. 1 steaming for auxiliary purposes and No. 2 warmed up. Ship darkened, in condition of Readiness III and Material Condition "B".

Signed: original by,
E. A. Parker, Ensign, USN

4 to 8

Moored as before. 0626 lighted ship.

Signed: original by,
G. H. Stone Jr, Ensign, USNR

8 to 12

Moored as before. 0830 mustered crew on stations: no absentees. 0908 YG-21 came alongside port side. 0926 YG-21 left the side of the ship. 0950 pursuant to the orders of ComCruPac dispatch 211900 of May, 1942, McCormack, J. R. 133-28-17 ACMM, Was transferred to the Receiving Station, Pearl Harbor, T. H. for further transfer to Naval Air Station, San Diego, California. 1128 water barge came alongside port side. Made daily inspection of magazines and smokeless powder samples; conditions normal. Conducted weekly test of magazine flooding and sprinkling system for airplane hangar and aviation storeroom; coniditions normal.

Signed: original by,
A. J. Burda Jr, Lieut. (Jg) USN

1200 to 1600

Moored as before. Pursuant to the orders of Patrol Squadron 41 letter VP-44/P16-4/00, Lt (Jg) W. L. M. Snead, A-V(S) USNR reported aboard with officers and personnel as follows:

Ensign J. M. Scott	Ensign R. R. Sparks
Ensign C. J. Bachtel	Ensign G. E. Hardeman
Ensign R. C. Trejo	

AMM3c Alford, L. H.	Y1c Andrew, E. X.
AMM2c Attanasio, E. A.	Sea2c Aune, K. R.
Sea1c Babb, C. E.	ARM3c Bacher, G. L.
OS1c Barruzo, B.	Sea1c Burns, W. W.
AOM3c Callaran, J. P.	ACRM Cavadini, C. V.
AOM3c Cekey, R. A.	ACRM Coffin, C. C.
Sea2c Cox, C. R.	AMM1c Degraw, E. R.
Sea2c De Lacruz, A. E.	PhM2c Dempwolf, R.
ACM Duncan, I. M.	AM2c Faulkner, F. E.
AMM3c Goovers Jr., G.	ARM3c Grove, G. W.
Sea2c Guy, W. T.	Sea2c Halquist, R. A.
ACMM Hammerstrand, L. F.	AOM3c Hitchhcock, G. W.
ACMM Janson, P. E.	Phm3c Johnson, J. P.

ACMM Leflar, S. L.
SC2c Mason, D. E.
AMM2c Meagher, J. E.
Sea2c Miller, R. G.
ARM3c Minervino, S. A.
Sea1c Mullenix, Hillard
AMM2c Munn, H. C.
AMM2c O'Daniel, W. C.
TM3c Ogeron, L. J.
CY(AA) Paine, R. D.
Sea1c Phillips, W. W.
Sea2c Proffitt, W. B.
Sea2c Rogers JR, H. H.
AMM1c Rowe, R.
Sea2c Selman, W. R.
AMM3c Stangl, M. E.
Sea2c Theuer, R. E.
AMM2c Tower, R. E.
Sea2c Tyler, H. E.
AMM3c Van Ness, H. A.

ACM Lippens, A.
ACMM McCardle, K. H.
AM3c Miller, C. E.
ARM3c Mills, J. C.
ARM3c Moore, S. J.
Sea1c Mullenix, Hilton
AMM3c Nicks, W. H.
Sea1c Odom, T. L.
ARM3c Olsen, E. L.
AM1c Panter, W. J.
AMM1c Pierson, W. H.
Sea1c Richmond, C. M.
Sea1c Rosson, W. W.
AM2c Saliger, H. F.
AOM3c Sewell, J. A.
Sea1c Studley, H. J.
AMM3c Threatt, C. E.
ARM3c Troland, C. V.
AMM1c Ulrich, K. A.
AM2c Vandergrift, C. C.

Sea1c Vey, C. D.
Sea2c Webber, L.
ACM Williams, R. F.
AMM1c Wolfe, C. O.
Matt2c James, J.
Matt3c Miller, J. R.
Matt2c Williams, R.

Sea1c Wade, R. L.
ARM3c White, J. G.
Sea1c Wilson, W. R.
Sea2c Zmak, J. H.
Matt3c Jones, L. T.
Matt3c Radcliff, J.
Matt3c Robinson, J.

1525

Completed taking on 2000 gallons of fresh water.

1530

Pursuant to the orders of the commanding officer of the U S S DIXIE the below officers and men reported on board for temporary duty. Records and accounts accompanied the men:

Lieut. Comdr J H Nivins, USN, (20 officers and men listed)

Original signed by

Approved _____

        G A Rood
        Captain USN
        Commanding

Original signed by

Examined _____

        J E Florance
        Lt. Comdr USN

Appendix 4

Logbook — Jack Reid
3 June 1942

Date	Type of Machine	Number of Machine	Duration of Flight	Character of Flight	Pilot
June 3.					On routine patrol out of Midway. Sighted first body of Japanese Fleet in the Battle of Midway. Fleet, consisting of 17 ships Battleships and Cruisers, Destroyers, Troop transports. Tracked for two hours and returned to Midway.
June 4.					On patrol out of Midway sighted same force as above. Fired on by 8 cruisers, Tracked and returned to Midway.
June 5					On patrol out of Midway sighted Japanese Force consisting of 2 Battleships, 4 heavy cruisers, 4 destroyers, and a burning carrier. Fired on by Battleships "AA" gallery.
June 6 & 7.					Searched and rescued survivors shot down during the Battle of Midway.
	Total time to date.				

PASSENGERS	REMARKS

June

PATROL SQUADRON 44

BROUGHT FORWARD			1764.1
THIS	FLGT. TIME	PASS. TIME	
MONTH	65.2	50.1	115.3
TOTAL TO DATE			1879.4

I CERTIFY THAT THE FOREGOING FLIGHT
RECORD IS CORRECT.

APPROVED
LT. COM. U. S. N.

Appendix 5

Aircraft Deployment
VP-44
21 May to 10 June 1942

Rear Admiral Bellinger War Diary, courtesy B. K. Vickrey

Date	Ford Island	Midway	Notes
21 May	12	0	Squadron reported to PATWING Two.
22 May	0	12	Squadron reported to Midway Commander.
(29 May	0	12	VP-23 Detachment reinforced.)
30 May	0	12	Two VP-44 planes engaged twin-engine enemy bombers and were damaged.
1 June	0	12	Two VP-44 planes engaged twin-engine enemy bombers. Total of four planes damaged.
2 June	1	11	One plane returned for repair.
3 June	4	8	Three planes returned for repair.
4 June	4	7	One plane shot down by enemy fighter float planes. Squadron strength 11 planes.
5 June	4	7	No change.
6 June	3	8	One plane returned to service.
9 June	1	10	Two planes returned to service.
10 June	10	1	Squadron transfered to Ford Island reporting to PATWING Two.

VP-44 was transferred to the Midway command on 22 May 1942. At that time, VP-23 had a detachment of PBY-5 planes operating out of Sand Island. On 29 May, the VP-23 detachment was increased to 12 planes. From 1 June to 10 June, detachments of squadrons VP-11, VP-12, VP-23, VP-24, VP-51, VP-72, and VP-91, at a level of from one to nine aircraft, operated from Eastern Island or Sand Island. In addition, VP-12, VP-24, and VP-91 vectored aircraft from Barking Sands, Kauai, westward toward Midway.

All personnel and aircraft of VP-44 were later transferred from the Midway command to the PATWING Two command and stationed for a short time on Ford Island.

Appendix 6

Officers and Crew

of the USS PATROL SQUADRON FORTY FOUR (VP-44) for the quarter ending 30 June 1942

Roster of officers courtesy B. K. Vickrey
Muster roll of the crew transcribed from copies of the original, courtesy B. K. Vickrey

OFFICERS OF VP-44
March 1942

5897* Lt. Cmdr. R. C. Brixner, Commanding
4189 Lt. W. L. Richards, Executive Officer
5436 Lt. D. G. Gumz
6247 Lt. (jg) C. E. Olson
6268 Lt. (jg) R. L. Summers
6481 Lt. (jg) R. S. Whitman Jr.

Lt. (jg) S. O. Cole NR**	Lt. Forest A. Roby
Ens. C. J. Bachtel NR	Ens. J. N. Andregg NR
Ens. C. D. Brislawn NR	Ens. C. D. Bauer NR
Ens. J. H. Camp NR	Ens. F. J. Buskirk NR
Ens. W. H. Cullin NR	Ens. E. D. Corckett NR
Ens. R. C. Donaldson NR	Ens. C. V. Dolan NR
Ens. G. H. Hardeman NR	Ens. G. W. Hantorn NR
Ens. R. B. Hays NR	Ens. R. L. Hayden NR
Ens. K. L. Howard NR	Ens. W. E. Headley NR
Ens. J. J. Lyons NR	Ens. R. Klinge NR
Ens. L C. McCleary NR	Ens. R. E. McCallister NR
Ens. J. A. Moflitt, Jr. NR	Ens. H. D. Metke NR
Ens. R. W. Neil NR	Ens. R. J. Molloy NR
Ens. J. L. Oppenheimer NR	Ens. H. S. Noon, Jr. NR
Ens. P. J. Post NR	Ens. S. R. Parker, Jr. NR
Ens. J. M. Scott, Jr. NR	Ens. W. E. Roy NR
Ens. R. A. Swan NR	Ens. J. L. Smith NR
Ens. R. C. Trejo NR	Ens. R. W. Talley NR
Ens. R. B. Felmeth NR	Ens. P. W. Vannoy NR
	Ens. J. G. Yoder

Commissioned April 1942:
Lt. (jg) Julius E. Cox	Ens. Fredrick S. Panetto
Ens. Jack H. Reid	Ens. Richard V. Umphrey

Came on board from VP-22 after 1 March 1942:
    Ens. Walter H. Mosley

* *Officers graduating from the Naval Academy were given personal serial numbers.*
** *NR = Naval Reserve.*

Muster Roll of the Crew
of the
USS PATROL SQUADRON FORTY FOUR (VP-44)
for the quarter ending 30 June 1942

Original prepared by
Lieutenant D. G. Gumz, U.S. Navy
Original approved by
Lieutenant Commander R. C. Brixner,
U.S. Navy, Commanding Officer

Forwarded 3 July 1942
From Pearl Harbor, T.H.

Source: National Archives
Provided by B. K. Vickrey

Ratings listed: AMM, AOM, AP, ARM, EM, & RM

Name		Rate	Service No.	Date on Board
Clifford	Adams	AP1c	320-99-40	9/17/41
John H.	Albers	AMM3c	321-61-49	3/21/42
Louis H.	Alford	AMM2c	274-40-22	6/3/41
Albert D.	Allen	AMM3c	346-86-71	3/41/42
Eldon P.	Allgood	RM3c	360-33-27	9/18/41
Gordon E.	Anderson	AMM3c	410-81-77	3/31/42
Emilo A.	Attanasio	AMM2c	207-24-61	3/31/42
Arthur J.	Arsenault	Sea1c	212-57-16	7/15/41
Glenn L.	Bacher	RM3c	616-01-62	12/11/41
Bert A.	Bankester	AMM3c	272-62-47	3/31/42
Robert M.	Barnes	AOM1c	385-74-05	6/8/41
Herchel P.	Barrington	AM3c	268-66-89	3/41/42
Norman E.	Bauer	ARM2c	414-47-04	6/9/41
Wallace J.	Baxter	AMM3c	385-91-78	3/31/42
William B.	Beck	AP2c	368-44-57	12/11/41
Dale A.	Berke	RM2c	411-14-85	6/19/41
Leo G.	Black	ARM2c	368-48-97	6/3/41
Harold O.	Blair	AOM1c	287-30-55	3/31/42
Jack L.	Bohner	RM2c	321-39-09	6/21/41
John W.	Brandon	AM2c	287-23-97	3/31/42
Richard E.	Brandt	ARM1c	243-64-09	6/4/41

Name		Rate	Service No.	Date on Board
Oliver ?	Braun	AMM3c	668-00-06	3/31/42
Edward D.	Brech	AM2c	295-34-93	6/22/42
Wendell (N.)	Brock	ARM2c	337-33-38	6/6/41
Earl F.	Bryant	ARM2c	510-01-21	8/22/41
Charles F.	Buchanan	ARM2c	414-48-92	6/24/41
Robert S.	Buckbee	RM2c	401-40-04	6/26/41
John P.	Callaran	AOM3c	321-10-55	10/1/41
Damon D.	Capps	ARM3c	510-01-77	8/22/41
Arthur T.	Carson	AMM2c	406-17-16	6/3/41
Cesare V.	Cavadini	ACRM	120-94-18	6/27/41
Charles C.	Coffin	ACRM	383-30-10	12/11/41
Hillis L.	Coker	AMM2c	321-12-80	6/6/41
Gordon H.	Crawford	AMM1c	261-82-62	8/11/41
George A.	Davies	AMM3c	411-23-23	3/31/42
Frank J.	Davis	AMM3c	616-00-30	3/31/42
Edwin R.	Degraw	AMM1c	214-90-53	8/15/41
Wilford M.	De La Mare	AMM1c	363-43-07	3/31/42
Raymond J.	Derouin	AMM2c	300-01-05	6/4/41
Roy D.	Doull	AMM2c	223-63-27	6/3/41
James W.	Downer	AMM3c	368-31-39	3/31/42
Ira M.	Duncan	ACM	290-90-87	3/41/42
Peter P.	Elko	AM3c	300-47-43	3/31/42
Donald F.	Elliot	AMM3c	382-41-58	3/31/42
Dahyle B.	Evans	AMM3c	368-49-53	4/17/42
V. R.	Evans	AOM1c	375-82-07	6/3/41
French E.	Faulkner	AMM2c	360-09-45	6/6/41
Dean A.	Ferbrache	AMM1c	393-05-77	7/7/41
James A.	Fielder	ARM1c	295-32-98	12/17/41
Patrick A.	Fitzpatrick	AMM3c	376-27-32	3/31/42
Francis E.	Ford	AMM3c	382-27-94	6/6/41
Anthony R.	Fornataro	AMM2c	234-29-96	6/16/41
Joseph E.	Forsythe	AMM2c	295-56-01	12/17/41
George	Frankiewich	AMM2c	223-63-15	6/4/41
Philip L.	Fulghum	AOM2c	393-34-45	6/3/41
John M.	Gadway	AOM3c	372-34-90	12/11/41
John F.	Gammell	AP1c	380-84-08	6/3/41
William L.	Garber	AMM3c	368-61-69	3/31/42
Edward E.	Garner	AMM1c	360-10-57	6/3/41
Omer D.	Goetz	AMM2c	385-04-85	7/14/41
George	Goovers, Jr.	AMM3c	311-70-95	3/12/42
Perry J.	Gregg	ACMM	161-98-04	6/3/41
John W.	Griffith	ARM1c	365-05-20	3/31/42
Robert A.	Grommett	AM3c	372-30-30	3/31/42
Noyes E.	Guess	ACOM	336-65-15	3/31/42
Leonard F.	Hammerstrand	ACMM	305-00-97	6/3/41
Carrel E.	Harmon	AMM2c	342-18-91	7/14/41
Thomas O.	Harward	AOM3c	368-61-34	9/18/41
Clifford F.	Hester	ARM2c	510-03-88	8/22/41
George W.	Hitchcock	AOM3c	394-41-31	4/29/42
Virgil A.	Hobart	AMM3c	614-00-08	11/10/41
Vernon T.	Holden	AMM2c	311-40-88	7/15/41
F. Sherwood W.	Holland	AM2c	262-45-33	3/31/42
Oris R.	Hollister	ARM3c	385-89-87	6/6/41
Pressley E.	Janson	ACMM	374-96-21	6/3/41
Alexander	Jocius	AMM2c	243-57-01	6/7/41
Victor A.	Jorgensen	AM3c	368-56-97	3/41/42
Loren G. H.	Judas	AMM2c	321-38-88	7/14/41

Name		Rate	Service No.	Date on Board
Frank	Kendra	AMM3c	300-44-89	11/10/41
William A.	Kerr	AM3c	274-56-77	3/31/42
John M.	Kiner	ACMM	316-08-48	6/3/41
William F.	Kinkella	AOM2c	376-02-16	2/8/40
John J.	Klopp	AMM3c	283-53-67	11/10/41
Wilbur V.	Lamson	AMM1c	201-48-13	6/3/41
Clarence R.	Lane	AMM3c	342-43-65	3/41/42
Joseph C.	Langowski	AMM3c	372-13-92	4/17/42
Stephen L.	Leflar	ACMM	375-22-34	6/3/41
Archie	Lippens	ACM	310-86-45	6/3/41
Jack L.	Loech	AMM3c	620-00-23	11/10/41
William E.	Lundberg	AMM2c	385-86-36	6/3/41
Carl E. W.	Lundquist	ACMM	327-94-34	3/31/42
Robert A.	Lux	AMM2c	381-30-47	6/10/41
Patrick J.	Mahon	AMM3c	337-60-55	10/27/41
Armido E.	Mancini	AP1c	250-45-57	6/3/41
Kenneth H.	McCardle	ACMM	367-83-34	6/3/41
Hugh	McIntosh, Jr.	AMM3c	266-39-62	3/31/42
Marion W.	McKiddy	AMM3c	365-52-60	3/31/42
Robert D.	McKiel	AOM2c	328-72-37	3/31/42
Edward K.	McKissick	AMM3c	243-90-29	3/31/42
Joseph E.	Meagher	AMM2c	382-19-18	6/6/41
Gordon M.	Merrow	AP2c	413-25-96	3/17/42
Clyde	Mersch	AMM1c	320-77-58	7/7/41
Charles E.	Miller	AMM3c	660-00-23	10/27/41
James C.	Mills	ARM3c	346-93-65	10/27/41
Samuel A.	Minervino	ARM3c	234-29-48	1/16/42
Walter E.	Mitchell	AMM3c	356-58-38	1/27/41
Sherman J.	Moore	RM3c	376-32-92	10/27/41
John F.	Morrison	RM3c	356-45-39	8/22/41
Harold C.	Munn	AMM2c	382-13-19	6/6/41
Francis G.	Musser	ACRM	328-05-89	6/6/41
John H.	Neiman	RM3c	412-00-04	6/22/42
Frank P.	Neufeld	AMM2c	385-88-86	3/31/42
George W.	Newcombe	AOM3c	356-58-29	10/27/41
Willard H.	Nicks	AMM3c	632-01-14	10/27/41
William C.	O'Daniel	AMM2c	287-35-29	6/4/41
Clifford A.	Olin	AOM1c	385-81-08	6/3/41
Edwin L.	Olsen	ARM3c	356-57-57	4/15/42
William E.	Oyens	AOM1c	380-50-63	3/31/42
Wendell J.	Paster	AM1c	295-35-32	6/3/41
Jim O.	Pearson	AMM3c	360-39-39	10/27/41
Vinton L.	Pease	ACRM	336-68-69	12/11/41
Frank A.	Pelroy	AMM3c	385-87-10	3/31/42
Wallace G.	Petrie	AMM1c	375-84-22	6/6/41
William H.	Pierson	AMM1c	320-92-11	7/7/41
Walter L.	Possage	AMM3c	383-49-60	4/29/42
Thomas F.	Reeder	MM3c	406-90-84	3/31/42
Edward C.	Roark	AMM3c	356-30-56	12/11/41
Earl H.	Robinson	ACMM	346-09-70	6/3/41
Roy H.	Robinson, Jr.	AP2c	382-01-78	9/17/41
Albert A.	Ronning	AP2c	385-75-67	12/8/41
Angus W.	Rose	ACRM	368-15-29	12/11/41
James J.	Roskowick	AMM3c	382-25-48	3/31/42
Raymond	Row—	AM2c	392-99-44	7/15/41
Henry F.	Saliger	AOM3c	382-51-76	12/11/41
Stanley	Schwartz	AMM3c	413-52-89	2/3/42

Name		Rate	Service No.	Date on Board
Francis O.	Scofield	AMM1c	375-66-81	3/31/42
James F.	Scott	AMM3c	360-33-58	12/6/41
Richard D.	Scott	AMM3c	628-00-29	12/6/41
James F. D.	Sewell	AOM3c	410-00-49	4/29/42
Maurice A.	Siesser	AMM2c	368-47-04	5/23/42
Ellis D.	Skidmore	ARM2c	393-35-07	6/3/41
Conrad E.	Smith	AMM2c	287-36-89	6/8/41
Morraine E.	Stangl	AMM3c	414-38-19	3/31/42
Edward A.	Steele	AMM3c	207-31-27	3/31/42
Wallace C.	Stephens	AM2c	346-77-26	6/3/41
Lowell A.	Stewart	AM2	295-57-92	6/3/41
Joel C.	Stoval	ACRM	375-37-87	6/3/41
Clifford L.	Studdard	AMM3c	360-40-38	2/3/42
Tatum B.	Taylor	AMM3c	360-39-29	10/27/41
Allen J.	Thompson	AMM2c	356-44-29	6/4/41
Cecil E.	Threatt	AMM3c	616-01-24	2/3/42
Charles	Tinc	AM2c	223-64-60	6/3/41
Roy E.	Tower	AMM3c	212-63-58	4/1/42
Arcia O.	Turner	ACOM	265-63-07	6/3/41
Melvin R.	Ubben	ARM1c	316-16-21	6/20/41
Peter E.	Ulbrandt	EM3c	223-77-07	4/16/42
Karl A.	Ulrich	AMM1c	380-82-81	12/8/41
Clarence C.	Vandergrift	ACMM	242-23-49	6/3/41
Harland A.	Van Ness	AMM3c	376-23-90	12/11/41
Mathias J.	Vopatek, Jr.	CAP	328-36-99	4/17/42
Dale L.	Wagner	AM3c	243-89-73	10/9/41
Ralph E.	Wallin	AMM1c	316-46-98	6/22/42
Thomas V.	Watkins, Jr.	AP1c	291-45-59	3/13/42
Richard G.	Watson	AMM3c	401-43-38	2/3/42
Julius G.	White	RM3c	385-97-63	9/18/41
Fredrick D.	Whitmeyer	RM3c	311-66-98	11/10/41
Samuel R.	Wideberg	AP1c	368-37-67	9/17/41
Keith K.	Wilkason	RM3c	337-60-65	11/5/41
Harvey G.	Wilkins	AMM3c	328-90-07	3/31/42
Ralph F.	Williams	ACM	227-93-99	12/9/41
Sheldon W.	Wilson	AM3c	376-24-53	10/13/42
Wilbur R.	Wilson	RM3c	668-00-31	10/27/41
Gerhardt O.	Wolfe	AMM1c	341-86-31	6/10/41
Lloyd D.	Wood	AMM3c	663-00-30	10/27/41
Frank A.	Young	AM2c	356-15-61	3/31/42
Zygmunt F.	Zydak	AMM2c	385-86-74	6/4/41
James W.	Adams	ACRM	320-85-61	9/1/41
Killed in action with enemy on 6/4/42 off Midway				
Clarence J.	Norby	AMM3c	372-19-10	??/??/??
Killed in action with enemy on 6/4/42 off Midway				
William H.	O'Farrell	RM3c	337-26-64	4/3/41
Killed in action with enemy on 6/4/42 off Midway				
Lyonal J.	Orgeron	AOM3c	274-62-18	??/??/??
Killed in action with enemy on 6/4/42 off Midway				

Ratings listed: Sea1c

Name		Rate	Service No.	Date on Board
Arthur J.	Arsenault, Jr.	Sea1c	212-57-16	7/15/41
Theodore L.	Beck	Sea1c	382-49-10	12/11/41
William E.	Bennet	Sea1c	386-02-66	3/3/42
Kenneth	Brown	Sea1c	376-31-47	3/31/42
Eldon G.	Brunelle	Sea1c	620-00-96	3/31/42
William W.	Burns	Sea1c	401-40-04	4/11/42
Kenneth E.	Cameron	Sea1c	408-70-26	3/31/42
Jack R.	Carroll	Sea1c	376-31-35	3/31/42
Ernest D.	Carveel	Sea1c	316-80-21	3/31/42
Frank J.	Cotita, Jr.	Sea1c	272-68-60	3/31/42
LeRoy H.	Cox	Sea1c	385-98-04	3/31/42
Orval W.	Davis	Sea1c	342-45-23	3/31/42
Harley C.	Ellis	Sea1c	376-21-92	10/10/41
Bernard W.	Fischer	Sea1c	316-78-03	3/31/42
Robert B.	Ford	Sea1c	632-02-40	12/11/41
William J.	Forrest	Sea1c	660-01-36	3/31/42
Stephen M.	Gail	Sea1c	382-44-26	3/31/42
William L.	Garrett	Sea1c	268-70-54	4/24/42
Leon	Glenn	Sea1c	360-38-60	3/31/42
Ellis P.	Greenfield	Sea1c	368-67-89	3/31/42
Earl R.	Haynes	Sea1c	360-38-69	3/31/42
Edward A.	Hemenway, Jr.	Sea1c	274-67-45	3/31/42
Russell L.	Hillard	Sea1c	360-43-55	3/31/42
Albert B.	Holmes	Sea1c	368-66-93	6/22/42
Louis R.	Houston	Sea1c	382-44-90	3/31/42
Luther A.	Hurst	Sea1c	342-45-70	3/31/42
Donald B.	Irvin	Sea1c	382-51-02	3/31/42
Howard J.	Irvin	Sea1c	250-63-81	3/31/42
William H.	Jackson	Sea1c	356-52-63	3/19/42
Lloyd S.	Janic	Sea1c	662-00-64	3/31/42
Donald V.	Jordan	Sea1c	393-54-09	3/41/42
William C.	Junck	Sea1c	238-77-27	3/31/42
LeRoy B.	Maxwell	Sea1c	616-01-80	2/3/42
Robert D.	McAdoo	Sea1c	662-03-16	2/3/42
James B.	McKinzie	Sea1c	356-64-15	12/11/41
Edwin C.	McLaughlin	Sea1c	382-51-38	2/3/42
David H.	Mechling	Sea1c	368-68-24	3/31/42
Cecil E.	Moore, Jr.	Sea1c	386-02-56	3/31/42
Hillard	Mullenix	Sea1c	376-34-50	3/31/42
Hilton	Mullenix	Sea1c	376-36-46	3/31/42
Frank W.	Mullick	Sea1c	376-33-87	3/31/42
Alfred L.	Mullikin	Sea1c	616-01-45	3/31/42
Donald B.	Mutz	Sea1c	372-33-38	3/31/42
Garth R.	Neikirk	Sea1c	662-01-51	3/31/42
Edward G.	O'brien	Sea1c	382-49-60	3/31/42
Charles H.	O'dell	Sea1c	346-95-10	2/3/42
Thomas L.	Odom	Sea1c	624-02-41	2/3/42
Orvil L.	Owens	Sea1c	382-47-28	3/31/42
David L.	Palmer, Jr.	Sea1c	356-62-24	3/31/42
Leland R.	Parker	Sea1c	376-33-16	3/31/42
Harry	Peterson	Sea1c	376-36-31	3/31/42
Woodward W.	Phillips, Jr.	Sea1c	356-60-10	3/31/42
Lonnie T.	Pool	Sea1c	382-48-83	3/31/42
Johnie C.	Powell	Sea1c	662-02-91	3/31/42
Bynum S.	Price	Sea1c	356-60-09	3/31/42
Wilbur B.	Proffitt	Sea1c	372-33-23	3/31/42
Carl E.	Reich	Sea1c	372-32-85	3/31/42
Cecil M.	Richmond	Sea1c	618-00-64	3/31/42
Elton E.	Siks	Sea1c	346-93-69	2/3/42
Walter C.	Stafford	Sea1c	300-41-48	3/31/42
Hillman	Studley, Jr.	Sea1c	662-04-61	2/3/42

Name		Rate	Service No.	Date on Board
Robert E.	Theuer	Sea1c	376-37-87	2/3/42
Robert E.	Thomas	Sea1c	662-03-22	3/31/42
Clifford V.	Troland	Sea1c	664-02-12	12/11/41
Robert L.	Wade, Jr.	Sea1c	360-43-54	9/26/41
Melbert M.	Wienschenk [sp.?]	Sea1c	321-69-89	11/18/41
Woodrow W.	Wilson	Sea1c	376-37-22	2/3/42
Joseph H.	Zmak	Sea1c	662-01-90	10/24/41

Ratings listed: Cox, Matt, Ptr, Phm, SC, and Sea

Name		Rate	Service No.	Date on Board
Edward W.	Andre	Cox	382-27-48	3/24/42
Kurt R.	Aune	Sea2c	654-17-51	2/11/42
Roy I.	Awan	Sea2c	386-02-53	4/12/42
Jay R.	Barker	Sea2c	654-18-40	2/11/42
Charles J.	Boucher, II	Sea2c	274-67-44	3/31/42
Norman F.	Cool	Sea2c	654-18-44	2/11/42
Charles R.	Cox	Sea2c	386-02-11	2/11/41
George F.	Dearborn	Sea2c	662-26-40	2/1/42
Arthur E.	De Lacruz	Sea2c	662-25-64	2/11/42
Frank	Delgado	Sea2c	662-25-13	2/11/42
Eugene H.	Dempekolf	Phm2c	321-36-94	2/18/42
Ernest W.	Dundas	Sea2c	632-20-56	3/8/42
John H.	Dyer	Sea2c	654-19-15	3/8/42
Gene A.	Ennis	Sea2c	660-09-83	2/11/42
Merrill P.	Faulk	Sea2c	604-02-35	3/31/42
William J.	Ferguson, Jr.	Sea2c	274-67-63	3/31/42
Theodore C.	Fletcher	Sea2c	632-01-81	3/20/42
John P.	Garavello	Sea2c	662-28-15	3/8/42
James F.	Gardner	Sea2c	664-04-44	3/31/42
Henry J.	Garth	Matt	3342-59-13	4/29/42
Thomas M.	Glass	Sea2c	632-17-75	3/8/42
O. W.	Glaxener	Phm1c	261-90-18	1/10/42
Edward E.	Gold———	Sea2c	382-76-00	3/8/42
Thomas L.	Gold———	Sea2c	356-67-33	3/7/42
Jesse W.	Go——er	Ptr1c	161-67-92	4/17/42
Raymond V.	Gossman	Sea2c	382-72-23	3/8/42
Frederick L.	Grahm	Sea2c	382-55-23	3/7/42
Robert T.	Green	Sea2c	368-69-33	3/7/42
Frank W.	Greene	Matt3	522-02-01	4/17/42
Frank N.	Grubb	Sea2c	664-12-77	3/8/42
Wilburn T.	Gut——	Sea2c	662-06-78	3/7/42
Mario B.	Gutteriez	Sea2c	624-05-44	3/7/42
Harvey T.	Hall	Sea2c	376-40-14	3/7/42
Henry F.	Halu	Sea2c	662-06-67	3/7/42
Orvie G.	Hamilton	Sea2c	356-66-65	3/7/42
Fred E.	Harper	Sea2c	660-10-24	2/11/42

Name		Rate	Service No.	Date on Board
James H.	Hatter	Sea2c	376-52-86	3/12/42
William J.	Henning, Jr.	Sea2c	386-02-81	3/31/42
Albert M.	Herbst	Sea2c	393-57-02	4/12/42
Casper C.	Hosang	Sea2c	662-25-12	2/11/42
Jesse	James	Matt3	356-20-32	7/4/41
George B. J.	Johnson	Sea2c	356-62-51	12/11/41
James P.	Johnson	Phm3c	272-29-34	3/31/42
Joe	Johnson	Matt1	272-69-82	9/17/41
Robert L.	Johnson	SC2c	632-14-74	3/18/42
Walter	Johnson	Sea2c	393-57-31	3/31/42
Horace M.	Jones, Jr.	Sea2c	382-49-04	12/11/41
Lawrence T.	Jones	Matt3	347-02-43	4/7/42
Walter H.	Jones	As	640-32-30	6/25/42
Roland A.	Lekey	Sea2c	628-08-91	3/31/4?
Charles M.	Marsh	Sea2c	662-00-69	12/11/41
Jesse I.	Martin, Jr.	Sea2c	386-02-39	3/31/42
Daniel E.	Mason, Jr.	SC2c	662-15-28	3/18/42
Edward F.	McCabe	Sea2c	368-68-77	2/26/42
Richard L.	McCoy	Sea2c	401-45-57	2/3/42
Richard G.	Miller	Sea2c	645-01-57	12/11/41
Paul F.	Ouellette	Sea2c	201-92-33	10/9/41
Johnny E.	Pannell	Sea2c	624-01-99	3/31/42
Earl A.	Peak	Sea2c	668-14-58	5/8/42
Jack	Poff	Sea2c	662-04-65	4/29/42
James C.	Price	Sea2c	311-64-41	7/15/41
Jacob	Radcliffe	Matt3	264-50-90	3/3/42
L. C.	Rayford	Matt3	347-02-46	3/3/42
Kennard	Reed	Matt2	356-75-13	3/3/42
James	Robinson	Matt3	644-19-07	3/3/42
Henry H.	Rogers, Jr.	Sea2c	268-84-71	3/31/42
Winferd R.	Selman	Sea2c	616-01-47	2/3/42
Robert C.	Sivertsen	Sea2c	662-00-73	12/6/41
Richard H.	Smith	Sea2c	376-35-86	2/3/42
John C.	Stark, Jr.	Sea2c	360-28-95	4/29/42
Arthur S.	Taylor	BM2c	380-77-92	3/31/42
Earl A.	Thompson	SF3c	628-07-22	3/31/42
Edgar R.	Toler	Sea2c	376-35-73	12/11/41
William E.	Towner	Sea2c	618-02-10	3/31/42
Thomas	Travis	Sea2c	372-34-29	2/3/42
Byrl S.	Troxel	Sea2c	382-58-81	3/31/42
Jack	Turner	Sea2c	265-63-07	6/3/41
Homer E.	Tyler	Sea2c	356-61-57	2/3/42
Robert	Tywer	Sea2c	654-05-00	4/21/42
Ralph R.	Vance	Sea2c	654-04-44	3/31/42
Nickolas P.	Vanderpol	Sea2c	386-05-35	3/31/42
Donald F.	Watson	Sea2c	375-35-52	2/3/42
Richard	Williams	Matt2	283-30-80	9/5/41

Appendix 7

VP-44 Flight Crews
June 1942

A partial reconstruction

44-P-3
Lieutenant Robert B. Hays
Ensign P. W. Vannoy
Clifford A. Adams AP1c (NAP)
F. O. Scofield AMM1c
R. A. Lux AMM2c
F. E. Ford AMM3c
R. E. Brandt ARM1c
D. D. Capps RM3c
G. W. Newcombe AOM3c

44-P-4
Ensign Jack H. Reid
Ensign Gerald Hardeman
Ensign Robert A. Swan
John F. Gammell AP1c (NAP)
Francis G. Musser ACRM
Raymond J. Derouin AMM2c
George Goovers, Jr. AMM3c
Patrick A. Fitzpatrick AMM3c

44-P-6
Ensign Jarloth J. Lyons
Ensign George W. Hanthorn
Ensign Fredrick S. Panetto
Ensign Frank H. Jarrel
Dean A. Ferbrache AMM1c
Zygmunt F. Zydak AMM2c
Richard G. Watson AMM2c
Charles F. Buchanan ARM2c
George W. Grove Sea2c

44-P-7
Ensign Richard V. Umphrey
Ensign Russel W. Neil
Ensign Robert R. Sparks
Mathias J. Vopatek CAP (NAP)
Edward E. Garner AMM1c
Conrad E. Smith AMM2c
Edward C. Roark AMM3c
James A. Fielder ARM1c
G. B. Johnson Sea2c
J. C. Mills ARM3c

44-P-?
Lieutenant (jg) Clarence E. Olson
Ensign Cornelius Brislawn
Ensign Robert L. Hayden

44-P-?
Ensign Carl D. Bauer
Ensign Harry D. Metke
Ensign Henry S. Noon

44-P-?
Lieutenant Shelby O. Cole
Ensign Richard Klinge
Ensign Ralph C. Donaldson
Roy H. Robinson AP2c (NAP)
A. O. Turner ACOM
E. H. Robinson ACMM
M. R. Ubben ARM1c
J. L. Bohner ARM2c
C. E. Harmon AMM2c
A. J. Thompson AMM3c

44-P-10
Lieutenant Forest A. Roby
Ensign Robert Felmuth
Ensign Harry A. Sorenson
Samuel R. Wideberg AP1c (NAP)
Wilbur V. Lamson AMM1c
Anthony R. Fornataro AMM2c
Richard D. Scott AMM3c
John W. Griffith ARM1c
John F. Morrison RM3c
Clifford A. Olin AOM1c

44-P-12
Lieutenant (jg) Robert S. Whitman
— KIA
Ensign Walter H. Mosley — KIA
Ensign Jack H. Camp — KIA
Ensign Lee C. McCleary
James W. Adams ACRM — KIA
Virgil R. Marsh AMM1c
John C. Weeks AMM2c
Philip L. Fulghum AOM2c
Clarence J. Norby AMM3c — KIA
William H. O'Farrell RM3c
— KIA

44-P-?
Ensign J. N. Andregg
Ensign W. E. Roy
Wallace G. Petrie AMM1c
Angus W. Rose ACRM

Appendix 8

Officers and Pilots of VP-44
October 1942

Commander R. C. Brixner, Commanding
Lieutenant Commander R. A. Rosasco,
Commanding (effective December 1942)
Lieutenant D. G. Gumz, Executive Officer
Lieutenant (jg) John N. Andregg
Ensign T. S. Atkins
Ensign C. J. Bachtel
Ensign Waite Bolden
Ensign Brchan
Ensign Bryce
Ensign Combs
Lieutenant E. A. Conrad
Lieutenant (jg) William F. Cullin
Lieutenant (jg) Lindsey Guehery
Lieutenant (jg) R. C. Donaldson
Ensign Diguillian
Lieutenant (jg) Robert B. Felmuth
Ensign Genuit
Ensign Granger
Lieutenant S. Greene
Ensign Hampton
Lieutenant (jg) G. W. Hanthorn
Lieutenant (jg) Robert L. Hayden
Lieutenant (jg) Robert B. Hays
Ensign Hayward
Ensign William John Hubbach
Ensign Chadron Hunter
Ensign J. K. Hutchinson
Lieutenant (jg) Richard Klinge
Ensign Lewis
Lieutenant (jg) J. J. Lyons
Ensign R. E. McCallister
Lieutenant (jg) Harry D. Metke
Lieutenant Thomas G. Monahan
Ensign Morris
Lieutenant (jg) R. W. Neil
Lieutenant (jg) Henry S. Noon
Ensign Oakley
Lieutenant Clarence E. Olson
Ensign Charles W. Pacey

Ensign Fredrick S. Panetto
Lieutenant (jg) Pettiet
Ensign Ramsey
Ensign Rees
Lieutenant (jg) W. E. Roy
Ensign Howard E. Rumrey
Ensign Schrieder
Lieutenant John Simpson
Lieutenant H. T. Skelley
Ensign J. L. Smith
Lieutenant (jg) H. A. Sorenson
Ensign Sparks
Lieutenant (jg) Leonard D. Sullivan
Lieutenant (jg) R. L. Summerell
Lieutenant R. L. Summers
Lieutenant (jg) Robert A. Swan
Ensign Thomas
Lieutenant (jg) Thorn
Lieutenant (jg) Ralph Trejo
Lieutenant (jg) Richard V. Umphrey
Lieutenant (jg) P. W. Vannoy

Aviation Pilots
Clifford A. Adams CAP
Reid E. Coble AP1c
John F. Gammell CAP
Harrison AP1c
Furman P. Jackson AP2c
Armido E. Mancini AP1c
Jim W. Martin AP1c
Gordon H. Merrow AP1c
Frank L. Michalek AP2c
Robert L. Ridle AP1c
Roy H. Robinson, Jr. AP1c
Walter D. Roll AP2c
Rossi AP2c
Arthur W. Snively AP2c
Mason L. Stitt AP1c
Thomas V. Watkins CAP
Samuel R. Wideberg AP1c

Appendix 9

Muster Roll of the Crew

of the USS PATROL SQUADRON FORTY FOUR (VP-44) for the quarter ending 31 December 1942

Original prepared by (not available).   Original approved by (not available).
From the Report of Changes records for December 1942

Source: National Archives

Name	Rate	Service No.	Place of Enlistment
Adams, Clifford August	CAP	320-99-40	Des Moines
Albers, John Henry	AMM3c	321-61-49	Des Moines
Allen, Albert Denver	AMM2c	346-86-71	Little Rock
Allgood, Eldon Paul	ARM3c	360-33-27	Houston
Anderson, Gordon Edward	AMM2c	410-81-77	St. Paul
Arsenault, Arthur Joseph, Jr.	AOM3c	212-57-16	Springfield, MA
Bacher, Glenn Lewis	ARM2c	616-01-62	Dallas
Ball, Richard James	AOM3c	328-83-23	Minneapolis
Barnes, Robert M.	AOM1c	385-74-05	Bremerton
Barr, Robert	ARM3c	622-03-72	Detroit
Bauer, Norman Ernest	ARM1c	414-47-04	Seattle
Beck, Theodore Lycurgun	AMM2c	382-49-10	Los Angeles
Blair, Harold Oren	AOM1c	287-30-55	Louisville
Blatherwick, George Walker	AOM1c	243-79-71	Philadelphia
Bowman, Robert Paul	AMM3c	621-08-38	Kansas City
Brandt, Richard Emerson	ARM1c	243-64-09	Philadelphia
Brown, Dale Ernest	ARM1c	346-76-78	Little Rock
Bryant, Earl Forest	ARM1c	510-01-21	Tacoma, WA
Buchanan, Charles Forest	ARM1c	414-48-92	Portland, OR
Bunch, James Richard	ARM3c	664-00-82	Seattle
Burns, William Wilbur, Jr.	AOM2c	401-40-04	Alameda
Capps, Damon D.	ARM2c	510-01-77	Tho Dalles, OR
Carson, Arthur Tell, Jr.	AMM1c	406-17-16	Macon
Coble, Reid Edgerton	AP1c	261-03-11	Raleigh
Coker, Hillis Leroy	AMM1c	321-12-80	Los Angeles
Cox, Charles Robert	ARM2c	386-02-10	Seattle
Crawford, Gordon Henry	ACM	261-02-62	San Diego
Derouin, Raymond Josey	ACM	300-01-05	Chicago
Downer, James Warren	AMM3c	368-61-39	Salt Lake
Fitzpatrick, Patrick Andrew	AMM3c	376-27-32	San Francisco
Ford, Robert Brooms	AMM2c	632-02-30	Los Angeles
Forsythe, Joseph Emear	AMM1c	295-56-91	Nashville
Frankiewich, George	AMM1c	223-63-16	New York
Gadway, John Marshal	AOM2c	372-34-90	Denver
Gammel, John Frank	CAP	380-84-08	Alameda
Gr—, Harry Leo	AM3c	632-31-48	Los ———
Griffith, John Willis	ARM1c	356-05-20	Dallas
Grove, George W.	Sea2c	337-32-34	St. Louis
Harty, Edward Patrick	ARM3c	328-94-26	———
Hitchcock, George W.	AOM2c	393-41-31	Portland
Hobart, Virgil Albert	AMM3c	614-00-08	Cleveland
Holden, Vernon T.	AMM1c	311-40-66	Detroit
Hubbard, Paul F.	ARM3c	321-66-60	———
Jocius, Alexander Clarence	AMM1c	243-57-01	———
Johnson, George B., Jr.	AMM3c	356-62-21	Dallas

Name	Rate	Service No.	Place of Enlistment
Judas, Loren George Henry	AMM1c	321-38-88	Des Moines
Junck, William Carl	AOM3c	238-27-77	Albuquerque, NM
Kallam, Robert Franklin	AOM1c	385-87-07	Seattle
Kammerer, Joseph Albert	ARM3c	348-00-42	Omaha, NE
Kinkella, William Francis	AOM2c	370-02-18	San Francisco
Klopp, John Joseph, Jr.	AMM2c	283-53-67	Cleveland
Leflar, Stephen Leonard	ACMM	375-32-24	Pensacola
Lippens, Archie	ACM	310-56-45	Kaneohe Bay
Loesch, Jack Lessenger	AMM2c	620-00-23	Des Moines
Lundberg, William Ellis	AMM1c	385-86-36	Seattle
Lundgren, Lewis Franklin	ARM3c	328-92-92	Minneapolis
Lutton, Carl V.	ARM3c	291-73-03	Indianapolis
Mahon, Patrick Jason	AMM3c	337-60-55	St. Louis
Mancini, Armido Elmer	AP1c	250-45-57	Pittsburgh
Marsh, Charles Marion	AMM3c	662-00-69	San Francisco
McCabe, Edward Francis	AMM3c	368-68-77	Salt Lake City
McCardle, Kenneth Henry	ACMM	367-83-64	Seattle
McKissick, Edward King, Jr.	AMM2c	243-90-29	Philadelphia
McLaughlin, Edward Cates	AMM3c	382-51-38	Los Angeles
Merrow, Gordon Mark	AP1c	413-25-96	NAS Pensacola
Michalek, Frank Albert	AP2c	207-25-63	New Haven
Miller, Richard Gunn	ARM3c	654-01-57	Portland, OR
Mills, James Cecil	ARM2c	346-93-65	Little Rock
Minervino, Samuel Anthony	ARM2c	224-29-18	Buffalo
Mullikin, Alfred Loren	AMM2c	616-01-45	Dallas
Neufeld, Frank Peter	MM2c	385-88-86	Seattle
Newcombe, George Webster	AOM2c	356-28-29	Dallas
Nicks, Willard Harvey	AMM2c	632-01-14	Los Angeles
O'Daniel, William Charles	AMM1c	287-35-29	Louisville
Olin, Clifford Alton	AOM1c	385-01-08	Seattle
Olsen, Edwin Leo	ARM2c	356-57-57	Dallas
Pearson, Jim Owen	AMM3c	360-39-39	Houston
Petrie, Wallace Gordon	AMM1c	375-84-22	Alameda
Pierson, William Henry	ACMM	320-92-11	NAS Pensacola
Reeder, Thomas Franklin	AMM3c	406-90-84	Miami
Robinson, Roy Hurst, Jr.	AP1c	382-01-78	NAS Seattle
Roskowick, James Joseph	AMM3c	382-25-48	Los Angeles
Rosson, William Wiley	AM1c	295-47-90	Nashville
Saliger, Henry Frederick, Jr.	AOM2c	382-51-76	Los Angeles
Schwartz, Stanley	AMM2c	413-52-89	San Francisco
Scofield, Francio Ohl	AMM1c	375-66-81	San Diego
Scott, James Foster, Jr.	AMM3c	360-33-58	Houston
Scott, Richard Daniel	AMM3c	628-00-29	Kansas City, MO
Sewell, James Fredrick Donald	AOM2c	410-00-49	Columbus, OH
Shafer, Robert Lee	ARM3c	279-83-96	Cincinnati
Siesser, Maurice Adrian	AMM1c	368-47-04	Salt Lake City
Sivertsen, Robert Carl	AMM3c	662-00-73	San Francisco
Stark, John Cecil, Jr.	AOM3c	360-28-95	Houston
Stitt, Mason LeRoy	AP1c	243-49-46	Philadelphia
Studdard, Clifford Leslie	AMM2c	360-40-38	Houston
Thompson, Allen Jordan	AMM2c	356-44-29	Dallas
Troland, Clifford Vernon	ARM3c	664-02-12	Seattle

(Trans. Flight School, St. Marys College, December 1942)

Name	Rate	Service No.	Place of Enlistment
Ubben, Melvin Rex	ARM1c	316-63-21	Omaha
Vandergrift, Clarence Clifford	ACMM	242-25-49	Pearl Harbor
Van Ness, Harland Arthur	AMM2c	376-23-90	San Francisco
Watkins, Thomas Vance, Jr.	CAP	291-45-59	Indianapolis
Watson, Richard Gould	AMM3c	401-43-38	San Diego
White, Julius Geaton	ARM2c	385-97-63	Seattle
Wideberg, Samuel Ray	AP1c	368-37-67	Seattle
Wilkason, Keith Kenneth	RM3c	337-60-65	St. Louis
Wilson, Wilbur Reid	RM3c	668-00-31	St. Louis
Wood, Lloyd Dale	AMM2c	663-00-30	St. Louis
Zmak, Joseph Harry	AOM3c	662-01-90	San Francisco

Appendix 10

VP-44
Pilot and Crew Organization — Kaneohe Bay

"A" Section

	Crew #1	Crew #4	Crew #6
PPC	Ens. Reid	Lt. Olson	Ens. Neil
2nd Pilot	Ens. Monahan	Ens. Pettiet	Ens. Hayden
3rd Pilot	Ens. Summerell	Ens. Schrieder	Stitt AP2c
4th Pilot	Jackson AP2c	Rossi AP2c	
PC	De La Mare	Doull	Harmon
2nd Mech	Roskowick	Fitzpatrick	Thompson
3rd Mech	Possage	Schwartz	Mullikin
1st Radio	Griffith	Hester	Buchanan
2nd Radio	Harty	Bowman	Grove
Air Bomber	Barnes	Blatherwick	Ball

	Crew #7	Crew #13	Crew #16 Super*
PPC	Ens. Swan	Ens. Donaldson	Ens. Roy**
2nd Pilot	Ens. McCallister	Ens. Sullivan	Ens. Klinge
3rd Pilot	Ens. Rees	Roll AP2c	Wideberg AP1c
4th Pilot	Snively AP2c		
PC	Scofield	Crawford	Coker
2nd Mech	Beck	Albers	Nicks
3rd Mech	McIntosh	Ford, R. B.	Wood
1st Radio	Ubben	Morrison	Cox
2nd Radio	Bunch	Barr	Lutton
Air Bomber	Olin	Newcombe	

"B" Section

	Crew #2	Crew #3	Crew #5
PPC	Lt. Hays	Ens. Noon	Lt. (jg) Lyons
2nd Pilot	Ens. Combs	Ens. Sparks	Ens. Bryce
3rd Pilot	Ens. Granger	Ens. Hampton	Ens. Thorn
4th Pilot		Martin AP1c	Merrow AP1c
PC	Judas	Jocius	Zydak
2nd Mech	Evans	Loesch	Allen
3rd Mech	Hobart	Scott, J. F.	Studdard
1st Radio	Brandt	Bauer	Brown
2nd Radio	Wilkason	Miller	Shafer
Air Bomber	Zmak	Sewell	Burns

	Crew #8	Crew #14	Crew #17 Super*
PPC	Lt. (jg) Andregg	Ens. Cullin	Ens. Vannoy**
2nd Pilot	Ens. Hutchinson	Ens. Smith	Ens. Trejo
3rd Pilot	Ens. Hayward	Watkins CAP	Adams CAP
4th Pilot	Harrison AP1c		
PC	Petrie	Carson	Frankiewich
2nd Mech	Neufeld	Garber	Downer
3rd Mech	McLaughlin	Marsh	McKiddy
1st Radio	Black	Mills	Olsen
2nd Radio	Conlon	Kammerer	Johnson
Air Bomber	Gadway	Junck	

"C" Section

	Crew #9	Crew #10	Crew # 11
PPC	Ens. Umphrey	Lt. Summers	Lt. (jg) Hanthorn
2nd Pilot	Ens. Bachtel	Ens. Ramsey	Ens. Morris
3rd Pilot	Ridle AP1c	Ens. Diguillian	Michalek AP1c
4th Pilot		Coble AP2c	
PC	Garner	Lundberg	Meagher
2nd Mech	McKissick	Van Ness	Siesser
3rd Mech	Scott, J. F.	Kendra	Anderson
1st Radio	Bryant	Buckbee	Brock
2nd Radio	Lundgren	Pittman	Allgood
Air Bomber	Arsenault	Kinkella	Hitchcock

	Crew #12	Crew #15	Crew #18 Super*
PPC	Ens. Felmuth	Ens. Metke	Ens. Panetto
2nd Pilot	Ens. Hardeman	Ens. Sorenson	Ens. Oakley
3rd Pilot	Robinson AP1c	Gammell CAP	Mancini AP1c
PC	Holden	Smith, C. L.	O'Daniel
2nd Mech	Klopp	Reeder	Mahon
3rd Mech	Watson, R. G.	Pearson	Pelroy
1st Radio	White	Wilson	Minervino
2nd Radio	Hubbard	Gerkin	West
Air Bomber	Saliger	Stark	

* "Super" was a special designation given by Lieutenant C. E. Olson when he reorganized the squadron in mid-1942. Meaning is unknown.
** Not qualified.

Original Signed by: C. E. Olson
Lt. U.S. Navy, Flight Officer

(No date given in copy of original. The document was effective at some point during the fall of 1942.)

Appendix 11

VP-44 Flight Crews
Espiritu Santo and Tulagi

*(Partial listing based upon action reports and photographs.
Individuals may have served on more than one crew.)*

44-P-1
Lieutenant Commander R. A. Rosasco
Lieutenant (jg) R. C. Donaldson
Ensign Waite Bolden
John F. Gammell AP1c (NAP)
F. O. Scofield AMM1c
Stanley Schwartz AMM2c
Theodore "Red" Beck AMM2c
Melvin R. Ubben ARM1c
Richard "Dick" Bunch ARM3c
George W. Newcombe AOM2c

44-P-2
Lieutenant (jg) John N. Andregg
Ensign Hutchinson
Loren G. H. Judas AMM1c
William C. O'Daniel AMM1c
John H. Albers AMM3c
Edwin J. McLaughlin AMM3c
Earl F. Bryant ARM3c
John M. Gadway AOM2c

44-P-3
Lieutenant (jg) Robert B. Hays
Lieutenant (jg) Leonard D. Sullivan
Clifford A. Adams CAP (NAP)
Loren G. H. Judas AMM1c
Patrick Fitzpatrick AMM3c
Virgil A. Hobart AMM3c
Keith K. Wilkason RM2c
Harold O. Blair AOM1c

44-P-4
Lieutenant (jg) R. W. "Russ" Neil
Lieutenant (jg) Lindsey Guehery
Ensign Thomas
M. L. Stitt AP1c (NAP)
C. E. "Bill" Harmon AMM1c
Allen J. Thompson AMM2c
A. L. Mullikin AMM2c
Charles R. Cox ARM2c
P. F. Hubbard ARM3c
Richard J. Ball AOM3c

44-P-5
Lieutenant (jg) Henry S. "Hank" Noon
Lieutenant (jg) Robert L. Hayden
C.E. Frye Ap1c (NAP)
A. C. Jocius AMM1c
Thomas F. Reeder AMM3c
James F. Scott AMM3c
Norman E. Bauer ARM3c
Orval W. Davis ARM3c
James F. Sewell AOM2c

44-P-6
Lieutenant (jg) William F. Cullin
Lieutenant (jg) Harry D. Metke
Ensign Johnson
Frank L. Michalek AP1c (NAP)
Arthur T. Carson AMM1c
Edward K. McKissick AMM2c
Charles M. Marsh AMM3c
Samuel A. Minervino ARM2c
George B. Johnson, Jr. ARM3c
William C. Junck AOM2c

44-P-7
Lieutenant Clarence E. Olson
Lieutenant (jg) H. A. Sorenson
C. E. Frye AP1c (NAP)
Gordon Henry Crawford ACMM
John H. Albers AMM2c
Robert B. Ford AMM2c
Edwin L. Olsen ARM2c
Robert Bowman ARM2c
George W. Blatherwick AOM1c

44-P-8
Lieutenant (jg) J. J. "Jiggs" Lyons
Lieutenant (jg) Thorn
Roy Hurst Robinson AP1c (NAP)
Zygmunt F. Zydak AMM1c
Albert D. Allen AMM2c
Clifford L. Studdard AMM3c
Dale E. Brown ARM1c
Robert L. Shafer ARM2c
William W. Burns, Jr. AOM2c

44-P-9
Lieutenant (jg) Robert A. Swan
Lieutenant (jg) "Harry" "Sully" Sullivan
Ensign Howard E. Rumrey
Samuel R. Wideberg CAP (NAP)
Frank P. Neufeld AMM1c
Patrick J. Mahon AMM2c
James J. Roskowick AMM3c
James C. "Jim" Mills ARM2c
Joseph A. Kammerer ARM3c
Arthur J. Arsenault AOM3c

44-P-10
Lieutenant E. A. Conrad
Lieutenant (jg) Thomas G. Monahan
Ensign E. D. Brchan
D. G. Grimwood AMM1c
J. W. Ward AMM2c
O. E. "Shorty" Evans AMM3c
George B. Johnson ARM2c
James J. Finn ARM3c
A. E. Downer AOM3

44-P-11
Lieutenant (jg) S. Greene
Ensign Charles W. Pacey
Paul Barker AP1c (NAP)
Elmer E. Conrad AMM2c
Luther Pinner AMM3c
Louie E. Lowinski ARM2c
Harry L. Gerkin ARM3c
Ward

44-P-12
Lieutenant (jg) Robert B. Felmuth
Ensign Chadron Hunter
Gordon H. Merrow AP1c (NAP)
Vernon T. Holden AMM1c
John J. Klopp AMM2c
Richard G. Watson AMM2c
Julius G. "Red" White ARM2c
Henry F. Saliger AOM2c

44-P-13
Lieutenant R. L. Summers

44-P-14
Lieutenant (jg) P. W. Vannoy
Lieutenant (jg) Pettiet
Thomas V. Watkins CAP (NAP)
G. F. Frankiewich AMM1c
J. O. "Jim" Pearson AMM2c
J. W. Downer AMM3c
W. Reid Wilson ARM2c
C. V. Lutton ARM3c
J. C. Stark AOM3c

44-P-?
Lieutenant (jg) W. E. Roy
Armido E. Mancini CAP (NAP)
Hillis L. Coker AMM1c
Willard H. Nicks AMM2c
Lloyd D. Wood AMM2c
Richard G. Miller ARM3c
Robert Barr ARM3c
Robert F. Kallam AOM1c

Appendix 12

25 December 1942

Copy by Jim Scott

Christmas Day

1942

✻   ✻   ✻   ✻

U. S. NAVAL AIR STATION
Kaneohe Bay, Oahu, T. H.

W. M. DILLON,
Captain, U. S. Navy,
Commanding

R. C. WARRACK,
Commander, U. S. Navy,
Executive Officer

H. R. COOKE,
Lieutenant (sc), USNR,
Commissary Officer

ANTHONY LORENZ,
Pay Clerk, U. S. Navy,
Asst. Comm. Officer

H. C. PUDCHUN,
CCStd., U.S.N.

✻   ✻   ✻   ✻

Menu

✻   ✻   ✻

Fruit Cup

Ripe Olives   Celery Hearts, Stuffed

Pickles

ROAST TOM TURKEY

BAKED SPICED HAM

Southern Corn Bread Dressing

Giblet Gravy   Cranberry Sauce

Mashed Potatoes   Peas

Asparagus Salad   Thousand Island Dressing

Hot Mince Pie   Ice Cream

Parker House Rolls   Butter

Coffee

Candy and Mixed Nuts

Cigars and Cigarettes

✻   ✻   ✻   ✻

Appendix 13

USS PATROL SQUADRON FORTY FOUR (VP-44) PAST COMMANDING OFFICERS
From Change of Command Ceremony, 1989, courtesy L. E. Lowinski

Lieutenant Commander V. D. Johnson, Jr. . . . . .July 1939-January 1940
Lieutenant Commander W. L. Erdman . . . . .February 40-November 1940
Squadron Redesignated
Lieutenant Commander W. C. Holt . . . . .June 1941-October 1941
Lieutenant Commander R. C. Brixner . . . . .October 1941-November 1942
Lieutenant D. G. Gumz . . . . .November 1942-December 1942
Lieutenant Commander R. A. Rosasco . . . . .December 1942-August 1943
Lieutenant Commander G. S. Bogart . . . . .September 1943-May 1945
Squadron Decommissioned
Commander L. T. McQuiston . . . . .August 1948-June 1949
Lieutenant Commander A. M. Ellingson . . . . .July 1949-August 1949
Lieutenant Commander C. J. Dobson . . . . .August 1949-October 1949
Lieutenant Commander A. M. Ellingson .October 1949-January 1950
Squadron Decommissioned
Commander F. H. Rand . . . . .January 1951-February 1952
Commander F. J. Grisko . . . . .February 1952-February 1953
Commander R. L. Ennire . . . . .June 1953-June 1954
Commander W. L. Laffey . . . . .June 1954-July 1955
Commander M. J. Burns . . . . .July 1955-July 1956
Commander M. E. Sotenson . . . . .July 1956-August 1956
Commander M. D. Macklin . . . . .August 1956-July 1957
Commander M. E. Haller . . . . .August 1957-July 1958
Commander C. Thompson . . . . .July 1958-July 1959
Commander L. W. Frawley . . . . .July 1959-July 1960
Commander E. E. Wilson . . . . .July 1960-July 1961
Commander R. L. Pierce . . . . .July 1961-July 1962
Commander A. Surrell . . . . .July 1962-July 1963
Commander J. L. Ball . . . . .July 1963-July 1964
Commander P. F. Hunter . . . . .July 1964-July 1965
Commander J. H. McDonald . . . . .July 1965-June 1966
Commander E. C. Waller, III . . . . June 1966-April 1967
Commander R. D. Synder, Jr. . . . . .April 1967-March 1968
Commander T. H. Warren, Jr. . . . . .March 1968-April 1969
Commander R. B. Olds . . . . .April 1969-March 1970
Commander T. D. Currey . . . . .March 1970-December 1970
Commander F. P. Gigliotti . . . . .December 1970-October 1971
Commander R. J. W. Smith . . . . .October 1971-October 1972
Commander J. R. Wyly, Jr. . . . . .October 1972-September 1973
Commander P. D. Smith . . . . .September 1973-September 1974
Commander W. P. Culhane . . . . .September 1974-August 1975
Commander J. Siembieda . . . . .August 1975-August 1976
Commander F. W. Carter, Jr. . . . . .August 1976-July 1977
Commander M. C. Roth . . . . .July 1977-July 1978
Commander W. L. Vincent . . . . .July 1978-July 1979
Commander D. W. Avery, Jr. . . . . .July 1979-July 1980
Commander R. E. Goolsby . . . . .July 1980-July 1981
Commander B. F. Folsom, Jr. . . . . .July 1981-July 1982
Commander R. T. Fuller . . . . .July 1982-July 1983
Commander V. L. McCullough . . . . .July 1983-October 1984
Commander J. L. Arnold . . . . .October 1984-February 1986
Commander R. Corn, III . . . . .February 1986-February 1987

Appendix 14

History of VP-44

From Change of Command Ceremony, 1989, courtesy L. E. Lowinski

Three past squadrons from Naval aviation's proud history have borne the designation VP-44 prior to the Golden Pelicans of 1989.

The first VP-44 evolved from VP-20 in Seattle, Washington. VP-20, under the operational control of Fleet Air Wing Four, was commissioned prior to 1939, and flew the PBY Catalina. The first commanding officer of record was Lt. Cmdr. W. D. Johnson, who commanded thirteen other pilots: 5 lieutenants and 8 aviation cadets. One of these lieutenants, R. A. Rosasco, was later to command the second squadron designated VP-44, described below. On 1 July 1939, VP-20 was redesignated VP-44. Lt. Cmdr. Johnson remained the Commanding Officer and thus gained the distinction of becoming the charter squadron commander. The squadron conducted intensive training exercises during the ensuing year, but the VP-44 designation was short lived. Redesignated VP-61 in November 1940, the command changed homeport to Alameda, California. In 1941 the squadron was moved to Norfolk, Virginia and subsequently redesignated VP-82, VB-125, and finally VPB-125, while conducting WWII operations in the Atlantic prior to decommissioning on 8 June 1945.

The second VP-44 of record, Patrol Bombing Squadron 44 (originally designated VP-44 but changed to VPB-44 in October 1943), was commissioned 3 June 1941 at NAS San Diego, California serving under Fleet Air Wing ONE, with twelve PBY-5a aircraft assigned. During early 1942 the squadron moved to Alameda in preparation for transfer to Pearl Harbor. By mid April all twelve aircraft had flown a successful transit to Hawaii. The average time of the crossing was 20.3 hours. On 23 May all planes arrived at Midway Island for extended operations and their first combat. Their War Diary states: When Ensign Jewell Harmon Reid, USN sent a contact report, "Main body", to Midway Island on 3 June 1942, he had made the most important patrol plane sighting of WWII. By this action he furnished the first positive information that a Japanese task force of imposing proportions was headed for Midway. Ensign Reid, who had taken off just before sunrise, made his first report about 9 a.m., relaying the sighting of two cargo ships some 470 miles from Midway. He came through just 21 minutes later with another report, stating that he had located the main body of the Japanese force — six large ships steaming in a column 700 miles from Midway. Then at 11 a.m., Reid sent a correction: there were 11 ships in the formation he sighted, not six.

On the night of the same day, four volunteer CATALINA crews, under the command of VP-44's Lt. W. L. Richards, USN, took to the air to deliver a night torpedo attack against the Japanese. The group included three aircraft from VP-24, which had arrived at Midway that afternoon. CATALINAS were not built for this kind of work, nor were their crews trained for torpedo attacks. Still, they managed to draw first blood. Three of the planes managed to locate the Japanese force, and Lt. Richards put a torpedo into the tanker AKEBONO MARU. In a 9 July 1942 endorsement of the battle report, Admiral Raymond A. Spruance stated: "This is a historical incident, being the first night torpedo attacks by our patrol planes on surface ships."

After Midway the squadron returned to Pearl Harbor and patrols were flown from Oahu and Johnston Island. Two crews participated in the special search for the Army B-17 lost with Capt. EDDIE RICKENBACKER aboard during October 1942. In February 1943 the entire squadron, under command of Lt. Cmdr. R. A. Rosasco (see above) deployed to the Solomon Islands. Through June they effected many survivor rescues during "Dumbo" operations, flew long scouting patrols, regularly flew in supplies to the island-chain coast watchers, staged and flew a six-plane night bombing attack on the enemy held island of Nauru, and engaged the enemy on numerous occasions. Then after 15 months in the Pacific, the squadron returned to San Diego in July 1943 for a well deserved rest and regrouping.

Lt. Cmdr. Gerard Schouler BOGART assumed command of the regrouped squadron on 29 September 1943, took custody of 15 new PBY-5a aircraft which were painted black, and began participation in the famous "Black Cat" organization. The Squadron deployed to the Pacific in February 1944 and arrived at Espiritu Santo, New Hebrides in March. While there they received detailed training in two new "technical aides in anti-submarine work — the sonobouy and a searchlight of 80 million candlepower." During the next months the "cats" participated exclusively in anti-submarine operations, participating in nine actual enemy actions. On 10 July the squadron was tasked to begin operations for which they had trained so hard: "BLACK CAT" ops. These night operations were normally formed together with small surface craft such as PT boats. On request from the boat, the plane would drop flares to light up a suspected target. Then both craft would carry out a coordinated attack against the enemy. These operations continued throughout the remainder of the year, and had much success around the New Britain and the Bougainville areas. During one such flight, a "BLACK CAT" PBY piloted by Lt. L. W GARISON of VP-44 was intercepted by a single-engine, twin float Japanese monoplane. During the ensuing action the enemy plane was destroyed by the PBY.

As the war moved north in the Pacific, so did VP-44. In January 1945 they were ordered north to participate in rescue operations in connection with the campaigns of Leyte and Luzon in the Philippines. After many successful rescue operations, the squadron was relieved by VPB-53 in mid-April

1945. Following its two highly successful 15 month deployments in the Pacific, the VP-44 "black cats" returned to San Diego where the squadron was "temporarily decommissioned" on 8 May 1945. The war ended prior to the recommissioning of the squadron.

Like the first VP-44, the third squadron to bear the designation evolved through a series of redesignations. This third command was commissioned as Patrol Squadron 204 on 15 October 1942 at Norfolk, Virginia. The squadron initially began with one PBM-3c "Mariner", but acquired six aircraft by December when they moved to San Juan, Puerto Rico. During the next 18 months the squadron operated from bases throughout the Caribbean and participated in sixteen attacks against German U-boats. As a result, six of their pilots were awarded Distinguished Flying Crosses. In 1945, as the European/Atlantic Theatre came to a close, the squadron was transferred to Coco Solo, Panama Canal Zone where they continued to conduct training flights and exercises. They were the first squadron to operate the PBM-5 in the Caribbean and to deploy with the aircraft to the Galapagos Islands, Ecuador. On 31 October 1946 the squadron designation was changed to Medium Seaplane Squadron FOUR (VP-MS-4). During the draw down years following the end of the war, the squadron conducted routine surveillance operations in the Caribbean, concentrating mainly on search and rescue. In 1947 the squadron began exercising with U.S. submarines with a new device called the "snorkel".

In June 1950, North Korean forces crossed the 38th parallel and the cold war became hot. On 31 January 1951, the fourth, and present, Patrol Squadron FORTY-FOUR was commissioned at Norfolk. Once again flying the PBM "Mariner", the squadron's primary mission was to be ASW.

In 1952, the squadron became the first VP squadron to receive the P5M-1 "Marlin" seaplane and the first to cross the Atlantic with the aircraft for a deployment in Europe. Barely 5 years in the fleet, the "Pelicans" received the first Battle Efficiency "E" ever given to a seaplane squadron, and followed the 1956 award with additional "E's" in 1957 and 1958. In 1959, after three consecutive "E's" VP-44 earned the Captain Arnold Jay Isbell Trophy for continued ASW excellence. This award, like the battle "E's", was also a first for an Atlantic seaplane squadron.

In 1960 the "Pelicans" completed their change of aircraft. Saying goodbye to seaplane aviation, the squadron transitioned to the land based Lockheed P2V "NEPTUNE".

In October 1961, VP-44 began its second Mediterranean deployment. Operating for five months from Sigonella, Sicily, the squadron played a major role in the "Project Mercury" space program in addition to general support of the Sixth Fleet and NATO operations.

One month after returning to Norfolk, VP-44 moved to NAS Patuxent River, Maryland where a third squadron aircraft transition began. In August, 1962 the first P-3a "Orion", christened "Rigel" taxied up to the VP-44 line. An intensive training program was immediately launched, one which was tested very quickly when the Cuban missile crisis erupted in October. Photos of a Pelican aircraft flying over a Soviet freighter carrying ballistic missiles made all the national wire services, and stood as a pictorial testimony to VP-44's contribution during the crisis.

Returning from a deployment to Argentia, Newfoundland in May 1964, Patrol Squadron FORTY-FOUR was awarded yet another Battle Efficiency "E" and the Captain Arnold Jay Isbell Trophy ASW excellence.

Operations in 1965 were diverse. A detachment was reestablished in Argentia early in the year, and operational exercises were flown out of Bermuda and Puerto Rico. For the second year in a row, the "Pelicans" earned another Battle Efficiency "E".

In recognition of its continued outstanding performance, VP-44 was designated Task Group Delta squadron in the spring of 1966. As the Delta squadron, VP-44 was responsible for an intensive program of equipment research and tactical procedure analysis. In the midst of Delta squadron assignments, VP-44 manned detachments in Argentia and Keflavik, Iceland through the summer months. In the fall, VP-44's research findings were presented to representatives of Atlantic Fleet ASW forces, which resulted in a new tactical syllabus for WING-SLANT patrol squadrons.

In July of 1967 the "Pelicans" relinquished Task Group Delta responsibilities to operate for a three-

month split deployment to Keflavik and Rota, Spain. In September, VP-44 returned to Patuxent River to resume Task Group Delta duties. After nearly a year of further research and short-term deployments, the squadron departed in late August of 1968 for a six month split deployment, between Keflavik and Lajes Field in the Portuguese Azores. The Golden Pelicans added their sixth Battle "E" for operations in 1967-68. In the fall of 1969, VP-44 added another first to its record with a four month deployment to Sigonella, Sicily, the first P-3a squadron to operate from that site.

After returning to Patuxent River, VP-44 made the move to its present home port at NAS Brunswick, Maine in July of 1970. Concurrently, crews deployed to Rota, Spain, Sigonella, Sicily and Souda Bay, Crete to operate as a patrol arm of the Sixth Fleet during the Jordanian crisis. For their work during this tense period, the Golden Pelicans were awarded the Meritorious Unit Citation.

The deployment site in the spring of 1971 was Bermuda where VP-44 crews flew anti-submarine missions throughout the North Atlantic and Caribbean. "Pelican" crews returned to Brunswick in June of 1971. Continuing to support VP operations with temporary detachments in Bermuda and Keflavik, the squadron concentrated on their next deployment in April 1972. This was a six-month split deployment to Rota, Spain and Lajes, Azores. Still flying their original veteran P-3a's, the "Pelicans" compiled an enviable ASW and maritime surveillance record.

Spending a welcome winter back home, the squadron now known to all as the "Golden Pelicans" began transition into newly configured P-3a "Orions". In June 1973 the "Golden Pelicans" returned to Bermuda and began a five month deployment. A year passed from their return from Bermuda in November and their deployment to Rota, Spain and Lajes, Azores.

In November 1974 , Patrol Squadron FORTY-FOUR deployed to Rota, Spain and Lajes, Azores. The "Golden Pelicans" participated in many interesting operations as well as varied exercises during this deployment. The squadron returned to NAS Brunswick in April 1975.

The Chief of Naval Operations Safety Award, for an east coast VP squadron was presented to Patrol

Squadron FORTY-FOUR in September 1975 by RADM Roy D. Snyder, Commander Patrol Wings Atlantic Fleet.

In mid-December 1975, VP-44 deployed to Bermuda and Lajes. The squadron enjoyed great success in ASW operations during this deployment, and later received a Meritorious Unit Commendation for operations out of NAF Lajes. In May 1976, the "Golden Pelicans" returned to Brunswick for a ten month period at home.

Upon its return to NAS Brunswick in September 1977, VP-44 began its initial preparation for transition to Navy's newest "Orion", the P-3c Update II. Extensive aircrew and maintenance training began in January 1978 and continued throughout the year. With the first Update II arriving in May, the squadron completed its transition and flew the last P-3a flight by an operational squadron in November 1978. With this flight, the Golden Pelicans became the first Navy squadron exclusively employing the Update II.

March 1979 saw VP-44 begin its long awaited deployment to Keflavik , Iceland with the Update 2 aircraft. The new aircraft exceeded its goals as the Golden Pelicans pushed it to its limits in their quest to maintain their excellence. Midway through the deployment, Vice-President Walter Mondale visited VP-44 while on a tour of Scandinavian countries. In July the Secretary of the Navy was guest speaker during the squadrons change of command. The squadron ended Keflavik deployment with a burst of activity in September 1979 and returned home for the CONUS training cycle.

1979 turned out to be a banner year for VP-44. Starting with the "Top Bloodhound" Award for top scores in torpedo placement accuracy, the squadron continued with the COMPATWINGSANT "Silver Anchor" for retention efforts and was runner-up for the "Golden Anchor" award for all VP squadrons. VP-44 also was awarded another Meritorious Unit Commendation for outstanding efforts during the Keflavik deployment, and capped the year by earning its seventh CNO Battle "E" for 1979.

At home in Brunswick, VP-44 continued its tradition of excellence. Regularly winning the NAS Brunswick "Betsy" Award for Ground Support Equipment excellence, the "Golden Pelicans" frequently had eight and occasionally all nine of their

aircraft flyable at one time, attesting to the outstanding effort put forward by the Maintenance Department. Official recognition of outstanding maintenance performance came in the form of the 1979 COMPATWINGSANT "Golden Wrench" Award for superior maintenance by an East Coast VP Squadron.

From September of 1980 until February 1981, the "Golden Pelicans" completed a highly successful deployment to Kadena, Okinawa. Operating throughout the Western Pacific and Indian Oceans, the squadron provided the first HARPOON capable aircraft in the Indian Ocean for battle group support. During the deployment the squadron won the "Platinum Link" award from the CTF 72 for excellence in data link operations, in addition to high praise for several first time ASW operations.

Returning to Brunswick, The "Golden Pelicans" faced a short seven month CONUS training period in preparation for a split deployment to Rota and Lajes.

Deploying to Rota and Lajes from October 1981 to March of 1982, the "Golden Pelicans" again distinguished themselves by winning the Sixth Fleet "Hook Em" award for ASW excellence and earning frequent praise for ASW prosecutions. Closing out on 1981 deployment, completed another banner year With the top "Bloodhound" award for torpedo placement accuracy and its eighth CNO Battle "E".

Returning home in March 1982, the squadron settled into the CONUS training cycle in preparation for a January 1983 deployment to Bermuda, looking forward to Christmas at home for the first time in three years.

The Golden Pelicans began 1983 with a 65-day detachment to WESTPAC while the remainder of the squadron deployed to Bermuda. The WESTPAC detachment experienced a highly successful deployment, culminating with the selection of Combat Air Crew Seven as the WESTPAC "Crew of the month", the first time an East coast squadron had ever won this coveted distinction.

During the short at-home cycle, the Golden Pelicans continued to set the pace for the patrol community while preparing for their 1984 deployment to Sigonella, Sicily.

In March 1984, VP-44 returned to Sigonella, Sicily for their first time since their involvement in the Jordanian crisis in 1970. With detachments in Rota and Souda Bay, the squadron carried out extensive operations throughout the Mediterranean and conducted coordinated ops with NATO and the Sixth Fleet. While in Sigonella, VP-44 conducted the single most successful prosecution of a Soviet nuclear submarine in Mediterranean history, for which they were awarded the prestigious Sixth Fleet "Hook "Em" award in June. In August the "Golden Pelicans" returned home for a well deserved rest before beginning CONUS operations and preparations for their next deployment to Rota, Spain and Lajes, Azores.

1985 was a banner year for VP-44. In addition to the normal training and maintenance milestones associated with CONUS, the Golden Pelicans blazed trails for COMPATWING FIVE in cross-decking and the Golden Orion Award for retention. Always a test-bed, VP-44 was the first Wing Five squadron to utilize the new Operational Readiness Examination (ORE) format, setting extremely high standards for the East coast squadrons. While still passing pre-deployment milestones (ORE/MRCI) in June, east coast Patrol Squadrons responded to the largest ever Soviet submarine deployment into the western Atlantic, and VP-44 played an integral role in successful prosecution. Over the course of the shortened at-home cycle, enlisted women were integrated into the squadron for the first time.

Patrol Squadron FORTY-FOUR spent a most enjoyable summer and fall in balmy Rota, Spain and beautiful Lajes, Azores. From July 1985 to January 1986, VP-44 participated in several exercises, tracked challenging targets, and enjoyed varied and interesting detachments to Panama, France, Keflavik, Crete, Italy, United Kingdom and the Ascension Islands. Always the Proud Golden Pelicans, the squadron thoroughly rehabilitated both sites prior to returning to Brunswick in 1986 for a slightly delayed but joyous reunion with family and friends.

The 1986 at home cycle was much welcomed, and training kept its high speed pace. Continuing total support to a flourishing professional cross-decking program, VP-44 routinely assigned personnel to other ASW communities including numerous submarines, carrier air wings, and Air Force surveillance commands. The squadron was the first organization to install and employ the evolutionary radar system AN/APS 137 (ISAR). In August, VP-44 participated in the most comprehensive and all encompassing Northern Wedding exercise in recent history. The squadron CO was OIC of six aircraft and crews on a detachment to Machrihanish, Scotland and conducted flawless operations throughout the North Atlantic for five weeks. With a rapid paced and short 9½ month at home cycle, the Golden Pelicans departed for deployment to Keflavik, Iceland.

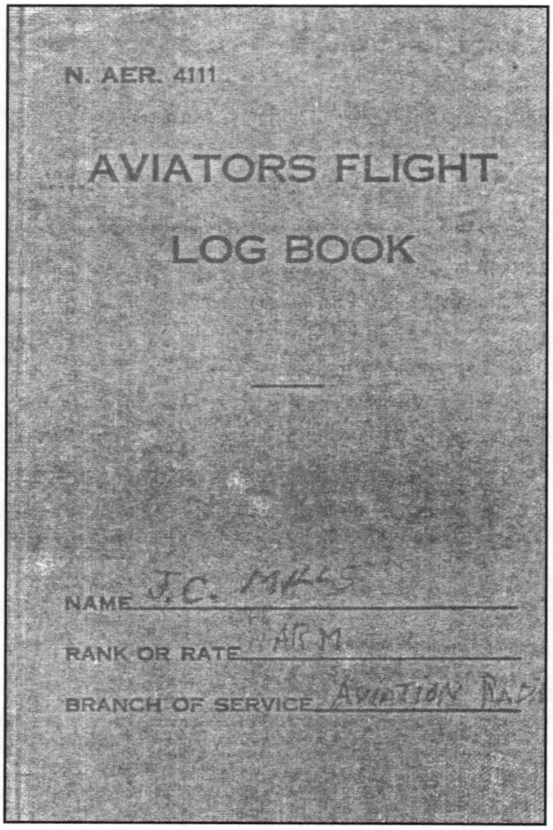

Appendix 15

Flight Log of James C. Mills

1 June 1942-June 1943

JUN 1942

Date	Type of Machine	Number of Machine	Duration of Flight	Character of Flight	Pilot	Passengers	Remarks
						Self	
1	PBY5A	04981	11.8		Ens. Umphrey	7	Had a helluva fight
9	PBY5A	04981	11.8	U	Ens. Umphrey	11	
25	"	7301	1.5		Lt jg Headley	6	
26	"	04978	11.9	J	" "	7	

Total time to date, 37.0

PATROL SQUADRON 44

BROUGHT FORWARD			431.8
THIS MONTH	PILOT TIME	PASS. TIME	TOTAL FOR MONTH
			37.0
TOTAL TO DATE			468.8

I CERTIFY THAT THE FOREGOING FLIGHT RECORD IS CORRECT.

APPROVED R C Brixner

LT. COM. U.S.N.

February 1943

Date	Type of Machine	Number of Machine	Duration of Flight	Character of Flight	Pilot	PASSENGERS	REMARKS
3	PBY5	8137	11.5	J	LT SWAN	SELF + 8	Buttons Patrol
6	"	"	11.2	J	"	"	Buttons to Vanikora
9	"	"	11.0	"	"	"	Vanikora to Buttons
11	"	8137	9.1	A	"	"	Buttons to Vanikoro
11	"	"	.3	X	"	"	Engine cut out change plane
12	"	8139	10.1	J	"	"	Vanikoro to Buttons
15	"	8140	11.3	J	"	"	Patrol by Tucopia
17	"	8137	12.1	J	"	"	Buttons to Vanikoro
19	"	8137	12	J	"	"	Vanikoro to Buttons
23	"	8137	11.1	J	"	"	Local Job. Lost Eng Reese
26	"	8130	3.1	J	"	"	Gun out Stop Vanikoro
26	"	8148	8.8	J	"	"	Vanikoro to Vanikoro
★ 28	"	8130	9.1	J	"	"	Vanikoro to Buttons Contact Mitsubishi Plane
			115.5	including the pilot			

TIME THIS MONTH 115.5
TIME BROUGHT FOR. 996.7
TOTAL TIME TO DATE 1112.2

PATROL SQUADRON 44

	PILOT TIME	PASS. TIME	TOTAL FOR MONTH
THIS MONTH			
TOTAL TO DATE			

I CERTIFY THAT THE FOREGOING FLIGHT RECORD IS CORRECT.

Total time to date, 1112.2

June 1943 — June 43

Date	Type of Machine	Number of Machine	Duration of Flight	Character of Flight	Pilot	PASSENGERS	REMARKS
1	PBY5	4563	5.3		LT (JG) SWAN	SELF + 15	Santo to Halavo B. Solomon Ils.
6	"	4426	2.3		LT CMDR GU	" " 9	Halavo to Banonogga
6	"	"	2.2		" "	" "	Banonogga to Guadalcanal
6	"	"	.3		" "	" "	Guadalcanal to Halavo
8	"	"	.5		LT (JG) Swan	" " 7	Halavo to Malaita
8	"	"	.5		" "	" " 8	Malaita to Halavo
13	"	"	1.8		LT CMDR GU	" " 8	Halavo to Segi New Georgia
13	"	"	2.5		" "	" " 14	Segi to Renell Isl.
13	"	"	1.7		" "	" " 18	Renell to Halavo
20	"	"	.5		" "	" " 6	Defense test Run
21	"	"	5.1		LT (JG) Swan	" " 15	Halavo to Santo
28	"	VP71	6.5	U	"		
29	"	"	8.3	U	"		
29	"	"	1.8	U	"		
30	"	"	8.1	U	"		
			52.4				

PATROL SQUADRON 44

BROUGHT FORWARD

	PILOT TIME	PASS. TIME	TOTAL FOR MONTH
THIS MONTH		1401	52.4
TOTAL TO DATE			1853.8

I CERTIFY THAT THE FOREGOING FLIGHT RECORD IS CORRECT.

APPROVED
LT. COM. U.S.N.

Total time to date,

Appendix 16

Dear Old Girl

Author unknown; courtesy Robert L. Hayden

To most of the world she is the PBY "Catalina" patrol plane, but her friends know her as *The Cat*. Back in 1941 when the war began there were those that looked at her and smiled wisely and said she was too old and tired and obsolete even then, and wouldn't last a month in the give-and-take of air-sea warfare.

Their smile grew wiser when in the Philippines the Japanese struck out of nowhere and caught her on the ground before she got her back up. They didn't know then that she had nine lives and would live to find her way to Australia and there grow strong and learn the tricks of fighting back.

She showed them she could fight, all right, when they backed her up into that little corner of the Southwest Pacific and she turned and swished her tail and shot a sharpened claw that cut a gash from Santa Cruz northward.

Yes, she showed them she could fight all right, and the stories of her victories will shine as long as the archives of World War II lie open. The men of the *CATS* — the pilots and crewman — they know her story. They know it but don't say much about it because it's kind of private, like a man's homelife or his girl. But they know it and feel it just the same.

They've sat behind her yoke and felt her purr as she rubbed against the tall white billowy clouds of the Caribbean.

They've swelled with pride as her cat's-eye reached through the blackness of the South Pacific night to spot her unwary prey a score of miles away.

They've laughed with her as she howled at night from the back fences of Munda and Rabaul and Paramisha [*sic*; Paramushiro] while their defenders threw their old-shoe ack-ack into the darkness.

They smiled and patted her nose when she donned her black cat garb and bad-lucked the path of the Japanese supply line to New Guinea.

Yes, hers is a story all right.

Remember the Bismarck? She found the Bismarck when the whole Allied world was looking for that scourge of the North Atlantic.

Remember Pearl Harbor? She spotted the submarine that was sunk that morning — the first Japanese casualty of World War II.

Remember Corregidor and Wake? She was the last to leave these besieged fortresses taking out people and equipment and information up until just before the enemy arrived.

Remember Midway? She discovered the air and sea fleet on its way to begin that historic battle — and then struck at that fleet in the dark in the first night torpedo attack.

Remember the Submarine War? She sent out that famous message, "SIGHTED SUB, SANK SAME."

And so it goes. Enemy battleships, carriers, cruisers, destroyers and transports have all felt the sharpness of her claws — claws that have reached out at night to rip a million tons of shipping out of the lifelines of Nippon's Pacific Empire.

But there is another side of the CAT, too. If you want to know about that side ask any of the hundreds of downed airmen who, floating helplessly on rubber life rafts on every one of the seven seas, have reached out their arms and cried "Thank God" for the Cat that found and rescued them.

That's how the story of the PBY CATALINA goes — The plane they smiled about and said she was too old when the Japanese first struck at Pearl Harbor — the plane that lived to <u>lead</u> the triumphant parade back to the Philippines.

That's the story the men of the *CATS* carry around inside them — the story they know but don't say much about. It's the story of their airplane, yes, but it's something more than that too — it's the story of their

"Dear Old Girl"

Appendix 17

Autographs of VP-44 Personnel

USS PATROL SQUADRON FORTY FOUR (VP-44) ASSOCIATION
THE BLUE CATALINAS OF WWII

Signature	Rank or Rate
(signature)	OAM 1/c
Howard R. Gurney	Lt.
Leonard S. Sucher	LtCdr
Jd Andrews	CDR Ret
Harold Koon	CDR R.T.
Bobby Robinson	Cdr Ret
Bob Swan	CDR Ret.
Jerry Hardison	LCDR Ret
Happy Hayden	LCDR
Owen L. Ryan	ACMM
Allen J. (Tommy) Thompson	ACMM
George W. Newcombe	AOC Ret.
James F. Scott	Amm 1/c Ret

On the occasion of the 50th anniversary of the return of the squadron to the United States in 1943 from actions in the Pacific Theater, during World War II, at Midway Island, Espiritu Santo, and the Solomon Islands.

Signature	Rank or Rate
(Charles) Warren Pacey	LCDR RET
Louie Townsle	ARM 1/c
Bill Cullen	CDR (ret)
Lloyd Word	AMM 1/c
Frank Reid	Capt USN Ret.
Pat Fitzpatrick	AMM 2/c
Lee McClung	Lcdr.
Jim Trim	ACM 2/c
Joseph Zmar	AK-2c
Jim Wills	ACRM
Dick Watson	LT. (J.G.) Ret.
Edward McKinnie	AMM 1/c
Reid Wilson	ACRM

Name	Rank or Rate
Glenn F. Bacher	enlisted as Apt Seaman Released to NA 1949 as LTJG 7
Mert Bourjer	Lieut.
Lloyd Baullard	CWO-3 (YN3c 1941) (Ret)
Charles T. Carl	LCDR USNR RET
Elmer Conrad	AMM 1/c ALSO VPB44
Ralph C. Dwaller	LCDR USNR Ret.
J. Monahan	Capt USMC Ret
Monroe Nelson	ATC. Retired
Lindsey de Gehry	Lt.
Jim Morgenson	LCDR-Ret · USNR
Clarence E. Olson	Capt. USN (Ret)
Ralph C. Rejo	LCDR USNR Retired
James A. Walls	SFC-E7 US ARMY RETIRED
Thomas V. Watkins	CDR. USN (RETIRED)
Julius G. White	ACRM (End of enlist. 1947)

Signature	Rank or Rate
Robert Barr	ARM 1/c LCDR-A(VN) USNR-Ret.
C. D. (Bud) Brislawn	CARM Ret. L.A.P.d. RETIRED.
Dale E. Brown	
Patrick J. Mahon	ACMM (PA)
M. R. (Ray) Ubben	ACRM

Glossary

Military Rank and Ratings

Navy

Adm.	Admiral
Vice Adm.	Vice Admiral
Rear Adm.	Rear Admiral
Comm.	Commodore
Capt.	Captain
Comdr.	Commander
Lt. Comdr.	Lieutenant Commander
Lt.	Lieutenant
Lt. (jg)	Lieutenant Junior Grade
Ensign	Ensign
CWO	Chief Warrant Officer
WO	Warrant Officer
AA	Acting Appointment
ACMM	Aviation Chief Machinist Mate
ACOM	Aviation Chief Ordnance Mate
ACRM	Aviation Chief Radio Mate
AM	Aviation Machinist Class 1,2,3
AMM	Aviation Machinist Mate Class 1,2,3
AOM	Aviation Ordnance Mate Class 1,2,3
AP	Aviation Pilot Class 1,2,3

ARM	Aviation Radio Mate Class 1,2,3
AS	Apprentice Seaman
BM	Bosun Mate Class 1,2,3
CAP	Chief Aviation Pilot
Cox	Coxswain Class 1,2,3
CPO	Chief Petty Officer
EM	Electrician Mate Class 1,2,3
Matt	Mess Attendant Class 1,2,3
NAP	Naval Aviation Pilot
PA	Permanent Appointment
PC	Plane Captain
Phm	Pharmacist Mate Class 1,2,3
PO	Petty Officer Class 1,2,3
PPC	Patrol Plane Commander
Ptr	Printer
RM	Radio Mate Class 1,2,3
SC	Ships Cook Class 1,2,3
Sea	Seaman Class 1,2
SK	Store Keeper Class 1,2,3
Y	Yeoman Class 1,2,3

Marine Corps and Army

Maj. Gen.	Major General

Brig. Gen.	Brigadier General
Col.	Colonel
Lt. Col.	Lieutenant Colonel
Maj.	Major
Capt.	Captain
1st Lt.	First Lieutenant
2nd Lt.	Second Lieutenant
Master Sgt.	Master Sergeant
TSgt.	Technical Sergeant
1st Sgt.	First Sergeant
Sgt.	Sergeant
Cpl.	Corporal
Pvt.	Private

Navy Aircraft Squadron Designations

The first letter indicates aircraft heavier- or lighter-than-air. The remaining letters indicate aircraft mission. Numerals following the last letter indicate squadron number.

VB	Heavier than Air, Bombing
VF	Heavier than Air, Fighter
VP	Heavier than Air, Patrol
VPB	Heavier than Air, Patrol Bombing
VO	Heavier than Air, Observation
VS	Heavier than Air, Scouting
VT	Heavier than Air, Torpedo

Marine Corps

The second letter "M" designates Marine. The letter designating manufacturer is dropped.

| VMF | Heavier than Air, Marine Fighter |
| VMSB | Heavier than Air, Marine Scouting Bomber |

General Abbreviations and Terms

BEF	British Expeditionary Force
CINCPAC	Commander-in-Chief Pacific
CNO	Chief of Naval Operations
CO	Commanding Officer
COMAIRPAC	Commander Aircraft Pacific
COMAIRSOLS	Commander Aircraft Solomons
COMAIRSOPAC	Commander Aircraft South Pacific
COMFAIRWING	Commander Fleet Air Wing
COMPATWING	Commander Patrol Wing
COMPATWINGSANT	Commander Patrol Wings Atlantic
COMPATWINGSPAC	Commander Patrol Wings Pacific
COMSOPAC	Commander South Pacific
CONUS	Continental United States
CW	Continuous Wave
FAW	Fleet Air Wing
IFF	Identify Friend or Foe
IJN	Imperial Japanese Navy
NAS	Naval Air Station
NATO	North Atlantic Treaty Organization
PATSU	Patrol Aircraft Service Unit
PATWING	Patrol Wing
PC	Plane Captain
PPC	Patrol Plane Commander
RAA	Royal Australian Army
RAAF	Royal Australian Air Force
RAN	Royal Australian Navy
RDF	Radio Direction Finder
WESTPAC	Western Pacific

Bibliography

Books and Articles

Blanding, Don. *Vagabond's House.* New York: Dodd Meade and Company, 1942.

Bogart, Gerald S. *The Black Cats of Green Island.* N.p.: n.d.

Campbell, Christy. *Air War Pacific.* New York: Reed Internatonal Books, 1990.

Cressman, Robert J., with Steve Ewing, Barrett Tillman, Clark Reynolds, and Stan Cohen. *The Battle of Midway 4-6 June 1942.* Missoula, MT: Pictorial Histories Publishing Company, 1990.

Crocker, Mel. *Black Cats and Dumbos.* Blue Ridge Summit, PA: Tab Books Inc., 1987.

Elson, Robert T. *Prelude to War.* Alexandria, VA: Time Life Books Inc., 1977.

La Forte, Robert S., and Ronald E. Marcello. *Remembering Pearl Harbor.* Wilmington, DE: Scholarly Resources Inc., 1991.

Lord, Walter. *Lonely Vigil.* New York: Pocket Books of New York, 1977.

"Naval Aviation Museum Foundation." *Naval Aviation Museum Foundation* 8.1 (Spring 1987).

Potter, E. B. *Bull Halsey.* Annapolis, MD: Naval Institute Press, 1985.

Prange, Gordon W. *Miracle at Midway.* Crawfordville, IN: Penguin Books, 1982.

Scarborough, W. E. *PBY CATALINA in Action.* Carrolltown, TX: Squadron Signal Publications, 1983.

Wernick, Robert. *Blitzkrieg.* Alexandria, VA: Time Life Books Inc., 1977.

The World Book Encyclopedia, Vol. 19. Chicago, IL: Field Enterprises Educational Corp., 1960.

Letters and Interviews

Andregg, John N.

Arsenault, Arthur J. 19 May 1993.

Brislawn, C. D. 23 Mar. 1994.

Brown, Dale E. 18 Apr. 1994.

Davis, C. D., Jr. 9 Aug. 1993.

Finn, James J. 21 July 1993.

Fitzpatrick, Patrick A. 15 Dec. 1992.

Hayden, R. L. 14 Feb. 1994.

Judas, Loren G. H. 27 Mar. 1993.

Klopp, James R. 22 Dec. 1992, 1 Sept. 1993, 19 Mar. 1994.

Lowinski, Louie E. 2 Mar. 1993.

Mahon, Patrick J. 26 Mar. 1993.

Marsh, Charles M. 18 May 1994.

McCleary, Lee C. 18 Feb. 1994.

McKissick, Edward K., Jr. 18 Feb. 1994.

Metke, Harry D. 11 May 1994.

Monahan, T. G. 3 July 1993.

Newcombe, George W. 16 Mar. 1993.

Reid, Jack H. 29 June 1993.

Scarborough, W. L. 12 July 1993.

Scott, James F. 17 June 1993.

Swan, Robert A. 15 Jan. 1994.

Thompson, Allen J. 6 Nov. 1992, 31 Jan. 1993, 1 Nov. 1993.

Vickrey, B. K. 17 Jan. 1993, 30 Jan 1993, 25 Aug. 1993, 15 Sept. 1993, and 21 Oct. 1993.

Watson, Richard G., Jr. 12 Apr. 1993.

Weems, Thomas H., Jr. Apr. 1994.

Wilson, W. Reid. 23 Oct. 1992.

Wood, Lloyd D. 7 Dec. 1993.

National Archives Documents

Muster Roll of the Crew: 31 Dec. 1940, 31 Dec. 1941, 30 June 1942, 30 Sept. 1942, and Report of Changes, 31 Dec. 1942.

Reports of Engagements: May 1942 and June 1942.

Flight Commanders Report of Night Torpedo Attack, 3 June 1942.

Daily Operations Reports, Halavo Beach, Florida Islands, Solomons: Feb. and Mar. 1943.

Contact Action Reports, South Pacific Area: Feb., Mar., Apr., May, and June 1943.

Flight Commanders Report of Attack on Nauru Island, June 1943.

Organizational Structures, VP-44, Midway and Espiritu Santo.

Index

by Lori L. Daniel

Other titles of Interest from

Sunflower University Press®

SOME EARLY BIRDS, by Joe Hill

*IT WAS MY WAR — I'LL REMEMBER IT THE
WAY I WANT TO!*, by G. William Sefton

CAMPAIGN RIBBONS, by John R. Simmons

A HISTORY OF AIRCRAFT PISTON ENGINES,
by Herschel Smith

*FRONTLINE AIRLINE: TROOP CARRIER PILOT
IN WORLD WAR II*, by John R. (Bob) Lester

*A WARRIOR FOR FREEDOM: ADMIRAL
ROBERT B. CARNEY*, by Betty Carney Taussig

*TWO YEARS BEHIND THE MAST: AN AMER-
ICAN LANDLUBBER AT SEA IN WORLD WAR
II*, by Harold J. McCormick

THE LOG OF AIR NAVIGATION, by Maj. Gen.
Norris B. Harbold, USAF